BULLS, BULLFIGHTING, AND SPANISH IDENTITIES

The Anthropology of Form and Meaning

BULLS, BULLFIGHTING, AND SPANISH IDENTITIES

Carrie B. Douglass

The University of Arizona Press • Tucson

The University of Arizona Press

© 1997
The Arizona Board of Regents

Manufactured in the United States of America

First printing

Library of Congress Cataloging-in-Publication Data

Douglass, Carrie B., 1948–
Bulls, bullfighting, and Spanish identities / Carrie B. Douglass.
p.   cm. — (The anthropology of form and meaning)
Includes bibliographical references and index.
ISBN 0-8165-1651-0 (alk. paper)
1. National characteristics, Spanish.   2. Spain — Civilization.
3. Fighting bull — Spain.   4. Bullfights — Social aspects — Spain.
I. Title.   II. Series.
DP52.D68   1997
946 — dc21   96-45806
CIP

British Cataloguing-in-Publication Data
A catalogue record for this book is available from the British Library.

The publication of this book was made possible by a generous grant
from the Program for Cultural Cooperation
between Spain's Ministry of Culture
and United States Universities.

CONTENTS

Part 3
Tradition:
The Bulls and Regional Identity
117

ILLUSTRATIONS

TABLES

ACKNOWLEDGMENTS

I wish to thank the National Science Foundation and the Program for Cultural Cooperation between Spain's Ministry of Culture and United States Universities for their support through several years of research.

In Spain many individuals went out of their way to help me with my work. I would especially like to thank Tomás Agrela Fernández (in the Sección taurina of the Ministerio del Interior), Francisco Martínez Llantado (in Asuntos taurinos of the Generalitat de Valencia), Jaime Miguel Adrada (Director of Social Studies, Gallup, Spain), Marcel Fournier (Director of Production of ALEF, S.A.), bull ranchers Fermín Bohórquez and Vicente Machancoses, and friends and family Carmen Vilá, Carol Harris, Jesús Echalecu, Raquel López Martínez, Roque Esteban, Maribel Asenjo, Conchita de Esteban, Juanita Maíllo, Luis Silva Vicente, Lola Maíllo, Lala Isla, Charo Martínez, Mariano Operé, José Luis Operé, and Rosario Santillana.

Several colleagues and teachers were instrumental in helping me define my direction and improve this work. Among those I especially want to acknowledge are Frederick Damon for his engagement with the data and probing questions and criticisms, David Sapir for his constant encouragement of my work with "the bulls," and Javier Herrero, distinguished Hispanist. I have also benefited greatly from the comments of David Gies, Richard Handler, and James Fernandez. I also thank Sonia Rodríguez-Jiménez and Virginia Invernizzi for reading and commenting on the chapters on Sevilla and Bilbao, respectively. Two colleagues and friends gave me very special help and must be mentioned separately. Results of my many conversations with Charles Piot and Eric Gable are scattered throughout the text and in some of its general orientation.

I am also indebted to Nancy Ehrenreich, Jackie Taylor, and Lydia Petersson, who gave me important editorial advice. Margo Leach (faculty secretary at Mary Baldwin College) and her student assistants, as well as Vickie Jo Einselen, helped get the manuscript into final form.

The person to whom I owe the most and who also helped me gain entry into many Spanish contexts, especially the traditionally male world of "the bulls," was my live-in Spanish informant and husband, Fernando Operé. Many times while I "observed," he "participated" by running with the bulls. A constant source of moral support and assistance, he also enthusiastically commented on every chapter in the book. I thank him. Finally, I must thank my three children—Philip, Peter, and Camila—who, one at a time or together, often accompanied me to bull ranches, fiestas and bullfights and who, I hope, came to love Spain and its cultures as much as I do.

BULLS, BULLFIGHTING, AND SPANISH IDENTITIES

INTRODUCTION

What in its substantial reality is that business of the bullfight? Why are
there bullfights in Spain in place of their not being there?
— Ortega y Gasset 1973:153

Modernity and Tradition

For many Spaniards and Hispanists of my generation, bullfights are a
minor, unimportant nineteenth century survival, part of an arcane
worldview associated with General Franco and his supporters. These
people—who identify with the liberal, modern, service-oriented, artistically avant-garde, culturally innovative, democratically open, internationally respected Spain of the 1990s—become irritated when they hear
the word "bullfights" in any analysis of "Spain." "Not more bullfights!" they cry. "This is not what Spain is."

Nevertheless, bullfights exist in Spain, and their numbers are not di-
minishing. This is because bullfighting, *los toros* (literally "the bulls"),
continues its role as a multivocal symbol with many contested meanings. If you are Spanish, it is almost impossible not to be involved in this
contest.

Bullfighting inevitably evokes political responses. Some Hispanists
see a red flag at the mere mention of bullfights ("tourist literature"),
granting agencies choose which "Spain" they want studied ("Not more
bullfights!"), and some Spanish officials are politically cautious enough
to deny access to statistics about taurine games in certain provinces.

I was once present in a debate between two Hispanists in the United
States as they discussed what to emphasize about Spain in a summer
seminar for high school teachers. One, an American, thought the
course should emphasize Spain's modernity: modern architecture, literature, film, and music, but definitely not "bullfights and the like."
The other, a Spanish citizen, retorted that Spain was also *fiestas* and
bullfights, with over 15,000 occurring in 1992. The American Hispan-

ist argued that everyone already thought that "Spain was bullfights, In-
quisitions, and flamenco." He wanted to go beyond these stereotypes
so that the teachers could see new Spain as the modern country it is.
The Spaniard wanted to emphasize Spain's traditions.

This, of course, is the problem some Spaniards have with the subject
of bullfighting. Many Spaniards, and Hispanists, fear that any study or
analysis of the bullfights will focus on them as the *essence* of Spain, as
much previous writing by Spaniards and foreigners tried to do. "This is
not what Spain is!"

Perhaps the problem lies with the English verb "to be." When we
talk about what Spain "is," does this mean "essentially is" (as if such a
core being existed in nature), or "sociologically is" (all the qualities and
characteristics that coexist within Spain's borders)? Or does "is" mean
"should be?" Is there a single description of Spain, or just a dominant
description? Does this imply homogeneity? If not, what about the other
parts of Spain? How does "is" deal with plurality? Does "is" refer to
the speaker's point of view, or does it pretend to have some objective
truth? Who decides what Spain "is"—a publishing elite, those in
power, social scientists, artists, a majority vote, insiders, or outsiders?
Does "is" refer to a metaphor or a metonym?

I make no claims that the bullfight, nor the bullfighting debate, defines what Spain is. But certainly, in talking about the bulls, one ends
up discussing some very important issues and relationships, both historical and contemporary, in Spain. These debated issues lie at the very
core of Spanish identity, and I discuss them to explain Spanish ambivalence about this institution and why it seems to be embedded in the
hide of Spain.

What I do not do in this book is talk about the morality or immorality
of the bullfights. Whether they remain in Spain or disappear from the
peninsula is not my concern. I am interested in them as a cultural phenomenon. Certainly many of these taurine games are, to my taste, excessively brutal. I have even walked out of one spectacle, a *toreo cómico*
(comic bullfight). At other times I have found myself moved by the
relationship created between man and beast. Yet, my only purpose here
is to explain how Spanish identities relate to the bull.

What I found interesting about studying bullfights in Spain was that
so many people showed irritation when I discussed my research. I frequently felt defensive and embarrassed to admit that I was investigating
such a tacky, "stereotypical" subject, as if I were single-handedly responsible for perpetuating myths about Spain. At the same time, in

most of Spain, there is hardly a patron saint festival without the bulls, hardly a street without a bar decorated with a bullfight poster or bulls' horns, hardly a conversation without a bullfight expression. Moreover, for all the Spaniards that threw up their arms in exasperation at the foreigner's interest in bullfights, other Spaniards assured me that the bull was the totem of Spain, that fiestas revolve around the bull, and that bullfights were a sublime art.

After General Franco's death in 1975, there was an almost immediate return to the historical discussion about nationality and national symbols. Scholars once again began to take seriously this institution that had been intimately tied to the dictatorship, yet which continued to thrive in democracy. In the past fifteen years, after almost two decades of silence on the subject, scholars have published a series of interpretations of the bullfight (Arauz de Robles 1978; Arévalo 1984; Caro Baroja 1984; Delgado Ruiz 1986; Douglass, C. 1984; García-Baquero González et al. 1980; Marvin 1988; Mirá 1976; Mitchell, T. J. 1986, 1991; Pitt-Rivers 1983, 1993; Serrán Pagán 1977, 1979; Serrán Pagán and Muntadas 1980). This deluge of articles seems to be a recognition of the bullfight's central role in Spanish culture, although even this aspect of it is disputed in these writings.

Most work on bullfights has dealt with one kind of spectacle, the *corrida de toros*. Anthropologists and others have tried to decipher the symbolic meaning of the corrida by examining the various steps, the role of the various performers, and the vocabulary employed, and then use these aspects as metaphors for other parts of Spanish life. Criticism of these studies often focuses on the invalidity of an analysis for all parts of Spain. Furthermore, the corrida de toros is just one of at least sixteen spectacles or games with bulls. It is the most well-known form, but not the most numerous. A few authors have dealt with other peripheral forms of bullfighting, locating their analysis in a specific town.

The analysis that follows discusses the whole phenomenon of los toros in Spain, not just one or another of its forms. My investigation suggests that these spectacles, taken in contextual relationship, create a dynamic discourse about significant cultural categories in Spain. Specifically, these different taurine formats are used to talk about male/female, urban/rural, national/local, class, and political relationships; hierarchy and equality; history; worldview; and most importantly for this work, the construction of the Spanish state and Spain's relationship with Europe. The idea that underlies all of these topics is the Spanish opposition between modernity and tradition.

Los toros is a semantic system that talks about "Spain" in the most profound and total sense. The meaning of los toros as a holistic phenomenon transcends the meaning of the individual games. Further, "Spain" is a disputed category within the nation-state called by that name. In a country with various and competing cultural and linguistic traditions, there is no consensus of what is "Spanish." Nor is there any agreement as to whether, or how, the whole (the nation-state) should take precedence over the many parts (the regions or ethnic nationalities). Should the regions be related in a hierarchical or in an egalitarian way? Put simply, there is an opposition between the *one* and the *many* Spains.

Complicating this debate is Spain's rapid transformation in the last forty years from a backward rural nation to a modern industrial one. On the one hand, many Spaniards define themselves as modern by denying that traditional customs, such as los toros, represent Spain. On the other, Spaniards identify with their particular region by clinging to and reproducing ethnic customs, which, after all, are historical or "traditional." These ethnic traditions often include specific forms of taurine games.

Modernity and tradition are seemingly self-evident oppositions to those that use them. Upon scrutiny, however, it is never clear what the exact referents of these terms are. Social science has a long history of opposing these two ideas, beginning with Max Weber's modernization theory. Moreover, modernity has become an extremely important notion in contemporary anthropology (Rabinow 1989). Nevertheless, recent work recognizes that as analytical tools the value of these terms has been obviated (Comaroff and Comaroff 1993; Mitchell and Abu-Lughod 1993). As many postmodern analysts note, in reality, each historical definition of "modernity" includes what could be called "traditional" elements and thus cannot truly be opposed to "tradition" (Mitchell and Abu-Lughod 1993). I use these terms because the Spaniards used them all the time in their conversations about "the bulls." Clearly, both "modernity" and "tradition" are social constructions. As such, each term has its own associations in Spain and will be used differently from the same words in other European cultures, even though the same preoccupations with something called "modernity," as opposed to "tradition," may exist elsewhere. Chapter 4, "The Bull that Ravished Europa," attends to the Spanish definition and use of the term "modernity."

Los toros, thus, serve as a vehicle to talk about two historical Spanish

debates about identity. The first is the place of "Spain" in Europe. This
has to do with modernity. For almost two hundred years, many Spaniards have seen the presence of los toros in their country as symbolic of
the obstacles to Spain's modernization and thus to acceptance into
the European community and worldview. Los toros symbolize non-
Europeanness and must be rejected. "Only the tourists go to the bullfights," say these Spaniards.

The second debate concerns regional identity and the place of the
various regions in the construction of the Spanish state. This debate has
to do with tradition. Although some regions view themselves as more
"European" than others, the "cultures" also define and reify themselves through their traditions. If they were all modern, they would all
be the same, while tradition differentiates one culture from another.
Thus, regions often identify with one taurine game and not another.
"I've never participated in a *sokamuturra*. I'm from Castile," one informant told me, for a sokamuturra is a Basque taurine game.

Nevertheless, the bull is the thread that ties all of the regions together. The games with bulls change as one moves across the tapestry
that is "Spain," but the animal remains the same. Although some places
in the south of France and Portugal also celebrate their fiestas with bulls,
the debate over the *toro bravo* (wild bull) is the truly significant Spanish
debate and thus can be said to signify "Spain."

One format is national, the corrida de toros. Attitudes about the corrida subtly reflect attitudes about a national culture. A cycle of important corridas de toros, celebrated from March to October, winds in a
clockwise direction throughout Spain. Each point (city) in the cycle
represents a different part of "Spain," while the cycle itself expresses the
concept of the whole. I chose five important points on this cycle to
study: Valencia, Sevilla, Madrid, Pamplona, and Bilbao. Five field sites
were necessary because it is through the whole cycle, not one part of it,
that the tensions between the "one" Spain and the "many" are tem-
porally played out.

Although there are many true fans *(aficionados)* and many convinced
detractors, I believe most Spaniards feel ambivalent about the bulls. As
one man commented, "The bulls don't make sense in the 1980s." In
the following pages I want to explain the many layers and levels of Spanish identities that determine *afición* for the bulls. No individual is one-
dimensional. Although regionalism is a strong determinant, so is age,
gender, political persuasion, worldview, and urban versus rural location.
Even the identity of one's audience can influence attitudes toward the

bulls. (Is the Spaniard speaking to a foreigner, a person from another region, a fellow townsperson while the town is in fiestas, or a fellow townsperson in an argument about European Economic Community [EEC] membership?) Attitudes also depend on which format of the bulls is being discussed. Spanish ambivalence is probably predicated on a perceived opposition between modernity and tradition, and the desire to have both.

Does one have to give up a one-thousand-year-old tradition to be modern? The theoretical analysis of these binary oppositions and their mediations through los toros is quite structuralist. According to Lévi-Strauss (1963), binary oppositions (e.g., North/South, national/local, hierarchy/equality, upper class/lower class, tradition/modernity, toros/*vaquillas*) are intrinsically unstable and require mediation. As will be seen, the fiesta cycle and fiesta of San Fermín in Pamplona seem to resolve the binary paradox and make the contemporary Spanish state possible by integrating its various parts.

Poststructuralist anthropology has criticized structuralism as privileging one voice relative to other voices. The so-called privileged voice is that of the anthropologist, who "sees" and analyzes elegant patterns and cultural structures, which may, nonetheless, be unrecognizable by the informants. The recent trend in anthropology is to let the informants speak for themselves. In this study, I believe it is the Spaniards who are the true structuralists. The oppositions and categories I use and explain in the following pages are a constant part of everyday discourse in Spain. They are used unselfconsciously in speech, film, literature, poetry, song, advertising, and politics. I also show that the mediations of these oppositions—like the fiesta cycle and Pamplona—are recognized on some level by many Spanish citizens as *models for* Spain.

Review of the Literature

Scholars in the eighteenth and nineteenth centuries were concerned with the origins of bullfighting. The Roman Circus theory competed with the theory of a Moorish origin. In 1900, Conde de las Navas (López-Valdemoro 1900) published his influential book *El espectáculo más nacional,* where he proposed a Spanish origin to the bullfight. However, in the early twentieth century, with the archaeological discoveries of the caves of Altamira and other prehistoric bovine artifacts, peninsular interest in bulls was placed back into prehistory. The modern bullfight was equated with the sacrifices ancient Mediterranean cultures made to their divinities. In the 1920s, the discovery of the bull-leaping frescos in the palace of Knossos on Crete seemed to confirm the Neolithic origin and sacrifice thesis of the bullfight in Spain. By the 1920s and 1930s, Spanish intellectuals had integrated the ritual sacrifice theme into their work. The poet García Lorca ([1954]1974:1077) saw the bull itself as a god and called the bullfight a "religious drama where, in the same way as in mass, a God is adored and sacrificed." The poet Machado (1967:1136) called it a "holocaust to an unknown God."

Also by the 1920s, Freudian psychology had entered the interpretation of the bullfight, building upon the sacrifice theme (Conrad 1957; Desmonde 1952; Fernández Flórez 1927; Frank 1926; Hunt 1955; Ingham 1964; Leiris [1937]1964). Those who followed a Freudian model usually stated quite clearly that the killing of the bull was the "killing of the father" (or some other authority figure or institution) and that in the spectacle the id was being amply gratified. Transgression was an overt theme.

A second Freudian theme concerned symbolic sex roles of the two principal protagonists: the *torero* and the bull. The essential femininity of the torero, or his feminine characteristics, has often been noted (Caba 1969; Delgado Ruiz 1986; Fernández Flórez 1927; Pitt-Rivers 1983). Others declare that the torero is locked in a homosexual battle with the bull (Ingham 1964; and Marvin [1982, 1988] speaks about the homosexuality of the torero). Still others have insisted upon the hypermasculinity of the torero, while noting the feminine qualities of the bull (Douglass, C. 1984; Tierno Galván 1961).

Freudian theory helped fuse the primitive sacrifice and sex act themes, which led to the idea that bulls were fundamental to rural magic fertility rites. The most important proponent of this idea was Alvarez de Miranda (1962), who wrote on rural Spanish folk legends and folk rituals concerning the bulls. He traced the modern bullfight to an Extremeñan wedding ritual, where the spilling of the bull's blood gave fertility to the couple (1962:115–31).

Ernest Hemingway began writing about the bullfight in the 1930s for an American public that knew almost nothing about the spectacle (Cambria 1991:206). His book *Death in the Afternoon* ([1932]1960) is generally considered excellent for its explanation of what happens in the corrida.

After the Spanish Civil War (1936–1939), which had interrupted both the bullfights and their interpretation, José María Cossío published the first volume of his encyclopedia *Los toros* (1943–1986). Before his death, Cossío had written or directed six of these massive volumes, full of erudite scholarship on every imaginable aspect of los toros. Although descriptive rather than interpretive, Cossío was the first to note that the context of the bullfight was the many patron saint festivals throughout Spain ([1943]1980[1]:637–88).

Until this time, the focus of all interpretation had been the corrida de toros. The sacrifice paradigms refer only to the corrida, since in many of the other taurine games the animal is not killed. Even Alvarez de Miranda, who wrote of the Extremeñan wedding bull (which was not killed), was proposing an origin to the modern corrida. After 1945 and the founding of the Revista de Dialectología y Tradiciones Populares (RDTP), Spanish folklorists began publishing descriptive articles on the other taurine fiestas, more in an effort to portray traditional folk culture before it disappeared than in a desire for global interpretation.

After the 1950s, with the exception of Alvarez de Miranda's important book (1962), scholars stopped their analyses of the bullfight. Spanish writers, especially, seemed to be totally indifferent (Cambria 1974:364). Not until the mid-1970s do we again witness scholarly interest in los toros. Two Spanish anthropologists have written about the place of local forms of los toros in small villages (Mirá 1976; Serrán Pagán 1977, 1979), and others have discussed the role of the *encierro* in Pamplona (del Campo 1980; Echeverría 1983; Serrán Pagán and Muntadas 1980).

Other anthropologists have written interpretations of the corrida and its meaning for Spanish culture (Delgado Ruiz 1986; Douglass, C. 1984; Marvin 1982, 1988; Mitchell 1986, 1988, 1991; Pitt-Rivers 1983). Pitt-Rivers and I both use the sacrifice paradigm, although Pitt-Rivers stresses that the object of *toreo* is for the virility of the bull to pass to its slayer. I posit that the relationship of torero/bull is similar to that of "male"/"female" in the Spanish honor code and that the ultimate message of the bullfight is about dominance and control. Marvin's (1982, 1988) thesis is also about control, self-control, and what it is to be "male" and "human" in Andalusia. Delgado Ruiz argues that the corrida symbolizes the necessary castration of men for the good of society, which he claims is matriarchal in Spain. Timothy J. Mitchell, on the other hand, in a 1986 article dismisses any metaphorical interpretation of the bullfight, seeing it merely as the progressive rationalization of a folk craft: the slaughter of a bull. Ironically, in his 1991 book, *Blood Sport,* Mitchell claims that the rise of modern bullfighting mirrors the uses and abuses of power in nineteenth and twentieth century Spain, thus truly making the bullfight a metaphor for Spanish society. All these anthropologists, except Mitchell and Delgado Ruiz, are careful to delimit their analysis to one specific area of Spain.

Thus, all anthropological or sociological analysis of los toros has focused on only one form at a time, either the corrida or some isolated, local format. No one has sufficiently analyzed the relations between the many forms. Furthermore, by focusing their studies on one village or region, ethnologists have usually avoided confronting the national meaning of the corrida, as well as the national significance of the whole phenomenon of los toros. Due to their common contexts—the patron saint festivals of towns and cities—my own data suggest that the different forms of los toros refer to and yet contrast with each other. Moreover, I assert that los toros serve as a vehicle to talk about and define the *relationships* that are "Spain."

This book is divided into three parts. Part 1, " 'The Bulls' in Spain," introduces the many taurine games, discusses the relationship between them, and relates these relationships to other well-known Spanish debates. Part 2, "Modernity: The Bulls and Europe," deals with the Spanish definition of modernity and describes the two-hundred-year-old debate about Spain's place in Europe. Los toros are used to signify one side of this debate, that Spain is not Europe. To be "European," Spain must eliminate los toros from its culture. The recent resurgence of interest in bullfights seems to be due to the obviation of this debate as Spain becomes officially part of the EEC. In Part 3, "Tradition: The Bulls and Regional Identity," I describe the corrida cycle and discuss how games with bulls, contextualized in patron saint fiestas, reflect ideas about national and local identity. The last three chapters in this part describe three different fiestas in Spain, showing the differing, yet pivotal, role bullfights play in each.

Field Sites and Methodology

Ethnographies of the nation-state were rare after the justified critiques of the national character studies of the 1930s and 1940s (Bateson 1972; Holtzman 1975; Mead 1953). However, now that anthropology posits the possibility of many, even contradictory and opposing, voices within a culture, studies at this level have been reappearing (Handler 1988; Herzfeld 1987; MacDonald 1993; McDonald 1990). Although I speak about Spain, it should be noted that I limited my study to only five provinces. Despite the small percentage of the population that I actually spoke with (in contrast to classical village studies), I was often astounded with the redundancy of the collective representations I found.

This book describes the complexities of identifications with and affection for taurine games in Spain, but I feel confident that what I have described are social categories. Spaniards will recognize themselves here.

Although most of my data comes from fieldwork done during the years 1983–1986, it is important to add that I lived in Barcelona from 1970–1978. Those years witnessed the decline of the dictatorship, the death of General Franco, and the transition to democracy under the constitutional monarchy. Furthermore, during those years citizens realized the extent to which the industrialization and urbanization of Spain had taken place: a new Spain was ready to be born. All of this I saw from the perspective of Catalonia, a prosperous, culturally distinct region located on the Periphery of Spain. Inevitably, my experiences and first-hand knowledge from that period have crept into this analysis of los toros.

Additionally, my husband and his family, who are from Madrid, have given me an intimate knowledge and many first-hand experiences of the Center. Over the past twenty years I have spent many weeks and months living in and visiting the central part of Spain. This knowledge, too, has inevitably seeped into my analysis of los toros.

My friendship and kinship networks, established in the 1970s, were used quite advantageously for my anthropological fieldwork in the 1980s. I often went to small towns or villages where I knew no one and simply plunged into my fieldwork. However, in the larger provincial capitals I contacted people who could serve as my hosts and guides. In all five of my research capitals, people invited me into their homes as the friend of a friend, or the in-law of a friend. Some of these people were professionals (doctors, bankers, nurses, teachers); others were farmers or housewives.

My anthropological fieldwork on los toros took place during several visits to Spain during the years 1983–1986. I visited bull ranches and interviewed at bullfighting schools. I obtained provincial statistics on los toros from the Ministry of Interior in Madrid, as well as in the Autonomous Governments. In these ministries, I spent hours talking to officials, clerks, and secretaries. I went to taurine clubs, art expositions, conferences, and symposiums. I worked in the Hemeroteca Nacional reading and analyzing coverage of los toros in the daily newspapers of the five research provinces for a period of six months (from March to June 1985).

I traveled to the capital city of each research province, interviewed, and attended the major festival (twice in some cases). I also attended fiestas in small villages in each province. In two provinces, I lived in villages for two months. Everywhere I interviewed, both formally and informally, as many different people as possible, taking care to include people of all classes, ages, and persuasions of los toros—from taxi cab drivers and bartenders to members of the aristocracy.

Even when I was not in Spain during these years, my fieldwork was able to continue. Not only do I have access to native Spaniards who are visiting, studying, or working here in Charlottesville, but I have several times telephoned Spain to obtain information that I realized was missing. Both Gallup Spain S.A. and Alef S.A. sent several of their polls on los toros to me. Friends and kin from all over Spain, who know of my research, have spontaneously sent me articles and books on the subject during the past ten years. I returned to Spain in the summer of 1989 and again in 1992 to do archival work as well as fieldwork on associated projects. During those years I continued speaking to people and studying los toros. I remain astounded that in all this time so little has changed in the conversation about "the bulls."

Part 1

"THE BULLS" IN SPAIN

Chapter 1

THE BULL AND BULL FESTIVALS

El Toro

Representations of the bull can be found in paleolithic paintings in the caves of Altamira, Celti-iberian stone statues of four small bulls in Guisando, Bronze Age bull masks from the Mediterranean coasts, bullfights in Madrid's Plaza Mayor, etchings of bulls by Goya, and bicycle-handle bull horns by Picasso. It has been the protagonist of countless poems, philosophies, books, and films. Expressions about the Spanish bull infiltrate the Spanish language. Mounted majestic heads of black bulls adorn innumerable bars, museums, and homes all over Spain. "The bull is the totem of Spain," is a statement voiced by many Spaniards and expressed in a variety of literature. However, it does not imply agreement with or acceptance of the bullfight.

The "bull" *(el toro)* refers to the animal of the breed *Bos taurus* L. *africanus,* popularly known as the toro bravo. Usually *el toro* refers to the uncastrated male animal, but there are times when *toro* also stands for a female cow *(vaca)* of this breed.[1] Although there are other breeds of cattle in Spain, which are used for both milk and meat, those uncastrated males—bulls—are usually called *sementales* (studs), or *machos* (males), words used with other species as well (e.g., horses and hogs).

Spaniards claim that the toro bravo descends from the original wild bull *(Bos primigenius)* that populated the plains and forests of northern, central, and southern Europe. This wild animal, called *aurock* by the Germans, or *urus* in the Latin languages, existed alongside the tame, domesticated stock. The last surviving example of the aurock supposedly died out in northern and central Europe between 1627 and 1700 (Ortega y Gasset [1950]1985:53).

According to Spaniards, the toro bravo is also wild, but in a cultural rather than natural sense. They have been raised on ranches in Spain since at least the mid-eighteenth century (Romero de Solis 1983). The word *bravo* when applied to animals means "wild and untamed."

"Tame" *(manso)* is not a positive characteristic in Spain. Mansos are those animals used for meat, milk, or labor,[2] and for a Spaniard there is nothing particularly admirable about an animal that lets itself be yoked to a cart or plow, or walks obligingly to its death in the slaughterhouse.[3]

Bravo, when applied to animals, also means "fierce," or "ferocious." This characteristic, translated into the willingness of the bull to spontaneously charge and gore a man, or any other object, is what Spaniards and *aficionados* think is peculiar and essential to the toro bravo. This characteristic is intrinsic, and breeders try to pass down this "behavior" through carefully monitored blood lines. This willingness to charge is celebrated in Spain and is the basis of the many taurine games. A bull's nobility *(nobleza)* is based on his "honesty." If the bull consistently charges the horse and the cape but does not try to gore the man's body, the bull is called "noble."

When applied to humans, *bravo/a* means "brave and courageous," "fine and excellent," "sumptuous and magnificent," "angry and violent," and "swaggering and blustering." There is much overlapping, however, between the human and animal spheres. After all, a "toro muy bravo" is very courageous, fine, sumptuous, and violent, as well as wild.

The toro, people emphasize, is indigenous to Spain. There is no other bovine like it anywhere.[4] Many Spaniards, both bullfighting fans and critics alike, said they thought the bull was the most beautiful animal in the world and that nothing is more attractive or imposing than a "brave bull."

The bull is the "totem of Spain" because it is identified with Spain and with Spaniards. The Iberian Peninsula was described by the Roman geographer Strabo in the first century as having the shape of a bull's hide *(piel de toro)*. This metaphor is constantly used to refer to Spain.

To hear a Spaniard say "The bull is the totem of Spain" should be riveting for an anthropologist. A great deal of anthropological theory (especially about identity) emerged from the study of totemism. In general, anthropologists use the term *totemism* to refer to a group's symbolic representation of its belief about its interrelatedness (in a genealogical or pseudogenealogical way) with particular plants or animals. Often this relationship forms the basis for ritual activities and ceremonies. Since the totem and the individuals of the group are thought to be of the same flesh, ritualistic dietary restrictions on eating the totem frequently exist. Some groups have rules against eating their ancestral totem. Others share the totem in a communal meal. Lévi-Strauss (1962) maintained, however, that totems were not only "good to eat, but good to think." Relationships between totemic animals often parallel social relationships between groups.

The bull has been a theme and metaphor in Spanish poetry and literature since the thirteenth century (Cossío 1944, [1947]1965[2]; Roldán 1970), but it is Rafael Alberti, the internationally respected Spanish poet, who created the specific symbol "Spain as toro." In several works published in the 1940s, this influential poet helped to establish the "Spain as bull" theme (Roldán 1970:346).

Many times people confided to me the following anecdote: "The toro bravo has the life for which every Spaniard secretly longs. For all his life, the toro lives in liberty in the countryside. He is given the best food and the best pastures. He does no work. He is free. At the end of his life, instead of walking placidly to the slaughterhouse, he is given a chance to display the wonderful characteristics of his breed and die in glory in the bullring." In Spain this anthropomorphism of the bull stresses freedom (lack of work), independence, and a moment of glory—all of which make life worthwhile (see Bennassar [1979] for more on the role of these qualities in Spanish culture). Often, I was not sure whether the informant was identifying with this description of the bull's life or implicitly criticizing other Spaniards and the so-called Spanish character.

Hispanist T. J. Mitchell (1986:410) has called the bull one of the "most powerful generators of cultural specificity Spain has known." The bull means Spain. Unlike the Spanish flag, the image of the black Spanish bull is used in many forms of advertising as a subtle symbol of identification. Many products from sherry to copy machines, sunflower seeds, and publishing houses are advertised using bulls in some form or another. The Spanish countryside is dotted with huge, black billboards in the shape of a bull, so lifelike that during my first years in Spain I thought these were real bulls standing in the middle of fields or on the crests of hills. Originally these billboards were advertisements for Osborne brandy; though billboard advertising is now prohibited outside of towns, these lifelike billboards are preserved as artistic national monuments (figure 1.1). Spaniards have also used the bull to represent Spain to the world. In 1982 a drawing of a bull was the official mascot of the World Cup Soccer Championships, and in 1986 a bull was the official emblem of the World Swimming Championships.

The bull is a totem, then, not in any strict anthropological sense, but because it stands for all of "Spain." Furthermore, informants often mentioned that the bull is ultimately eaten. The animal is butchered

Figure 1.1. Bull billboard that has been "pardoned" by the Spanish state. The name of the brandy that the billboard originally advertised has been painted out. (Postcard courtesy of Gráficas Siete Revueltas; photographed by Javier Andrada)

right after the fight and sold (or given away) at a special stand at the market. Thus, this "totem" is "sacrificed" for general consumption.

Los Toros

In English the term *bullfight* usually calls to mind an image of one spectacle: the *corrida de toros*. There are actually many different kinds of games with bulls in Spain, at least sixteen. The term *los toros* (literally "the bulls") can at once refer to all the bovine spectacles, or, depending on the speaker and context, to just one of them, la corrida de toros. In the sentence "Two basic elements of national folklore, the religious themes and los toros are repeatedly found in the *fiestas*" (Garrigues 1984:76), *los toros* clearly refers to all the many forms of taurine spectacles. However, the expressions *"vamos a los toros"* (let's go to the bullfight) and *"a los toros"* (to the bullfight) refer specifically to the corrida de toros.

Given these two different references of the term *los toros,* Spaniards sometimes seem to contradict themselves. Javier, a university student from Barcelona, made a typical comment. He told me that he did not like los toros (meaning corrida) and yet later in the same conversation told me he was going to go to Pamplona that summer to fulfill a lifelong ambition: to run with los toros (meaning *encierro*).

Although *los toros* is the general encompassing reference to the bulls, another series of expressions is used to refer to taurine spectacles. These expressions all include the word *fiesta:* for example, *la fiesta de toros, la fiesta del toro, las fiestas de toros, la fiesta taurina,* and *la fiesta nacional.* Furthermore, in many taurine contexts, one simply says "la fiesta." *Fiesta* refers to any celebration and is frequently translated as "public rejoicing," "festival," or "holiday." *Fiesta* is a cognate of *feast* in English, and eating plays an important role in all fiestas. Historically the taurine spectacles have always been referred to as fiestas (i.e., fiesta de toros). Moreover, the verb translated as "to have" in the expression "to have a bullfight" has always been "to celebrate" *(celebrarse).* These expressions, like the expression *los toros,* can either encompass all the taurine spectacles at once or refer to just one: la corrida.

However, one of these expressions, *la fiesta nacional* (the national fiesta), deserves further comment. *La fiesta nacional* is much more polemical than any of the other "fiesta" expressions. The problem lies not with the term *fiesta* but with the word *nacional,* an adjective associated with la corrida de toros since at least the seventeenth century. Before its present form (a man on foot fighting a bull), when it was still a spectacle of mounted aristocrats spearing bulls from horseback, the corrida was already known as a "national" spectacle. By the eighteenth century, scholars began to debate the use of the adjective *nacional* with the bulls, and this debate has continued to the present time. The objections to the adjective *nacional* are related to Spain's internal and external definition of itself: Is the "bullfight" truly national? That is, does it exist in all parts of Spain? And does the "bullfight" appropriately represent "Spain?"

Polemical or not, the term *fiesta nacional* is used to refer to the corrida de toros: *ABC,* the conservative monarchist national newspaper, titles its section dealing with corridas de toros, "La fiesta nacional." The expression is often used to encompass and describe all the taurine spectacles in Spain. Yet because of the word *nacional,* this expression is not used in certain regions or by those who dislike the bullfight. In summary, *la fiesta nacional* is in many ways more of a politically motivated choice of terms than *los toros,* but in other ways the expressions function similarly.

Later in this chapter, I describe fifteen different categories (called *modalidades*) of taurine fiestas in Spain: *corrida de toros; corrida de no-*

villos picados; corrida de toros de rejones; corrida de novillos de rejones; corrida de novillos sin picador; becerrada; toreo cómico; festival; recortadores; tienta; encierro; capea; vaquillas; suelta de reses; and *toro de fuego.* A sixteenth category, which I label miscellaneous, groups all of the unique fiestas that are specific to a single locality. I divide these sixteen categories into three formats: "national formats," "local formats," and "intermediate formats," a combination of national and local formats (table 1.1).

In the "national" format each fiesta's rules are defined and regulated from Madrid through the Ministry of Interior (see *Reglamento de Espectáculos Taurinos* [1962]1982). The same thing will happen in a novillada whether in Madrid, Sevilla, or Teruel. These categories have national rules. The central government through its local representatives

Table 1.1 Categories of los Toros

National Formats	Intermediate Formats	Local Formats
corrida de toros (4–5-year-old bull, fight on foot)	becerrada (2-year-old calf, fight)	encierro (run through town to ring with bulls or calves)
corrida de novillos picados (3–4-year-old calf, fight including picador)	toreo cómico (comic calf fight)	capea (cape work, male calves)
	festival (charity benefit calf fight)	vaquillas (female calves freed in ring)
corrida de toros de rejones (4–5-year-old bull, fight on horseback)		
	recortadores (cow dodgers)	suelta de reses (animals in streets)
corrida de novillos de rejones (3–4-year-old calf, fight on horseback)		
	tienta (calf tests on ranch)	miscellaneous (unique forms)
corrida de novillos sin picador (2–3-year-old calf, fight not including picador)		toro de fuego (man and fireworks)

(Gobierno Civil, or since 1981, the Gobierno Autónomo) grants permission to hold these fiestas.

On the other hand, "local" formats have rules defined only by citizens of the town holding the event. The same thing will not happen in an encierro in Navarra and in one in Madrid. The regional government supposedly grants permission to hold these fiestas, but apparently many small towns never bother to get this permission. For example, the ranch owners that provide the animals for the many local fiestas gave me numbers that were much higher than the official figures. Others also describe the spontaneous organization of a *suelta de vaquillas,* on the day it occurs, without first seeking permission from anywhere (Mirá 1976). These fiestas are not spectacles, but rather communal activities.

A definite hierarchy exists among the various taurine fiestas. The hierarchy is an implicit ranking, from more important to less important, from more "serious" *(serio)* to less serious.[5] This ranking can be elicited in several ways: by asking the national or local government officials in charge of taurine affairs, by comparing fees charged for holding a taurine fiesta, or by talking to "people on the street," who could spontaneously name several categories, always beginning with the corrida de toros and ending with vaquillas or some isolated, unique, local form. The intermediate categories had various orderings, according to the speaker and province (table 1.2). Dedicated corrida fans always ranked the corrida first and would hardly even consider the lower "local" forms: the capeas, for example. "They aren't serious," these aficionados said. Or, "They are barbarous." However, even where people told me they preferred vaquillas or encierros, they inevitably, if reluctantly, ranked the corridas as "more important" or "more serious."

Context

Fiestas

National bullfights are called shows or "spectacles" *(espectáculos),* but they are not spectacles like cinema or soccer.[6] Most of the time los toros are embedded in other celebrations and holidays. The vast majority of taurine fiestas take place exclusively within the context of the patron saint festivals *(fiestas patronales)* or major festivals *(fiestas mayores)* of the many cities and villages throughout Spain.

Madrid, Sevilla, Valencia, and a few other big cities are exceptions in that they offer many taurine spectacles outside of their fiestas mayores.

Table 1.2 Hierarchy per Province

	Sevilla	Navarra	Madrid	Valencia	Vizcaya
National Formats					
corrida de toros (bullfight on foot)	1. corrida de toros	1. corrida de toros	1. corrida de toros	1. corrida de toros	1. corrida de toros
novillada picada (3–4-year-old calf, fight inc. picador)	2. novilladas picadas	2. novilladas picadas	2. corridas de toros de rejones	2. novillada picada	2. novillada con picador
corrida de toros de rejones (bullfight on horseback)			3. corrida de novillos picados	3. corrida de toros de rejones	3. corrida de rejones
corrida de novillos de rejones (calf, fight on horseback)			4. corrida de novillos de rejones	4. novillada picada de rejones	
novillada sin picador (2–3-year-old calf, fight not inc. picador)	3. novilladas sin picador	3. novillada sin picador	5. corrida de novillos sin picadores	5. novillada sin picar	4. novillada sin picadores
Intermediate Formats					
becerrada (2-year-old calf, fight)	4. festival	4. becerradas	6. corrida de becerros	6. becerrada	5. becerrada
toreo cómico (comic calf fight)	5. becerradas	5. festivales taurinos	7. becerrada–toreo cómico	7. cómico taurino	6. cómico
festival (charity benefit)	6. cómico	6. festivales cómico–taurinos		8. festival benéfico	7. becerrada benéfica
recortadores (dodge female calves)	7. rejones				
tientas (tests on ranches)					
Local Formats					
encierros (run through town to ring)		7. encierros–vaquillas	8. encierro	9. encierro de reses bravas (vaquillas and toros embolados)	

Table 1.2 (*Continued*)

	Sevilla	Navarra	Madrid	Valencia	Vizcaya
Local Formats (cont'd)					
capeas					
(cape work,					
male animals)					
vaquillas	8. vaquillas		9. toreo de		8. suelta de
(female calves			vaquillas		vaquillas
freed in ring)					
suelta de reses			10. festival		9. sokamuturra
(animals in					
streets)					
miscellaneous					
(unique forms)					
toro de fuego					
(man and					
fireworks)					

They have their own "seasons." However, their best and most important schedules of bullfighters and bulls (*carteles,* literally, "posters") are arranged for the week and/or weeks of their big fiestas, for example, Valencia during Las Fallas (March), Sevilla during Feria de Abril (April), and Madrid during San Isidro (May–June).

Other than in a few big cities, taurine fiestas usually take place exclusively within the context of a town's major festival (fiesta mayor), as is true for Bilbao and Pamplona. A *fiesta taurina* is thus not an entertaining spectacle, but is instead an integral part of a town fiesta. Except in a few capital cities, to have los toros means the town is in fiestas. Although many towns cannot afford to have a bullfight, or choose not to have one, those that do have bullfights hold them during their town fiestas only *once* a year.

During the days devoted to a town's fiestas, bullfights are just one of many activities offered. Depending on the size and traditions of the town, there are dances, fireworks, art expositions, music, bicycle races, cooking contests, theater, folk dances, street vendors selling food and souvenirs, and parades. The bigger the town, the more activities there are offered. If the fiestas commemorate a saint or virgin, masses, processions, and offerings will also honor the saint (see table 1.3 for the schedule of a town's fiesta activities). In some provinces these other activities are considered mere padding and los toros are the truly defining char-

Table 1.3 Activities during Fiestas in Guadalajara and Pamplona

Guadalajara May 31, 1985		Pamplona July 11, 1986	
10:00	Encierro	6:45	Music, dianas
	Suelta de vaquillas	8:00	Encierro
11:00	Encierro "chico"	8:30	Encierro txiki
11:30	Children's activities	9:30	Parade of Giants
12:00	Jogging: The Urban Mile	10:30	Mass: San Fermín
12:30	Regional folklore parade	12:00	Concert: regional music
13:30	Bicycle race	12:30	Parade of bands
14:00	Hour to rest	17:30	Parade of the mules
17:00	Viva la Música (5 groups)		to the bullring
18:00	Corrida	18:00	Corrida
22:20	Fireworks	18:30	Children's Festival Theater
23:00	Dance with band	20:00	Children's party
		21:00	Regional music
		22:00	Toro de fuego
		23:00	Fireworks
		24:00	Parade of bands
		24:30	Popular dance

acteristic of the fiesta. Even the religious saints being honored play a secondary role, and there is much less participation at the masses and saints' processions than at los toros.

Although a town has los toros because it is in fiestas, in many ways it is possible to say that a town is in fiestas because it has los toros. This is especially true of small towns and cities that include the local, lower-level taurine categories in their fiestas. Anthropologist Joan Mirá says of the north of Valencia, "The fiesta and 'the bulls' almost become identical; the days of fiesta are the days of 'the bulls' and everything else passes to a secondary plane" (Mirá 1976:112, my translation). This was also my impression in many of the small towns where I attended los toros.

However, a schoolteacher in his mid-thirties told me he knew nothing about los toros and he thought they lacked significance for most people these days. He thought soccer was more important to people of his generation. Although the man worked in Valencia city, he was originally from a small, nearby town. When asked about his town fiestas, he admitted that there were toros during the fiestas. I then asked if he could imagine the fiestas without los toros. The question seemed to surprise him. He looked at me and could not answer. He thought a second, I suppose trying to imagine the fiesta without toros, and concluded that it would be strange. Of course, this man reacted at first to my questions about los toros, assuming that I meant la corrida as a spectacle unto itself. Los toros contextualized as vaquillas or toro embolado in his town's fiestas evoked a different response.

Even in larger towns, though, los toros mean fiestas. Although it is not possible to say of large cities that "la fiesta is los toros," for most people in these cities los toros are a significant symbol of the fiestas, a necessary part of the many elements that make up the fiestas.

During the month of May, enormous posters announcing the bullfight schedules of Madrid's San Isidro fiesta are plastered all over the city: in every subway stop, in the buses, in the streets, in the store windows, in bars. Madrid's newspapers, which also have a national distribution, dramatically increase their space devoted to the bullfight, from one-half or one page daily to two to four pages daily. In Madrid in 1985 and 1986, many other events having to do with the fiesta nacional were held during this time, for example, colloquiums about los toros, bullfighting poster expositions, taurine art expositions, and conferences on various aspects of the corridas. It is possible for the vast majority of Madrileños to ignore these important bullfights, but most people probably know these corridas are going on. On June 7, 1985, during the San Isidro fiestas, one *torero*, Antoñete, was carried out of the Main Door (Puerta Grande) of the bullring on his fans' shoulders, a sign of triumph. The next day the five major newspapers in Madrid carried the story and pictures on the front page. Radio and television also had stories about Antoñete's "afternoon of glory." Thus, even without the slightest interest in los toros, most Madrileños would be able to associate San Isidro with corridas de toros.

Depending on the number of days the festival lasts, a town may offer one or more taurine fiestas. Large urban centers usually offer a selection of only upper-level national spectacles. However, some provincial capitals also offer lower-level, local taurine fiestas. In smaller towns, the fiesta mayor most often offers only lower-level, local taurine spectacles. Table 1.4 shows examples of the kinds of taurine spectacles offered.

In the 1970s the numbers of corridas began to drop. Many people said these fiestas were dying out in response to a new, modern Spain. However, people were comparing the drop in numbers to the large

Table 1.4 Kinds of Taurine Spectacles Given during Fiestas

Year	Province	Town	Population	Spectacle	Date
1984	Sevilla	Ecija	34,619	corrida	9/22
				toreo cómico	9/23
	Sevilla	Paradas	6,408	nov. sin pic.	5/12
				suelta de vaquilla	5/13
	Sevilla	Lebrija	24,744	suelta de vaquilla	9/8
				rejones	9/9
				toreo cómico	9/11
	Navarra	Fitero	2,186	nov. con pic.	9/15
				nov. sin pic.	9/9
				8 encierros	9/9–16
	Navarra	Tudela	24,629	nov. con pic.	7/28
				toreo cómico	7/27
				6 encierros	7/25–30
	Madrid	Pozuelo de Alarcón	29,495	4 nov. sin pic.	9/3–8
				2 becerradas	9/6–7
				6 encierros	9/3–8
	Madrid	Aranjuez	35,936	2 corridas	9/5, 8
				nov. con pic.	9/9
				becerrada	9/2
				4 encierros	9/2, 5, 8, 9
	Madrid	Brunete	1,068	nov. sin pic.	9/15
				toreo cómico	9/16
				becerrada	9/17
				3 encierros	9/15–17
	Vizcaya	Orozco	2,092	2 nov. con pic.	9/1–2
				becerrada	9/4
1985	Valencia	Játiva	23,755	corrida	8/16
				nov. con pic.	8/15
				toreo cómico	8/19

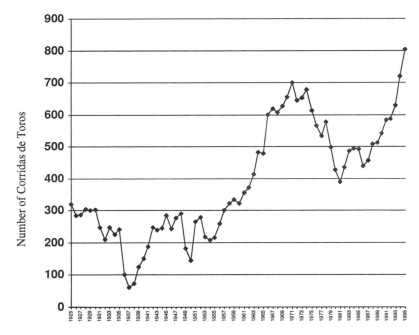

Figure 1.2. Corridas during the twentieth century in Spain (*"Los toros en el siglo XX en España"* 1995 : 3)

number of corridas celebrated during the 1960s. Partly in response to European tourism, corridas de toros had almost tripled in number from 145 in 1950 to 645 in 1970 (figure 1.2). Bullfights were given in small tourist towns all along the Mediterranean coasts, where they had never before been celebrated. Other cities on the coasts dramatically increased their number of corridas, offering them outside of their traditional fiesta contexts, obviously for tourist consumption. Interior cities, however, which have never depended on tourism, barely changed the number of corridas offered during these dates (table 1.5). Thus, what was truly happening in the 1970s was an elimination of the extra tourist corridas and a return to the context of corridas solely within the fiesta mayor. Surprisingly, since 1982, corridas and other taurine fiestas have again grown in number, this time for internal consumption, as towns have added more days to their fiesta celebrations.

Seasons

With few exceptions, taurine fiestas are celebrated between March and October. Most aficionados agreed in saying that the season *(tempo-*

Table 1.5 Number of Corridas de Toros

City, Town, or Village	Location	1960	1970	1984
Gerona	Costa Brava	0	6	0
San Feliu		11	8	0
Lloret		1	11	5
Tarragona		2	5	7
Viñaroz		2	4	1
Benidorm		0	13	6
Malaga	Costa del Sol	10	20	8
Torremolinos		0	11	2
Marbella		0	13	6
Velez-Malaga		0	6	0
Fuengirola	Basque Coast	0	8	3
Ondara		1	7	1
Palma de Mallora	Baleares Islands	18	32	6
Ibiza		0	3	0
Santa Cruz de Tenerife	Canary Islands	0	2	0

rada) really begins in Valencia the week of its fiestas, Las Fallas, on March 19. The bullfighting season ends around October 12 with Zaragoza's fiestas. These dates refer specifically to corridas rather than any of the other spectacles.

Besides the March to October dates, some people gave me a different set of months for the bullfighting season. When I interviewed in the Gobierno Civil in Pamplona, I was told that "the season goes from July to September." In Sevilla, people said "the season runs from Easter Sunday to June." In Madrid, almost everyone told me the season was from March to September. Only later did I realize that these "seasons" corresponded with the traditional dates of corridas celebrated in that specific city or province. In other words, there was a national season and a local season. Many people followed the national corrida season to a greater or lesser degree, tracking toreros' performances in the various fiestas around Spain from March to October, but in some places it was also possible to talk about one ring's local temporada. Most Spanish cities and towns, however, do not have a "season," but rather celebrate taurine fiestas only once, perhaps twice, between March and October.

Most taurine fiestas take place during August and September, as this is when most Spanish *pueblos* and towns celebrate their fiesta mayor. During these months, especially between August 15 (the feast of the Assumption, the most important of the Marian fiestas) and September 8 (another Marian fiesta, the Birth of the Virgin), twice the number of towns celebrate fiestas than during any other months (Velasco 1982b; tables 1.6 and 1.7).

When asked why there could not be a fiesta taurina in November or December, people answered that a fiesta de toros needs sun *(hace falta sol)*. When I pointed out that there was sun in winter, people then said it had to be sunny *and* hot. Sure enough, in March and April especially, corridas were often canceled because of bad weather—rain, wind, and cold. And on the day of a corrida, a common comment among friends is, "Let's see if there is sun today." In Bilbao in May 1985, the newspaper critics blamed poor attendance at the bullring on the cold and lack of sun: "Not much bullfighting ambience due to the cold and gray skies" ("Novillada" 1985:45). The lack of sun was also given as the reason for why there is no *afición a los toros* in Galicia. In this part of

Table 1.6 Calendar of Taurine Fiestas

1984	Sevilla	Madrid	Navarra	Valencia	Vizcaya
January	1	5	0	13	0
February	2	14	0	21	0
March	5	12	18	31	0
April	9	32	13	50	0
May	22	98	17	44	2
June	5	84	19	83	5
July	3	51	70	151	15
August 1–15	8	45	66	517	6
August 16–September 15	20	275	317	492	31
September 16–30	6	61	44	266	4
October	0	82	28	74	2
November	0	0	0	11	0
December	0	0	0	2	0

Table 1.7 National Figures of Taurine Fiestas

	Corridas	Novilladas
January	1	1
February	2	3
March	10	11
April	24	20
May	50	25
June	52	34
July	73	96
August	137	79
September	121	116
October	23	13
November	0	0
December	0	0
Totals	493	398

Spain, known as "green Spain," it rains a lot. One evening in Madrid a group of middle-class professionals agreed that Galicia lacked sunshine, an essential ingredient for the bullfight. Sun, like the bull, is intimately associated with "Spain."[7]

The reason given for the shorter "seasons" in Navarra and Sevilla was heat. Navarrans said there were no toros before July because the weather was not warm enough until then. For "los toros you need hot weather," but Navarra is in the north of Spain and includes the Pyrenees Mountains. On the other hand, in Sevilla the season of corridas lasts only until June.[8] There I was told that after June it gets "too hot." Only the most dedicated aficionados will go to los toros in the intense heat of Sevilla's summer. Sevilla is in the southern and hottest part of Spain. Thus, in Navarra there is not enough heat until July for a corrida, while in Sevilla there is too much heat in July.

Day/Time

Tourist literature about the corrida generally says they take place on Sundays. However, since most taurine spectacles are celebrated during the week of a town's fiestas, they actually end up falling on every day of the week. Therefore, to say the Spanish have bullfights on Sundays (Marvin 1982; Pitt-Rivers 1983, 1993) is to describe just corridas in a few urban centers. This is not the predominant pattern.

Furthermore, this same literature says that los toros take place in the afternoon. Pitt-Rivers (1983, 1993) thought it significant that the corrida takes place on Sunday afternoon, after morning mass. However, this social fact corresponds only to the corrida. The other taurine fiestas take place in the morning or afternoon, and the hour varies from place to place. The encierro of Pamplona begins at 8:00 A.M. and in Manzanares (Madrid) at 9:00 A.M. In some towns an animal is let loose to run in the streets in the morning and later again in the afternoon. In Valencia, lighting of the torches on the toro embolado takes place at midnight.

Categories: Las Fiestas de Toros

National Formats

Corrida de toros. This form of "bullfighting" was established in the eighteenth century in southern Spain (Andalusia), following the decline of a centuries-old tradition of aristocratic bullfighting from horseback.[9] The two principal characters in a corrida de toros are the torero (the bullfighter) and the toro (the bull).

In the corrida, three professional toreros each kill two bulls, one at a time. To become a torero a boy must spend many long years of training and practice and work his way up through the rank of *novillero.* Since 1976 it has been legal for women to be professional bullfighters, but it took twenty years for one to attain the rank of *torera.* The "graduation" to torero depends on the boy's successes in the lower national-format taurine fiestas (i.e., becerradas, novilladas). It used to be said that aspirants to torero came from the lower classes and that becoming a bullfighter was a way to change one's social status. Since the 1980s middle-class boys also attend the various taurine schools.

In the bullring the torero dresses in a silk suit, embroidered in gold or silver threads, called a "suit of lights" *(traje de luces).* The torero directs a team of men *(picadores* and *bandarilleros)* whose job it is to help him dominate and kill the bull. A well-known behavior etiquette governs the relations between a torero and his team *(cuadrilla)* and between one torero and another. Deference to seniority and generosity are key values that reign in the relations between the men in the ring.

Grace, skill, intelligence, and courage are the values looked for in the relationship between the man and the bull. A torero should never show fear, should always stand his ground, should never have to "run away," should never be ungraceful (i.e., lose his balance), and should always dominate and never be dominated. The names of successful toreros are well known all over Spain, and for a torero to die in the ring almost immediately ensures hero status.

The bull must be a certain age (four to five years old) and/or a certain weight (470 kilograms in first category rings) before being sent to the bullring. The bull must be a physical virgin, as well as a "virgin" to the cape, which the torero uses to attract the bull and make it charge.

A bull's defensive and offensive weapons are his horns, and an authentic fetish has built up around the bull's horns. To ensure the element of danger, which is said to be the true essence of the corrida, the Spanish government is in charge of overseeing that a bull's horns are "intact" (i.e., have not been cut, filed, or shaved, thus giving the torero an advantage).[10] The ring president or the public can reject a bull and have him taken out if his horns are not intact.

A bull is also rejected if his appearance *(presencia)* is judged unfit for a particular ring. Such a bull is called *defectuoso,* which is a matter of collective aesthetics. In Madrid during the 1985 San Isidro fiestas, the veterinarians rejected many bulls long before the animals entered the ring. The public rejected many more in the ring for the slightest perceived flaw, such as a damaged horn or a slightly dragging hoof.

The toro bravo used in a corrida is bred on only certain accredited, registered ranches, which are known collectively as the Unión de Criadores de Toros de Lidia, and long genealogies of each animal attest to his "purity." As a yearling, the bull is tested for his fighting spirit. Those who fail the test are sent either to lower-level taurine fiestas (i.e., novilladas) or to the slaughterhouse.

The process of the corrida itself follows strict canons of time and style. It begins with a ceremonial parade of the ring officials followed by three toreros and their assistants. Each of the three toreros has twenty minutes to fight and kill one bull, and then each kills a second bull. When the bull enters the ring, colored ribbons representing the ranch adorn his back. The bull's head is initially held high, but it must come down for the torero to be able to kill the bull from the ground. During the first part of the corrida, the bull runs excitedly around the ring and the torero learns about the bull by "passing" him with a cape *(capa)* and watching others pass him to see if he prefers one part of the ring to another, and to judge whether the bull tends to gore to one particular side or the other. At this point, if the bull does not charge or if he retreats, he is enticed out of the ring.

Each fight is divided into three parts *(tercios)*. The first tercio is that of the picador. Two horsemen enter the ring on blindfolded draft horses that are padded to protect them from the bull's horns. While the bull charges the horse, the rider (picador) uses a long lance to spear the muscle on the back of the bull's neck, which tires the muscle, and thus begins the work of lowering the bull's head. According to the rules, the bull must charge the horse three times, although sometimes the torero instructs the picador not to spear the bull hard three times, so as to save the animal's strength.

The second tercio is signaled by a horn. The horses and riders leave the ring, and the placing of the *bandarillas* begins. The bandarillas are beribboned, short, barbed spears. This time men on the ground, sometimes the torero, but usually two members of his team, place the bandarillas from directly in front of the bull into the hump of the charging bull's neck.

The last tercio is the high point of the corrida, when the torero will thrill or disappoint the public with the relationship he establishes with the bull. Although ostensibly preparing a bull for the kill, this part of the corrida is an end in itself and composes the "artistic" portion of the fiesta. The torero works with a small, stiff cape held out on a stick *(la muleta)*. The animal is tired and slower now, but still very dangerous. The torero bravely "passes" the bull, exposing himself to the sharp horns as much as he dares. The public looks for long, slow turns by the bull both past and around the stationary torero. The style, the rhythm, and the number of consecutive passes are the true essence of the corrida. Control is the torero's goal. The passes show whether the torero is controlling the bull or if the bull is intimidating, and thus controlling, the torero. The torero must work within the time limits to dominate the bull artistically.

When the bull has been stopped and his head lowered sufficiently, the torero calls for his sword *(estoque)*. After lining up the bull's feet, the torero is ready for the kill. With the muleta in his left hand, he lures the bull's head down further, while his right hand and sword go between and over the horns and penetrate the *cruce* (cross, crossroads, junction), the route to the aorta, the severance of which spells instant death for the bull. This is a very dangerous moment, called the *hora de la verdad* (moment of truth). If the bull does not follow the cape and instead raises his head, the torero almost certainly will be gored. A bull that falls dead on the first attempt signifies a well-fought, risk-filled bullfight. Most bulls, however, require a second or third try and often must be finished off by having their spinal cord cut with a knife once they have collapsed to the ground.

Corrida de novillos picados/novilladas picadas. Novilladas follow the exact same rituals and process—dress, time limits, etc.—as the corrida de toros except that instead of bulls (toros), calves *(novillos)* are used, and instead of a torero killing the animal, a novillero kills it. Otherwise the same "seriousness" and order pertain as in the corrida de toros. A novillo is a male animal between three and four years old that does not weigh more than 410 kilograms.[11] A novillero is an aspirant to the profession of torero who has not yet attained that rank.[12] The term *picadas* in this category means the picador performs in this spectacle.

Corrida de toros de rejones. Although this spectacle is relatively new, having reappeared in Spain in the 1920s after a century's absence, fans see it as a continuation of the aristocratic tradition of fighting bulls on horseback. The riders, in contrast to toreros, are often members of the aristocracy, or are at least landed gentry.

The rider *(rejoneador)* does not wear a "suit of lights" like the torero, but rather wears a "country outfit" *(traje campera* or *traje corto):* a short, dark leather jacket; leather chaps; and wide-brimmed hat. This is the outfit of a southern Andalusian gentleman. An important aspect of these outfits is that they look "used," as if the riders actually wore them while working on their ranches. The horses are also an Andalusian breed, raised on ranches, like the bulls, by these wealthy gentlemen.

In this spectacle, a rider takes a bull through the various stages astride a horse. The rejoneador may use three different kinds of spears before he tries to kill the bull with the longer *rejón de muerte* (sword), shot out of a springlike mechanism. The rejoneador executes all the tercios by himself, although he has a team to help him. Rather than debilitating the bull excessively, the many weapons serve as an excuse for an exhibition of horsemanship. The rejoneador tries to kill the bull from horseback but may use only two rejones de muerte. If necessary, he must get off his horse and kill the bull on the ground. This spectacle is frequently inserted in the middle of a corrida de toros. At other times the entire fiesta consists of bulls killed by rejoneadores.

Although mature bulls are used, the public does not consider this spectacle as "serious" as la corrida. In fact, in some ways *rejoneo* is considered a bit effeminate, and men say it is a spectacle for women. The press also refers to it that way.

The difference for Spaniards between rejoneo and corrida is the measure of "risk" involved. First, the horse rider does not expose himself to death or serious injury, as does the torero on the ground. Second, in rejoneo the tips of the bull's horns are usually blunted or covered, thus again reducing the risk and "seriousness" of the spectacle.

Corrida de novillos para rejones. This spectacle is exactly the same as the above, the only difference being the substitution of the younger animal (novillo) for the bull (toro).

Corrida de novillos sin picador/novilladas sin picador. In this spectacle, picadores do not participate. The animals, between two and three years old and not weighing more than 210 kilograms, are even less expensive than those used in novilladas with picadores. The novillero, dressed in a "suit of lights," performs in these fiestas.

Intermediate Formats

Corrida de becerros/becerradas. Becerradas are the lowest level of spectacles with a national format and are the center axis between the national and local formats. There are three types of becerradas: by students of bullfighting schools; by professional toreros, usually for charity; and by aficionados. In this spectacle the male calf, *becerro,* must be no older than two years.

There are several bullfighting schools *(escuelas taurinas)* where young boys are formally taught to fight bulls, located in different parts of Spain. A school periodically offers an exhibition with calves. The boys dress in their traje de luces and, except for the absence of the picador, the becerrada is organized with the same "seriousness and order" as a corrida de toros.

In a second type of becerrada, a torero offers to fight a becerro for no monetary compensation, and any profit made on this spectacle goes to charity. Such fiestas are usually called *festivales* (see below). The torero never wears his "suit of lights," but rather dresses in street clothes or a "country outfit." Since the torero is not paid for his performance, the points on the animal's horns have often been blunted, lessening the risk to the torero and the "seriousness" of the spectacle.

The third type of becerrada, where aficionados confront the calf in

the ring, is quite common. In many cities or towns with strong bullfighting traditions, there are clubs dedicated to los toros, or to specific
toreros. These clubs serve as a forum to discuss taurine topics, watch
bullfighting on television, and listen to lectures. They often sponsor
trips to corridas or novilladas in other towns. Periodically the club or-
ganizes a becerrada so that club members can have the opportunity to
cape a calf in a plaza, which frequently takes place on a private ranch.
They are often held in the morning, and the calf's horns have usually
been blunted, both elements of which lessen the "seriousness" of the
event. A professional torero or novillero must be present to "protect"
the amateurs from any real harm and kill the animal at the end, but
otherwise this is a nonprofessional fiesta.

Toreo cómico. The protagonists in toreo cómico are clowns, or clownlike
people (e.g., dwarfs), who perform humorous sketches with one-year-
old calves (becerros). Circus elements such as acts, tightrope artists, and
bands are often added to the show, but the part with the calf must be at
the beginning of the program. Several toreo cómico troupes tour Spain
offering these spectacles.

The plaza is full of young children, and the clowns' antics obviously
provoke laughs. The clowns do not dress in "suits of lights," nor are
they graceful or aristocratic. Instead, they jump over the calves, fall
down under them, or get hit by them. The clown troupe is accountable
to the Interior Ministry for some aspects of the shows, yet each troupe
makes up its own sketches.

Festivales. A festival is put on to benefit a charity. Although in festivales
any age animal may be used as long as it is male, festivales are generally
considered a subcategory of becerradas because normally two-year-old
males are used. A torero, wearing his "country outfit" rather than the
"suit of lights," performs and kills a calf without compensation.

In small villages the festival may be the only taurine event in the year.
However, in most towns, the festival is only one of several taurine fiestas
offered during the patron saint celebrations.

Recortadores. In this spectacle teams of two men, recortadores, have
one minute in the ring to dodge *(recortar)* and/or jump over the female calf (vaquilla). Each "dodge" is rated artistically by three judges.
Then the teammates have two minutes, working in tandem, to see how
many three-inch rings they can slip over the cow's horns. Two prizes are

awarded: one for the most artistic dodge and one for the highest number of rings.

This is supposedly an old form of taurine spectacle that has reappeared as an event during fiestas. It combines national and local forms. In 1984 and 1985, recortadores took place only in certain parts of Spain and in this way seem like local formats. It is a spectacle because the public pays to watch the two-man teams perform. However, the teams are composed of amateurs whose members dress alike but otherwise do not wear uniforms (i.e., both boys may wear the same color T-shirt and jeans). This event takes place in the morning, rather than in the afternoon like the "serious" taurine fiestas. Finally, recortadores use female calves (vaquillas), like many of the local categories, rather than bulls.

Tientas. Not a state controlled category, tienta refers to the testing of the baby calves *(erales)* on the ranches that raise bulls for the corrida. The tests take place in the spring when the animals are approximately a year old. These are tests for bravery. Out in the fields men on horseback use long poles to knock over the male calves. If the little animals get up and charge the horses, they pass the test. If they get up and run away, they will not be used in a corrida. Only female calves are caped and tested in a ring. If she is willing to charge the cape, then she passes the test and will go on to become a mother for potential "toros." If she fails, she goes to the slaughterhouse.

Ranch owners have traditionally used this spring rite as an excuse to invite friends to the ranch during the several days of testing. The tienta is a prolonged party. The owner hosts his guests, who often try caping the young calves.

The tienta is another intermediate category. It is a spectacle, yet no one pays to get in because it is private, by invitation only. The guests watch, as well as participate as amateur toreros. It takes place in the field and the ring. In contrast to all other fiestas, a tienta is located in the middle of the countryside. Like the taurine spectacles with local formats, tientas have no relationship to the central government.

Local Formats

Local format fiestas change from being primarily "spectacles" to being primarily "activities," where more and more nonprofessionals take part. At the same time, there is a movement from the plaza to the street. Furthermore, the national government loses "control" over these activities, and each format tends to be local in origin. There are no national rules for these formats. Although the animals must still be registered in a secondary category of ranches (Asociación Nacional de Ganaderías de Lidia), they are thought to be of inferior quality.

Encierros. An encierro is a function of a national-level fiesta (corrida, novillada) in a bullring. Originally an encierro occurred before every taurine fiesta. Bulls or calves were driven across the countryside to the edge of the city where they were going to be fought. There they were put into corrals to rest. The night before their appearance in the ring, usually around 2:00 or 3:00 A.M., the animals were driven through the streets of the town to the ring, which was done at night to avoid the possibility of hurting people. Young men, however, sometimes tried to run with, or in front of, these animals to test their own skill and bravery.

The necessity for the encierro died out at the end of the nineteenth century when trains and trucks could unload bulls at the ring. The tradition continues, however, in small towns and villages. (Today no big city, except Pamplona, has an encierro.) Now the running of the animals is an event in itself. The streets are barricaded, and store windows are protected by slabs of wood or iron bars. Many towns have post holes built into their streets and sidewalks to facilitate setting up the course.

There are no written rules about who may run in an encierro, although each town has its own traditions about age (no children, married men generally do not run) and gender (in Pamplona no women run close to the bulls; in Guadalajara I saw a couple of teenage girls run the encierro, but the animals were only novillos). It is not necessary to be a town resident.

Although the encierro's underlying objective is the same in each town, to drive the animals to the ring, the overt objective is to run with the bull, and this, every town does differently. In Falces (Navarra) the vaquillas are run down a mountain path into the town, in Segorbe (Castellón) the boys and men are on horseback, in Manzanares (Madrid) the run through the town is very straight, while in Pamplona the course makes two distinct turns.

While the other fiestas vary in name according to the bovine's age, sex, and kind of bullfighter (e.g., professional, amateur), encierro is a kind of generic category that can occur in the morning of, for example, a corrida, novillada, becerrada, or capea. Consequently, the encierro numbers are much higher than those of any other category of spectacle. Moreover, several of the miscellaneous forms get labeled as encierro for "official" records and administrative purposes.

Sometimes towns offer *encierros-chicos,* where both boys and girls under fourteen years old run yearling calves through the streets. Later the children are allowed to play with the calves in the ring like in vaquillas (see *suelta de vaquillas/toreo de vaquillas/vaquilla* below).

The final categories of taurine fiestas include so many different kinds of activities that one must check each town to see what it means by the term. Much of the Spanish literature refers to these fiestas as "primitive forms" (Cossío [1943]1980[1]:679), and sometimes it is assumed that these are the origins of the other national fiestas (Serrán Pagán 1977). The opposite view also exists: that these primitive forms are a bastardization of the medieval aristocratic games with bulls, the ancestor of the corrida. Nevertheless, when the historical archives first make mention of taurine fiestas in the eleventh century, they record the existence of both the aristocratic and village games. Further descriptions constantly applied to these local fiestas are "anarchy" and "disorder." Although they are always recognized as something "authentic," with "deep roots" in the Spanish pueblo (people, common people), these taurine fiestas are also judged "cruel" and "barbarous" by many corrida fans.

Capeas (capings). Capeas only take place in small towns (pueblos). There is no such thing as a capea in a capital city. In a capea many young men in a "ring" try to "cape" a bovine. The plaza most often is truly the town square *(plaza)* that has been closed off to make a ring. A real *(permanente)* bullring may be used or a temporary one *(portátil)* may be hauled in and set up. In earlier times a ring was created by drawing carts and trucks together to form a plaza on the outskirts of town. The boys, equipped with jackets, sweaters, or even newspapers for capes, tease the animal mercilessly, pull its tail, jump over it, call its attention, or throw soda cans to get it to charge their way. The animal is not killed in the ring. If it is killed, it is killed outside the ring after the capea by a professional bullfighter or a slaughterhouse employee. Despite a rule requiring the animal's sacrifice, quite often its life is spared.

The animal used in capeas is never a toro bravo, although it is usually male and referred to as a toro. Sometimes an older animal is used, but more often young two-year-old calves are used.

Suelta de vaquillas/toreo de vaquillas/vaquillas (freeing of cows; fighting cows; cows). This official category includes unique fiestas that cannot be easily categorized. Vaquillas is a taurine fiesta similar to capeas, where female animals are used instead of males. Vaquillas, as an activity, means something different in each locality and may take place at any time of day.

Vaquilla means female calf, at least two years old, but often older. The calf has well-developed horns, and in many places (e.g., Pamplona) the tips of the horns are covered with leather balls to reduce the harm the vaquillas can do, though not all towns cover the horns of their vaquillas. Since uncovered horns means the possibility of death in the ring, those towns brag that their fiesta is more dangerous (more "serious") than fiestas in other places. In my experience, vaquillas were never killed, neither in the ring nor afterward, although the Reglamento requires it.

In towns with bullrings, the vaquillas are freed *(sueltas)* into the ring one, two, or three at a time. The rings are literally full of young men or boys. The cows run around butting and charging the boys who must keep track of them. The vaquillas are not caped, rather, the boys run away from or jump over their charges. Often the boys escape getting caught by jumping up and clinging to the sides of the plaza. Nevertheless, many boys get caught by the vaquillas and are flipped up into the air. Even with covered horns, the animals can break the boys' ribs and other bones.

A suelta de vaquillas takes place in a ring. If a town does not have a bullring, portable rings may be set up, which are metal plazas with bleachers. If the ring is used for other taurine spectacles, the fences marking off the arena are solid, like the wooden fences in a bullring *(barrera)*. Where vaquillas are the only ring fiesta, for example in Valencia province, the plaza is formed by a series of vertical metal bars that are twelve inches apart so that the young men can slip out through the bars, but of course, the animals cannot. The public bleachers begin six to eight feet above the ground, and the boys are, thus, under the spectators when they escape through the bars.

The location of these temporary plazas varies from town to town. Sometimes they are set up in the center of town, sometimes right outside of town. In some coastal towns on the Cantabrian and the Mediterranean Seas, the suelta de vaquillas takes place on the beach or down on the dock. One side of this "plaza" is the sea itself (figure 1.3), as in Denia (Alicante).

Suelta de reses para fomento y recreo de la afición (the release of cattle for the promotion and recreation of the public). In this category, the animal or animals are played with in the streets, not in a ring. It differs from an

Figure 1.3. A vaquillas fiesta in Denia (Alicante). The rectangular bullring is set up by the port so that one side of the ring is water. The cow is chasing the boys, who jump into the water to escape. (Postcard courtesy of Postales Hermanos Galiana, S.L.)

encierro in that the animals are not on their way to the ring, but rather stay in the streets to chase the men for one to two hours or more. Either females or males may be used.

In small villages, only the exits of the town are blocked off and the bull runs through the whole town. In larger towns, some streets are blocked so that the animals do not escape into other parts of the town. Usually the animal runs in what is the oldest and central part of town.

One type of suelta is the toro embolado. The name *embolado* originally referred to protective leather balls or coverings put on the horns of animals to prevent fatal gorings. Today, however, *toro embolado* refers to bulls with balls of fire on their horns (figure 1.4).

These fiestas take place at midnight. Torches are screwed to the animal's horns, and the animal is freed in the streets at the moment the torches are lit. The young men are chased by, chase, slap, dodge, and run away from the animal. Most towns prefer a bull, but they may use a cow because it is less expensive. The law requires the sacrifice of these animals, but usually this is not done. These fiestas have various names according to the locality: *toro jubilo* in Medinaceli (Soria), *toro de ronda*

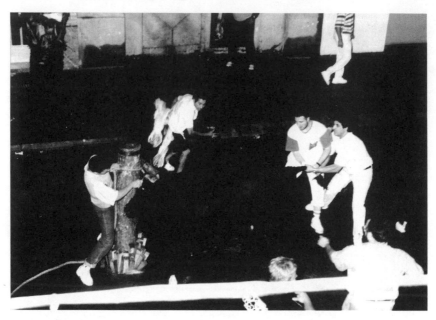

Figure 1.4. Toro embolado of Valencia. The burning torches have been affixed to the bull's horns. The young man is about to cut the rope that ties the bull to the post, freeing the animal to run in the streets. (Photographed by Juan Martínez)

in Carineña (Aragón), *de los hachos* in Navalcarnero (Madrid), and *bou emboulat* in Valencia.

In the *toro enmaronado/toro ensogado/toro gallumbo* a huge rope is tied around the horns of the animal. The animal is freed in the streets, and the young men pull on the animal or drag it by the rope to certain parts of town. The names and objectives vary in this category. In Grazalema (Cádiz), where the fiesta is known as *el lunes del toro,* the rope is used to pull the bull to different parts of town, representing different competing factions of young men. In Chinchón (Madrid) it is called *toro aguardiente;* in Benavente (Zamora), *toro de cuerda;* in Guadalajara, *baco.* In the Basque Country this form is called *sokamuturra.* There the fiesta takes place in an enclosed, fenced off space and cows are used.

Another form of the suelta is *suerte de banasta* (*corre de boi* in Catalan). In this fiesta a young man gets into a huge hamperlike basket, full of straw or rags. When the toro charges the basket, the boy ducks inside it.

Miscellaneous. Some locales have fiesta taurinas that are so unique they cannot be grouped with any other. For example, in *toro de la vega* of Tordesillas (Valladolid), a bull is run through town and across the bridge over the Duero River. When the animal arrives at a large open field, young men either on horseback or on foot attack the bull, throwing spears and lances. They must kill the animal before it reaches the other side of the field. In Coria's (Cáceres) *el toro de San Juan*, a bull is set free in the streets. It is "tortured" by jabbing it with knives, scissors, sharpened sticks, and darts until it collapses. The testicles are then cut off while it is still alive.

Toro de fuego (bull of fire). This is not a bull at all, but rather a man under a long, rectangular-shaped wooden box that forms the body of a bull and a head with real bull horns affixed to the top of the box. The man bends over slightly when he runs so that the box / body is in a more horizontal than vertical position. A series of fire crackers are attached on the back of the "bull." The toro de fuego appears in a crowd at a designated time at night and runs through the crowd as the firecrackers rocket off toward the crowd with loud explosive noises, scaring young children and causing a ruckus.

This "event" shares the contexts of the other taurine fiestas, and informants often gave it as their local form of los toros. In Basque this event is known as *zezensusko*.

Chapter 2

"MENTAL CONSTRUCTIONS"
OF "SPAIN"

National Identity in Spain

On the cover of *Euskadi,* a magazine published by a conservative Basque political party, was the question, "Are we Basques Spanish?" Shown below were a series of "Spanish" images: flamenco dancers and singers, Easter week processions, the Civil Guard, and most prominent of all, a *torero.* All of these images are easily recognized stereotypes of Spain *(España tópica).* The magazine's obvious answer was, "No. We Basques are not these things. Thus, we are not Spanish." To make the answer even more evident to the readers, the torero's hat *(montera)* had been replaced by a Basque beret, creating a jolting juxtaposition of categories. Here the phenomenon of bullfighting—in the person of the torero—is used to talk about Spanish nationality.

In this chapter, I describe what Amando de Miguel (1976:311) calls the "mental construction" of Spain. Although I often make reference to scholarly works of history, economics, politics, and sociology, I am more interested in capturing "mental constructions," Durkheimian collective representations—the ways people think and talk about "Spain"— than any objective reality.[1] Thus, this description of "Spain" is not definitive, nor all inclusive. Moreover, it is an oversimplification of reality. My purpose is to delineate those Spanish categories with which one must be familiar to understand the language and multiple meanings of los toros.

Spain is a recognized sovereign state located in Europe. Within the country called Spain (España), however, the concept "Spain" has been called an "enigma," "problem," "labyrinth," and "puzzle." Although everyone in Spain acknowledges the existence (if not the legitimacy) of the Spanish state *(estado español),* the definition of "Spain" *(España,* referring to the nationality, or culture, and therefore, "Spanishness") is debated. The debate is not merely about semantics, it has ultimately to do with the very social and political structure of the country.

Spanish history provides multiple interpretations. Some find a con-sciousness of being "Spanish" since Visigothic times (A.D. 400–700) (Sánchez-Albornoz [1956] and school) or before. The Roman, Seneca, is often called the first Spanish philosopher. Probably the most popular view (led by Américo Castro [1954]) is that "Spanishness" was created during the Reconquest, the wars of the various northern Christian king-doms against the Islamic south. Although the relationship between the many parts of the peninsula has varied through time, a unified state had been created by 1515.[2] Nevertheless, since its formal union, there has been a tension inherent in the concept of the state, generated by the need to balance "an efficient central government and the imperative of local autonomy" (Brenan 1962:ix). How the country should be struc-tured today is most often justified in terms of one of the visions of the "past." There are three basic positions on the question of national iden-tity in Spain: "Spain," "not Spain," and "the Spains."

"Spain"

"Spain" as a nation, or nationality, is accepted by many. In this case, "Spain" as a nationality is posited in nature, and one sometimes hears of the Spanish race *(raza española; estirpe española)*. Furthermore, reli-gion (Catholicism) is often coterminous with Spanishness (Saiz Barbera 1982:406). Regionalism is accommodated, but the existence of a series of basic characteristics that are "Spanish" is maintained. In this view, the regions become subsumed within the concept of "Spain." Region and nation are two different levels of identification.

Since before the beginning of this century, this concept of the nation and culture of "Spain" has often been identified with the political forces known as the Right (de Miguel 1986:8). During the Spanish Civil War (1936–1939) the Right (the rebels) called themselves Nationalists be-cause they perceived themselves as fighting those who would destroy "Spain." The Right called the Republicans, and the political Left, the "anti-Spain." The anti-Spain were those who denied the oneness and cultural values of "Spain." The short lived, center-leftist Second Republic had proved it was anti-Spain by granting limited autonomy to some regions. The Nationalists' battle cry was *"¡Arriba España!"* (Long live Spain!).

Even long after the Civil War in the 1970s and 1980s, the pragmatics of politics required the political Left, especially the ruling Socialists, to balance carefully the granting of political autonomy to the "regions." They had to emphasize the indissolubility and sacredness of "Spain" and its symbols (e.g., the flag and the monarchy), especially with respect to some particularly sensitive, powerful groups, such as the armed forces and police.

"Not Spain"

Those who say they do not share the culture of "Spain" insist that it coincides almost exclusively with only one region, Castile. People who take this position argue that it is Castile's culture and nationality that is imposed upon the rest of the differentiated "nationalities." In essence, these people (usually "Basques" and "Catalans") accuse Castile and especially the capital city of Madrid, which is located in Castile, of cultural and political imperialism. By assuming the existence of "España" (as Castile), the essence of the other *naciones* (nations) in Spain is denied, creating an unjust asymmetry of power relationships.[3]

Since "region" implies an asymmetry within the relationship nation/ region, the term *region* is not used in this argument. Rather, these groups insist upon the terms *nación* and *nacionalidad*. Their political demands range from self-government in many issues to a federated association with "España" to outright separation and creation of a new, sovereign nation-state. The arguments in favor of these "nationalities" also often posit them in nature. For some people, identification with their nacionalidad (e.g., "Basque" *[vasca]*) precludes any identification with España. The Spanish philosopher, Ortega y Gasset, referred to this "particularism" in his influential book, *Invertebrate Spain* (1937:44), by saying that "Spain is not so much a nation as a series of water-tight compartments."

In the above contexts, speakers often try to avoid the terms *España* and *español*. Instead a series of substitutes are used: the state *(el estado)*, the Spanish state *(el estado español)*, or the peoples of the peninsula *(los pueblos de la península)*. To speak about the team that represented Spain in the European Soccer Cup, which was composed of the best players from all over Spain, the press had to resort to the expression *selección del estado español* in contrast to the expression *selección española*. In these social contexts, no one speaks of Spanish (español) as a language; rather, it is called Castilian. Not even foreigners are allowed to make this mistake.

Thus, the words *nation, national,* and *nationalist* differ in meaning for these two visions of the Spanish state, "Spain" and "not Spain," and not much social communication bridges these two contexts. *Policía nacional* belong to "Spain" and are considered imperialist, occupying forces by some Basques. Meanwhile, *partidos nacionalistas* are regional political parties from the perspective of "Spain" and are seen as a threat to national unity by other Spaniards. The argument is over the social structure of the state and its cultural components and symbols of identity.

"The Spains"

A third vision of the "nation" is located somewhere between these two poles. Since the beginning of this century, this position, along with the separatist positions, has been associated with the political Left. Nevertheless, compared to the other two positions, the Right (only one "Spain") and the separatists ("not Spain"), this is a mediating position. It is also the basis of the 1978 Constitution.

This position changes "Spain" into "the Spains" (las Españas). It assumes a unity while permitting, even emphasizing, diversity. Since 1978 the state has been officially composed of seventeen Autonomous Communities *(comunidades autónomas)* rather than fifteen regions (maps 2.1 and 2.2). This new nomenclature avoids the asymmetry of nation/region and implies equivalence between all the Autonomous

Map 2.1. Autonomous Communities after 1978.

Map 2.2. Research provinces and their Autonomous Communities.

Communities, while maintaining an underlying Spanishness. The "nationalities" point out that this equivalence still ignores their distinctiveness as a people with a different language, history, and culture from many of the other communities. In other words, they say some of the Autonomous Communities are "nations," while others are merely regions of Spain.

In the context of the bulls, the problem with the expression *fiesta nacional* is now evident.

History and the Majority View Today

All three of these definitions use history to support their point of view. All three groups believe there is an original essential reality, and one need only peel back like an onion skin all the polluting ideas and occurrences to get to the pure, original, authentic essence. This essence can and should be recreated in the present. Some members of the Autonomous Communities claiming to be nations, those who hold the "not Spain" view, project back to times before the creation of the Spanish state (1515) or before their incorporation into it. In contrast, the "one Spain" view glorifies the deeds of the Spanish empire under Philip II and the perceived single direction and "will" of all the Spanish peoples. The middle position declares that true "Spain" was merely a union of the many "Spains" before the tendency toward centralization inaugurated in 1700 by the French Bourbons, who took over the Spanish throne. Before this, Madrid was the capital of the country, but the king was considered ruler of "las Españas" and not "España."

Each position harkens back to an interpretation of a certain moment in time, ignoring other moments where the evidence does not speak to, or support, that vision of "Spain." During the nineteenth century, for example, there was no organized, mass sentiment in the Basque Country to the effect that the Basques were not "Spanish" (García de Cortázar 1984).

It is unclear what percentage of the country's citizens supports each vision of "Spain." During General Franco's regime (1936–1975), the "one Spain" ideology was dominant. All other particularistic visions of Spain were repressed and censored. Since 1978, Spain has had a formal constitutional monarchy. As stated above, the Constitution was drawn up acknowledging the inherent rights of the "historic nationalities" to some forms of self-rule, while at the same time insisting upon the indissolubility of "Spain." The Constitution was submitted to a national referendum and approved overwhelmingly, even in the Autonomous Communities that consider themselves "nations" (Linz 1986:227). The Francoist Right can now be counted in votes: in 1982 the extreme Right received only 2% of the national vote and since then has effectively disappeared as a political party.

In the three Autonomous Communities that claim to be nacionalidades (Basque Country, Catalonia, and Galicia), not all citizens participate in national elections. Separatist political parties urged people to abstain. In 1979, sociological surveys showed that between 47.7% and 52.3% of the people in the Basque Country did not think of themselves as "Spanish."[4] Although a citizen in the Basque Country may feel only "Basque" and not "Spanish," this citizen may desire to have one of several different possible relationships with Spain—from a federated association to total separation. The rest of the citizens divide up between the other two visions of "Spain."[5]

Whatever the actual numerical strength, these three categories most certainly exist as social representations. The minority views carry great weight in the collective consciousness. Rightly or wrongly, the army, the Civil Guard (paramilitary police), and what is left of the landed gentry are associated with the "one Spain" concept. The "not Spain" concept is associated primarily with the Basques but also to some degree with the Catalans, Galicians, and even the Valencians (all those areas that claim to be "nationalities"), no matter what the actual breakdown of ideas and voting patterns are in those communities. In fact, "the Basques" quite often means "separatists" in colloquial speech.

Since the elimination of censorship after Franco's death, the question of how to justly come to terms with the question of "Spain" and the other nationalisms has been the preoccupying issue in Spanish politics. Terrorist acts by extreme Basque separatists have kept this a very emotional and bloody issue. Many conferences and seminars on the subject have been organized, while the press has been literally inundated with articles, editorials, and letters to the editor dealing with these questions.

The interesting characteristic of this country in Western Europe is precisely that Spain is a *relationship* between these many points of view. Furthermore, individuals identify with different definitions of "Spain" according to different contexts in which they find themselves.

Accepted Cultural Assumptions

Despite these differences, a series of cultural assumptions, or categories, are employed and understood by all those who live in Spain. The first assumption is that the regions/nacionalidades form a basis of essential differentiation among Spaniards. A second assumption is that "Spain" can also be described as if it were composed of just two different, and sometimes opposing, parts. Each region/nacionalidad identifies with one side of two opposing divisions, called either North and South or Center and Periphery. One division (North/South) implies egalitarian relationships between the regions, while the other (Center/Periphery) assumes hierarchical and asymmetrical relationships. A third historical, cultural category also divides Spain into two parts, based not on a division of the regions but rather on worldview or social class. This is known as the "two Spains." Finally, all Spain's citizens seem to share the objective of finding and reproducing the "real, authentic culture" of their vision of national identity.

Regions

Anthropologist: Do you like los toros?
Woman: I'm from Galicia.

It is a well-known social fact that people from Galicia do not like "the bulls."

The first shared cultural assumption is that the regions and/or "nations" within Spain form one of the primary contexts of differentiation among the people of Spain.[6] The seventeen regions/nacionalidades, although constructed administrative units, are also often assumed to be natural, separate entities. That is, they exist in nature, and in this sense each entity is equal to the others. (The regions' boundaries were redrawn in 1978; these administrative units are now called Autonomous Communities.) Each geographical area (region/nacionalidad), due to its differentiated history, culture, and sometimes language, imprints upon people born there a kind of "character" or "identity" that is antithetical to all the other areas in Spain. Although other influencing contexts such as class, political ideology, sex, age, and education are not denied, where a person is born is assumed to be the overriding influence on personality. Changing one's place of residency does not change one's regional identification.[7] I constantly heard about someone's "Basque friends," "Andalusian neighbor," or a "Catalan student." Often a trait was explained simply in terms of one's region of birth: "Berlanga always has fireworks in his films. He's from Valencia." Thus, stereotypes about each region's purported "personalities" have been generated. Exceptions to the rules can be found, but there is always something inexplicable about contradictions, such as a Catalan torero or an Andalusian *empresario* (businessman). All this assumes a working knowledge and a social communication across regions/naciones about the traits, characteristics, and "differentiating elements" of each.[8] For example, supposedly regions either have bullfighting traditions, or they do not. Otherwise the answer "I'm from Galicia" to the question "Do you like the bulls?" would make no sense.

North/South

In the North, the verse is about the bull, not the bullfighter. . . . In contrast, the South is where the bullfighting figure is exalted.
Martínez Remis 1963:12, my translation

In the categorization of the person by region/nacionalidad, the regions are assumed to be different but equal. Although Andalusia has eight provinces and a population of 6.4 million, and Navarra consists of one province and a population of 507,000, they are qualitatively equal. However, the regions/nacionalidades are conceptually organized into two groups in two different ways.

The first way the regions are divided up is into North and South. Although North/South are descriptively different, they are conceptually equal. A third category, Center, often emerges to mediate between

North and South, and a fourth category, the Levante (or Mediterranean coast), is used to further explain "Spain." But the primary divisions are North and South; there is no East or West.

What is meant by North and what is meant by South varies. When asked to name the regions/nacionalidades included in the North, some people distinguished northeast (Catalonia) and northwest (Galicia) from the North, while others included all the regions north of Castile and Leon in "North." In Sevilla, a local government official said everything north of Sevilla was the North, specifically naming Madrid and Valencia. However, the core of the North seems to be the Basque Country, Cantabria, and part of Navarra. The South, in contrast, refers to all of Andalusia, sometimes Andalusia plus Murcia and Extremadura, and sometimes everything south of Madrid. However, the core of the South is Andalusia, especially Sevilla.

The North is often called "humid" Spain because of its abundant rains and is contrasted with "dry" Spain (four-fifths of the peninsula), which is the South. Another contrast is "green" Spain with "dry" Spain. The North is mountainous, while the South has flat, rolling plains interrupted by high mountain chains.

Spaniards believe that the North and South refer to different historical experiences. In the fourth century B.C. the Celts invaded and settled basically in the North, while the Iberians had settlements in the Southeast. In the second and first centuries B.C. the Romans heavily colonized the South but never really colonized parts of the North. In 711 the Moslems invaded and conquered all of Spain except the mountainous North. Since, as the story goes, the Romans and Moslems never "invaded and conquered the North," it is often considered the original, most "pure" (castiza) part of Spain. Many peoples in the peninsula retreated there to avoid the Islamic invasion. The Basques, especially, with their pre-Indoeuropean language are often spoken about as the "most pure" Spanish, the "least contaminated" by the various invasions of outside cultures (Algañaraz 1984:53).

At a collective level, it is always said that the Reconquest of Islamic Spain began in the mountains of the North in Asturias. At the beginning of the Reconquest at least seven different Christian political entities (called kingdoms [reinos] or counties [condados]) emerged, speaking Basque and Romance languages, and were related through royal marriages and treaties. The land to be conquered was the "South," Islamic-held territory. The Reconquest lasted some seven hundred years (718–1492). Different northern kingdoms reconquered and influenced different southern areas. The largest areas were conquered by the kings of Castile (originally a small central country in the North) after the twelfth century. Thus, it is said, Castile reconquered the South, which explains its ties to Castile and its language, *castellano*.[9]

Agriculturally, small land parcels *(minifundios)* characterize the North, while large land tracts *(latifundios)* characterize the South. Many of these large landholdings, originally awarded by the kings to their nobles upon reconquest, survive relatively intact today. It is on these latifundios that the fighting bulls are raised. In the North, rural farmers work their own land, while typically in the South landowners employ wage laborers to work the land. The North raises various subsistence crops, as well as corn for animal fodder. Cultivation of a single large crop for the market, traditionally wheat, wine, or oil,[10] typifies the South. In the mountainous North, cows produce milk products (and oxen are draft animals), while in the South cattle are raised exclusively for meat. Rural human settlement in the North is often based on single, isolated farmhouses *(caserios, masias)*, a pattern that is absent in the rest of Spain, where the *pueblo* (or village cluster) is the norm.

Urban settlement size is another important difference between the North and South. Characteristic of the North are small towns of two thousand people or less. This size town makes up the majority of the municipalities (about 80%) in this part of Spain (Floristán 1972).[11] The small villages, with their populations of peasant landowners, parallel strong egalitarian sentiments (Douglass, W. 1969:13; Freeman 1970: 5).[12] Although such towns exist in the South (Pitt-Rivers' Grazelema [1971] is the most well known in anthropology), they are not representative of the South for Spaniards.

The South, on the other hand, is characterized by "agro-cities," with populations between ten thousand and thirty thousand people,[13] where the landless proletariat who work on the large surrounding farms live. These towns, composed of owners and laborers, are often torn by bitter class antagonisms and hierarchy.

Although Spain is a Catholic country, the North is known as the most religious part (de Miguel 1986:122), while the South has the largest number of nonpracticing Catholics.

Industrialization is another difference between North and South. It is associated with the North, due to the presence of the first two great nineteenth-century industrial centers in Spain, Bilbao (Basque Country) and Barcelona (Catalonia). Although Madrid and several other central cities (Zaragoza, Valladolid) have industrialized since the 1960s, the

North still represents industrial Spain, while the South represents agricultural Spain.

Due, in part, to its industrial character, the North is also described as the most "European." By contrast, the South is "not European." These two classifications imply an opposition of value systems, sometimes posed as "modern versus traditional," sometimes "work ethic versus status ethic," or sometimes "bourgeois versus seignorial Spain."

Both parts of Spain have large proletariats: the North has an urban proletariat, while the South has a rural proletariat. The Center emerges here to mediate these two "Spains" with a third, "middle class" *(clase media)*, meaning the part of Spain characterized by service and administrative classes.

Madrid, the representative of the Center, has recently undergone tremendous industrial growth and demographic expansion. Although always large and important, before the 1950s Madrid was characterized as a typical Castilian administrative city, full of the "comfortable classes" *(clases acomodadas)*. Madrid's idealized lifestyle was in many ways the archetype for "Spanishness." It has always been described as castiza (pure Spanish). Madrid had some light industry but was not an industrial city like Barcelona and Bilbao. In fact, there was something very rural and rustic about Madrid (Linz and de Miguel 1966:290). From 1940 to 1970, however, Madrid tripled in size. Despite its status now as an industrial city, people all over Spain still talk about Madrid as if it were unproductive and only an administrative city.[14]

In the vocabulary of the North/South dialectic, Center emerges as a truly middle and mediating third category. When Center is used in this context, no hierarchy is implied. In contrast, in the following discussion of the dialectic Center/Periphery, Center is the privileged category in a power hierarchy. It is important to discern which meaning of Center a speaker is using, since Center can mean a relation of difference but equality in some contexts (as in North/Center/South), while it may signify a relation of hierarchy in other contexts (as in Center/Periphery). Center is the ambiguous category that unites the two models.

In taurine contexts, people make constant reference to North, Center, and South. Although North and South are often opposed, as in the quote at the beginning of this section about *afición* for the bullfighter and the bull, one category is not necessarily valued over the other.

Center/Periphery

A second set of categories is also used to speak about "Spain." Again the regions/nacionalidades are grouped into two parts: Center and Periphery (Centro y Periferie). Implicit in the relationship Center/Periphery is the idea of hierarchy. Center is assumed to be favored politically, linguistically, and culturally over Periphery. The Center is unduly favored due to its claims to be "authentic, pure Spain." When one uses this symbol, Center/Periphery, to speak about "Spain," most likely the speaker is discussing inequalities between the regions/nacionaldades. For many the use of "Center" is pejorative; it is a criticism of these inequalities.

The regions/nacionalidades that compose the categories "Center" and "Periphery" also vary by informant. The Center always means the city of Madrid, sometimes Castile, and sometimes all of the interior (provinces not touching the coasts). The western part of Spain along the border of Portugal is always Center. On the other hand, the Periphery is sometimes described as a literal periphery, that is, provinces around the outside of Spain. Others define the Periphery as the nacionalidades, the regions with their own language, culture, and "personality" (Basque Country, Navarra, Galicia, Catalonia, Valencia). Still others call the Periphery the industrialized regions of Spain (Basque Country, Catalonia, Valencia, Asturias), although often only the capital cities of the regions are industrialized, existing side by side with a very conservative, pastoral, rural tradition. The historian Jaime Vicens Vives (1970:xxx) defined the Periphery by high population density, thus excluding Navarra, Aragón, Castellón, Murcia, and Huelva from the Periphery but including all the other coastal provinces. When Periphery is meant literally, Andalusia obviously must be included. When it refers to the non-Spanish regions or industrialized areas, Andalusia is not implied.

Although Center and Periphery imply spatial and geographical categories, they do not necessarily involve spatial relationships in their use in Spain. In other words, people use geography to discuss different kinds of moral and social relations. However, center/periphery does not just apply to the social geography of the regions. It appears in other contexts as well. For example, each city has a center that is always its oldest, original part and a periphery composed of the apartment buildings on its fringe. It always costs much more to live in the city center, as this is the most valued area. Consequently, the upper class lives in the center and the lower class lives in the periphery. All cultural and political demonstrations occur in the center, again underlining its social importance. The most important city rituals and fiestas also take place there, emphasizing the idea that "center" equates with "original" and "authentic culture."

It is very possible that the hierarchy in the categories Center and Periphery corresponds to the relationship inherent between the two verbs for "to be" in Spanish: *ser* and *estar*. *Ser* is used to express a perceived essential, permanent characteristic such as gender (I am a woman: *Soy mujer*), color, or significantly, *nationality*. *Ser*, from Latin *esser*, means essential. *Estar* is used to describe a temporary, transitory state such as mood (I am sad: *Estoy triste*) or health. For location, *ser* always expresses *origin* (I'm from Castile: *Soy de Castilla*), while *estar* expresses placement (I'm in Madrid: *Estoy en Madrid*). *Ser* is thus central to the person, while *estar* is peripheral.

The Spanish linguist Angel López García (1985:123) specifically links the use of Spanish (called castellano [Castilian]) in regions/nacionalidades that have other languages with the "estar" of a person and not the "ser," which would be the use of the mother tongue. Furthermore, he recommends looking to the past for the answer about language priorities in Spain today. "The only intelligent thing we can do is assign to the past what belongs to the past, and reask the question of how it came about originally, because it is the *origin that makes up the true essence of things* and not the accidental mutations of later development. People, like individuals, are made in childhood and should return to their childhood memories each time they are in danger of losing their identity" (A. López García 1985:98, my translation and emphasis).

Origins, true essences, central cores, and ser have a positive valuation. Accidental mutations, temporary states, peripheral characteristics, and estar have a negative valuation. The hierarchy implicit in the categories Center/Periphery is established through these connections. *Ser* as Center is positive; *estar* as Periphery is negative. All four important languages in the peninsula (español/castellano, *vasquense, catalan*, and *gallego-portugués*) use an opposition like *ser/estar* to express "to be," which is rare in other European languages (A. López García 1985:55).[15]

Since the relationship Center/Periphery is not only a spatial relationship but a moral one, a problem arises when it is transferred from one context to another. For a Catalan to talk about the "center" or the "periphery" of Barcelona will not seem problematic because these moral categories seem to "make sense," to be "in nature." However, once Barcelona is placed in the Periphery of "Spain" and Madrid in the Center, the relationship becomes problematic for the Catalan from Barcelona. There are two implied solutions to this "problem": admit to one's moral/spatial inferiority (and Madrid's superiority) and be alienated from the center of social life and production in "Spain," or use the Center/Periphery label as a critique of unjust relations with the Center and refuse to participate in them.

Again, the Periphery turns out to be those regions/nacionalidades in the North that were political entities at the beginning of the Reconquest in the eighth century. Castile, which was a rather late political invention, was then just another small, not necessarily important, kingdom. The history of "Spain" usually coincides with Castile's rise in eminence, its leadership and role in the Reconquest, its growth as it added conquered territories, and its sponsoring and control of the American adventure and wealth. The other kingdoms remained as separate entities from Castile with their own rights and autonomy but were allied with Castile as dependents after 1515. Not until the nineteenth century did laws and administration, decreed from Madrid, became uniform for all Spain. These separate "histories" differentiate the Periphery from the Center. "Periphery" implies a different culture, a different language (though not in every case or for every citizen), different economic structure, and different views of history from Castile. Moreover, at some point people began to refer to only Madrid (as if it were separate from Castile) as Center.

In the nineteenth century, political Liberals tried to rationalize the state. The short lived 1812 Constitution of Cádiz inaugurated a century-long struggle to modernize Spain. This political rationalization included a uniform administration for all of "Spain," which would be run by a national parliament located in Madrid. Thus, in the nineteenth century centralization was an idea of the political Left.

By the twentieth century, with the rise of the "regional question," and the nationalist movements in the Periphery, the political Right had become associated with the Center. The Right supported the "one Spain" idea and felt their concept of Spain was threatened by the Periphery's autonomy demands. The Left, on the other hand, was willing to grant some form of autonomy to the Periphery's historic nationalisms. In the Civil War, with the exception of Madrid, the provinces that declared themselves, or were initially won by, the Nacionales (the Right) correspond to the traditional Center, while the provinces that remained loyal to the Republic (Left and Centrist) correspond to the traditional Periphery.[16]

Another important difference between the Center and the Periphery is that between industrialized Spain and agricultural Spain, which repeat themes from the North/South dialogue. The first northern industrial centers, Bilbao and Barcelona, are also located in the Periphery. Industrial production also implies material wealth, so the Periphery represents rich Spain, while the Center represents poor Spain. Again, because of industry, the Periphery seems "like Europe." It supposedly has a worldview that is "more European" and more "modern" than that of the Center.

The Center, on the other hand, was traditionally known as agricultural Spain. Nevertheless, the land-owning classes lived in the midsized cities with the administrative and the professional classes. The countryside provided these cities with food but did not provide much work for the poor, landless laborers. Much of the land lay idle, since larger landowners could live well without cultivating all of it. This "agrarian problem" (idle land, idle peasants) has preoccupied Spanish lawmakers and governments for 150 years. At any rate, the lack of industry, in general, and the dependence upon agriculture made the Center seem "less European" and in turn, was defined by some as more "Spanish," more castizo. Castizo, which derives from the word *casta* (chaste, pure), becomes the antithesis of "European."

Thus, collective representations arose of two different personalities. The Periphery worked: the people were industrious, productive, and concerned with money, acquisition, and material gain. The Center, with its idle poor and idle rich, did not work.[17] Many people in the Periphery accuse the people in the Center of being lazy: a Cambridge-educated Catalan economist once explained to me that Castile was poor because "the people there do not work, like the Catalans do." The collective representation for the Center's personality was one of aristocratic concern for honor (status) and relationships, spiritual life, style, and substance, but not for material gain. The Right has called the personality of the Center the "spiritual reserve of the West." These collective representations were still actively used in the 1980s.

Until the 1950s Spain was considered an agricultural nation, since the majority of its laborers were engaged in agriculture. In the 1960s, Spain changed from an agricultural to an industrial nation.[18] Laborers left the countryside (Center) and flooded to the industrial areas (Periphery) in search of jobs and a better life, while agriculture itself also industrialized. Although cities all over Spain took in rural populations, people often imply that Spain is an industrial nation today because the Center literally migrated to the Periphery.

The origin of the asymmetry between the Center and the Periphery, however, is in the continuing perception that the Center governs (*"sabe mandar,"* as Ortega y Gasset said) while the Periphery produces (de Miguel 1976:283). Certainly all the data supports the collective representation that the Periphery produces industrially (Tamames 1986). The problem for Spanish nationalism is that the relatively rich and industrially productive parts of Spain (the Periphery) feel alienated from political power, and thus, "Spanishness." For not only is the seat of power located geographically in the Center of Spain, Madrid, but the perception in the Periphery is that men from the Center rule Spain (and thus define "Spanishness").[19] People feel that Spain's rulers (political, military, and religious) for the last 150 years have primarily come from the Center. (Ironically, the one exception was the forty year dictatorial and centralizing rule of Franco, born in Galicia.)[20] However, the real problem is not why the social leaders' origins do not correspond more closely to the population's geographic distribution but rather the disjunction between the center of material production (Periphery) and the center of the production of "Spain" (Center).

With the new 1978 Spanish Constitution and the Socialists' triumph in the 1982 national elections, a more federal form of government was instituted. Some political powers were transferred to the regions. This gives the individual Autonomous Communities somewhat more control over themselves, but it does not give the Periphery, as a whole, more political control over the Center. Many still feel that national policy, affecting all of Spain, emanates from the Center; and physically this is true.[21]

Because many of the oppositions between North and South are repeated between Center and Periphery, in many conversations people talk as if the Periphery is the North and the Center is the South.[22] In this way Andalusia becomes part of the "Center." Thus, the North/South relationship of equality is converted into the Center/Periphery relationship of hierarchy.

Intellectual Division: The "Two Spains"

El mañana efímero
The Ephemeral Tomorrow

La España de charanga y pandereta
    Spain of the military brass band and the tambourine
cerrado y sacristía
    closed and [religious]
devota de Frascuelo y de María
    devoted to Frascuelo and Maria
de espíritu burlón y de alma quieta,
    with a mocking spirit and quiet calm soul,

. . . .

esa España inferior que ora y embiste
   this inferior Spain that prays and charges
cuando se digna usar de la cabeza
   when it deigns to use its head
aún tendrá luengo parto de varones
   will still give birth for many years to men
amantes de sagradas tradiciones
   lovers of sacred traditions
y de sagradas formas y maneras;
   and of sacred forms and manners;

. . . .

Mas otra España nace,
   But another Spain is being born,
la España del cincel y de la maza,
   Spain of the chisel and mace,
con esa eterna juventud que se hace
   with that eternal youth which is made
del pasado macizo de la raza.
   of the massive past of the race.

. . . .

España de la rabia y de la idea.
   Spain of rage and of ideas.

Antonio Machado 1913; 1967:828–29, my translation

Spaniards not only talk about the North/South or Center/Periphery, but as shown below, historically they have spoken of a third division: the "two Spains." The "two Spains" are purely ideological divisions, with no spatial or geographical implications, and refer to two antithetical worldviews, sometimes called traditional and modern, sometimes posed as hierarchial and egalitarian, sometimes Right and Left. The ideological "two Spains" crosscuts all other spatial divisions.

In 1836 the essayist Mariano José de Larra (1960) in reference to the first of the bloody Carlist (civil) Wars, wrote, "Here lies one half of Spain. It died at the hands of the other half." Some take this to be one of the first references to the idea of two Spains existing side by side, while others project two Spains much further back in history. The "two Spains" *(las dos Españas)* have been described as "the battle between two social forces, each wanting to have ideological hegemony over the nation, since the beginning of Spanish history in 1808" (Tuñon de Lara 1973:27).

It was the Generation of 1898—that group of intellectuals and scholars galvanized by the Spanish loss of colonies in 1898—that first used the term and wrote incessantly of the "two Spains." In 1914 Ortega y Gasset wrote of "two Spains that live together and that are perfect strangers to each other: an 'official' Spain, which obstinately prolongs the gestures of a perished age and another Spain, aspiring, germinal, a Vital Spain, perhaps not very strong, but vital, sincere, honorable, which blocked by the other, cannot fully enter into history" (cited in Tuñon de Lara 1973 : 149). Others would say the "two Spains" represented a battle between capitalist and precapitalist forms and ideologies.

Only one of these "two Spains," however, admits to dualism. The early theory of the historian Menéndez Pidal (1951) does not suppose "two Spains," but only one "authentic" Spain. The other part of Spain, if it exists, is marginal and antinational.

Implicit in this idea of the "two Spains" is the disjunction between the "real" Spain and the "official" Spain. At the end of the nineteenth century, the Catalan Valentí Almirall spoke of the *"España real,"* as opposed to *"España convencional,* invented by tourists" (Almirall 1972 : 38). Other labels have been "real versus fantastic," "real versus symbolic," and "real versus official." Throughout the 1970s and the 1980s the search for the "real" Spain (versus "official" Franco Spain) was realized in countless sociological surveys. Even the democratic elections can be considered a vindication of "real" Spain.

The "two Spains" is in many ways a euphemism for the idea that Spanish political life for the last 150–200 years has been a clash between the Left and the Right. A Centrist position in politics was said to be absent or weak. In the political Transition Period after General Franco's death in 1975, the creation of a Center in politics was a topic of much discussion. A Center, it was said, was necessary to solve Spain's historical problems. Analysts say that the Socialists' (PSOE) success in the 1982 elections was due to the perception that it now occupied the Center rather than the Left in the political spectrum.[23]

As in the past, all political parties in the current Spanish democracy are categorized as either Right, Left, or Center. Historically, the Left has been associated with democratic and parliamentary governments (since 1812), while the Right has often preferred nondemocratic governments, such as monarchy, military juntas, and dictatorship. Since 1975 most of the Right claims to uphold the Constitutional Monarchy. Coup attempts by the military were nevertheless a real threat at least until 1983 and were still being "uncovered" by the press in 1986. Thus the Right's nondemocratic image still persists.

Beyond the typical European economic and moral configuration of conservatives and liberals, the Right and Left in Spain are identified with specific positions on religion and nationality. The Right, in general, believes Spain is a Catholic (confessional) state, while the Left since 1812 has always wanted to separate religion from politics. Furthermore, since the beginning of this century, the Right, as stated above, has been associated with a rigid "one Spain" view of the nation-state. The Left, on the other hand, has encouraged various forms of local government and cultural diversity. For Antonio Machado, the influential poet who wrote before the 1936 Civil War, the oppositions between the "two Spains" were those of the *señorito* (landed gentry) and the *hombre del pueblo* (common man) (Tuñon de Lara 1973:159). The clash between the upper classes and the lower classes crosscut the whole country. The Right was always perceived as Spain of the señorito, and the Left claimed to represent the common man.

A further division implicit in the "two Spains" is the opposition between urban and rural Spain. In Machado's confrontation of señorito and hombre de pueblo, the señorito also represented the city, while the pueblo represented the backward, rural villages. In many ways, even in the 1980s these were two different worlds. According to the 1981 census, villages with fewer than one thousand inhabitants make up 58% of Spanish municipalities. Yet 50% of the population lives in municipalities of over twenty thousand people. Although fewer people than ever live in small pueblos, they still play a large role in the collective representations of Spain. Some pueblos have even been made into national monuments, effectively freezing them in time.

Although the oppositions inherent in the "two Spains"—reactionary versus liberal, Catholic versus anticlerical, authoritarian versus anarchist, backward rural versus modern metropolitan—are the same as those implicit in the moral division Center/Periphery, the "two Spains" does not usually refer to the geographical space on the map but rather to two mentalities that permeate all Spain: North and South, Center and Periphery.

The bulls are associated with one of the two Spains. For the Left, the bulls are one of the symbols of the Right, of archaeological, official Spain, of Spain invented by the tourists, Spain of the *pandereta* (tambourine). The Right, on the other hand, has often accused the Left, the anti-Spain, of being *antitaurinos*.

Throughout my research (1983–1986), many Spaniards insisted that there were no longer "two Spains." What they meant was that "official" Spain was numerically so small and unimportant that for all practical purposes it was dead, thus reassuring me of the stability of the modern Spanish democracy. Nevertheless, the collective representation of the "two Spains" is still in use, both in informant speech and in the press, if only to refer to the past, if only to deny its present importance. The following appeared in an editorial in the national newspaper *El País* on the fiftieth anniversary of the outbreak of the Spanish Civil War (July 18, 1986). "The other Spain, the one that lost the war and today is reviving with democracy, is precisely the one that does not think that there are two Spains confronting each other, but rather a multicolored Spain that is not debated between life and death nor does it play 'bulls' with politics" ("Opinión" 1986:8).

For both conceptions of "Spain," the "real" Spain is the ser (essence); anything else is simply estar (peripheral). "Real" Spain becomes the heart of the problem. What is the "real" Spain? Is real Spain merely a statistical description? Or is "real" Spain "pure" Spain? (In the North/South dialogue pure Spain is the North, while in the Center/ Periphery dialogue pure Spain is the Center. In the "two Spain" dialogue pure Spain is non-European Spain.) Or is there no Spain? And if the bulls and the bullfight are identified with Spain, which Spain is it? Recall that los toros are called the fiesta nacional by many. Thus, the bulls immediately become more than a spectacle. The label *fiesta nacional* implies a political vision of Spanish nationality resented by many.

Vitoria, capital of the Basque province of Alava, was in fiestas, celebrating its patroness, the White Virgin. It was the early 1980s. As was typical, various young men's clubs were marching in the streets in the early afternoon. Each club was wearing different-colored long "blouses," which give the clubs their collective names: *las blusas*. They were on their way, following a team of mules to the bullring, where they usually sat together to watch the afternoon *corrida*. While parading to the bullring, someone yelled that the corrida was the "fiesta nacional de España." An argument ensued over the implications of the phrase. In response, the blusas arrived at the ring and en masse refused to go in, thus refusing to participate in this non-Basque spectacle. From then on, the blusas parade to the bullring but do not go in. Every year this morality play about Spanish nationality is repeated.

Chapter 3

FROM RENTED COWS TO VIRGIN BULLS: RELATIONS BETWEEN THE VARIOUS FIESTAS TAURINAS

In March 1985, the respected Spanish film director Luis G. Berlanga finished the culminating film of his career. The film's opening was covered extensively in the press. The film, which went on to be the Spanish box office hit of 1985, was titled *La Vaquilla* ("The Little Cow"). Most films about the Spanish Civil War have tended to blame one side or the other. *La Vaquilla* was hailed as the first film that laughed at both sides. It was about the foibles of mankind as a whole, thereby superseding the division of "Spain" into the "two Spains" of the Spanish Civil War and obviating any question of guilt or moral superiority.

The story takes place in a small town under Nationalist control. The town is going to celebrate its fiestas with the typical festive events: a dance, festive meal, religious procession, and bullfight with a vaquilla (cow). The vaquilla becomes the focal point of this very humorous film. The film's humor, however, depends on some very basic understandings and assumptions about the semantics of los toros.

The Asymmetry between Cows and Bulls

The Spanish National Library contains over 4,228 works about los toros, most of which deals with only one spectacle: the *corrida de toros* (Cossío 1980[5]:458). Almost all analyses of los toros by Spaniards in the last two hundred years (1780–1980) have focused on the corrida (see Cambria 1974, 1991 for a review of this literature). Information about the other taurine fiestas is usually tucked inside books or articles dedicated to la corrida or exists as picturesque descriptions within trav-

Table 3.1 Number of Taurine Fiestas in 1984

Categories	ADETA Total Spain	Sevilla South	Navarra North	Madrid Center	Valencia Levante	Vizcaya North
National						
corrida de toros	485	22	22	71	11	7
novillada picada	252	16	14	83	18	4
rejones, toros rejones, novillos		4	0	13	7	1
novillada sin picador	1506	11	12	191	15	3
Totals:	2243	53	48	358	51	15
Intermediate						
becerrada	1537	10	22	124	4	3
toreo cómico	298	8	10	36	7	1
festival	203	6	8	61	2	1
Totals:	2038	24	40	221	13	5
Local						
encierros	1755	0	472	336	1051	0
capea	0	0	0	0	0	0
vaquillas	1559	7	0	57	0	58
miscellaneous	—	—	—	—	—	—
Totals:	3314	7	472	393	1051	58
Totals	7595	84	560	972	1115	78

elogues or novels. Typical of this phenomenon is José María Cossío's colossal eight-volume work entitled *Los toros* (1943–1986). With over 8,000 pages dedicated to the corrida, only 128 are written about all the other taurine fiestas.

Despite this literary emphasis, the corrida de toros represents a very small part of the total taurine fiestas. In 1985 there were at least 7,595 *fiestas taurinas* in Spain.[1] Only 485 were corridas de toros. The vast majority were various local formats (table 3.1).

The corrida and the other fiestas refer to each other. Any analysis of los toros must include both the upper-level national formats and the lower-level local formats. It is a mistake to think that los toros means la corrida. By doing so, one is missing such Spanish debates as the "two Spains," North and South, Center and Periphery, urban and rural, and Right and Left.

Table 3.2 Structural Oppositions of Corridas and Vaquillas

Corridas	Vaquillas
Animal	
bull	cow
male	female
mature	immature
horns intact	horns covered/none
de muerte	de vida
sacrificed	recycled
virgin	used
owned	rented
expensive	cheap
People	
adults	children
spectators	participants
aristocrats	pueblo
professionals	amateurs
one on one	many on many
Place	
ring/inside	streets/outside
tickets	no tickets
urban	rural
South	North
national	local
Values	
hierarchy	equality
order	anarchy
control/domination	identification
culture	folklore
arte	barbarie
slow	fast
Right	Left
Franco	Socialists/democracy

To refer to the differences within the hierarchy of taurine formats, Spaniards collapse all the many formats into the two extreme poles: the corrida de toros (bullfight) at the top of the hierarchy and *las vaquillas* (games with cows) at the bottom. Although both bulls and cows appear in fiestas, the toro, not the cow, represents "Spain," for it is never said that the cow is the totem of Spain. These forms represent the oppositions between the national and the local forms (table 3.2). The corridas and vaquillas thus stand for more than simply two different kinds of games with bovines. The differences between corridas and vaquillas are associated with opposing people, places, and ultimately values. This chapter explores these meanings. I first discuss the different roles of the animals in each fiesta and then move on to the role of people, places, and values.

Animals

The animals associated with each pole of the taurine hierarchy are the bull *(toro bravo)* in the corrida and the cow (vaquilla) in the fiesta of vaquillas. The toro bravo is a mature (four to five year old) male animal, while the vaquilla is a young (one to two year old) female. Besides the usual asymmetry of sex and age, these two animals differ in several other ways.

Horns

One of the toro's most important symbols is his horns, which in the corrida must be "intact" (for *seriedad,* seriousness). To reduce the risk to the *torero,* horns were filed or "shaved" quite regularly in the 1950s and 1960s.[2] The government then stepped in to insure "intact" horns. Ranchers are fined if their bulls are discovered with "shaved" horns. After each corrida the horns are checked, and any suspicious-looking ones are sent to Madrid in a sealed box for inspection by veterinarians. The opposite of the intact horn is the covered horn *(cuerno embolado).* A protective leather ball or cover is tied onto the horns or the points of the horn may be filed off. In vaquillas, the cows let loose to butt and charge the boys usually have their horns covered. However, not all vaquillas have covered horns. Some towns are very proud that the cows in their fiestas still have sharp, intact horns as this lends prestige to the fiesta. Neither do all toros always have intact horns. In bullfights on horseback the bulls usually have their horns filed off. In general, however, the categories "intact versus covered" horns correspond with the categories "toro versus vaquilla."

Life/Death

The toros in a corrida are sometimes referred to as "bulls of death" *(toros de muerte)* because they die in the ring. The animals in the lower-level fiestas, for example vaquillas, are called "bulls of life" *(toros de vida)* because these animals, especially the cows, do not die during the fiesta. Therefore, a town must *buy* a bull. Cows, however, are merely rented for the day from a local rancher. The next day they may be re-cycled and used again in the next town down the road. Moreover, the toros are "virgins" to the cape (i.e., never caped before), and the rancher must guarantee this or he is liable for punitive fines by the government.[3] Obviously, vaquillas are not held to this rule since they are often used over and over again throughout the summer. In contrast to the "virgin" bull, vaquillas are valued for their experience. Experienced cows are called "sharp" or "smart" and according to villagers make better fiestas because they know exactly how to charge and flip people in the air.

Breed

The male toro for the corrida should be a purebred animal: a toro bravo. It must come from an accredited ranch that can attest to the animal's genetic purity. Each bull's genealogy is considered of utmost impor-tance. Fans go to a specific corrida because of a ranch's good reputation, which means its bulls are noble and will charge. The breeder receives applause if his bulls perform well and is shamed if his bulls do "badly." Purity and good breeding are exalted.

The lower-level fiestas use animals from a secondary organization of ranches. These animals are of inferior quality. Sometimes they are bulls of mixed breeds. A rancher who raised vaquillas around Valencia contra-dicted himself when he claimed that he kept the breed "pure" but also spoke quite openly of crossing lines within the breed, "although the law said you couldn't do this."

Price

Its age and other characteristics make the toro bravo very expensive to buy. A rented vaquilla is not as expensive. This economic consideration is thought to be the only reason some towns would choose an animal (or spectacle) other than a toro bravo (or corrida de toro). Nevertheless, people insisted they would never give up their "typical" fiesta, even though it involved a "lesser" animal, since that fiesta defines part of their town's identity.

People

Age and Participation

By law, only people over fourteen years old may attend corridas. (However, in every corrida I attended outside of Madrid, I saw many children accompanied by adults.) On the other hand, vaquillas are for families and children. In a corrida the public watches the torero, who is paid to entertain and work for them, while the people are merely spectators. In vaquillas the townsmen chase the cows, thus the people are participants. This probably explains their loyalty to their local form.

Social Class

The corrida has a definite aristocratic air. It has a reputation of being patronized by aristocrats and landed gentry from southern Spain. On the other hand, the *pueblo* participates in vaquillas. In Spanish, *pueblo* has three meanings. First, it means "town or village," in contrast to city. This contrast immediately elicits a hierarchy where urban (city) is valued over rural (pueblo), sophistication (city) over brutishness (pueblo), and culture (city) over folklore (pueblo) (Caro Baroja 1963). Second, in the expression *el pueblo español* (the Spanish people), *pueblo* refers to "a people," a culture. *Pueblo* also means "the common people," the "people," "plebe," and finally, "the lower classes." So while *pueblo* implies lower class, it is also where the true values of "Spain" are posited, where the "essence" of Spain is to be found. When I say "the pueblo participates in vaquillas," the meaning of both "village" and "plebe" is elicited. The rural people and the "common man" are the protagonists in vaquillas. One young woman explained why her father, a university-educated lawyer who had inherited land in the village, never let his sons participate in the town vaquillas. "Only the *populacho* (a pejorative word for 'common people') run in vaquillas," he used to say.

Professionals versus Amateurs

In the corrida the man who fights the bull is a professional (torero), while in vaquillas the men who tease the calves are strictly amateurs (sometimes called *toreadores*). The torero must belong to the Bullfighters Union and upon retirement can collect Social Security.

The corrida pits one man against one bull, thus underlining the man's individuality, while vaquillas pit many men against many calves. The many men clearly represent the community, and in this sense a lower-level fiesta is a ritual about community identity (Mirá 1976; Serrán Pagán 1979). The corrida, on the other hand, forges an individual identity, that of the torero.

Place

Ring versus Street

Corridas take place in a plaza de toros, while vaquillas and *encierros* can take place in makeshift rings, or even more typically, in the village streets.[4] This is a key difference between the vaquillas and corridas. In encierros and vaquillas the animals run in and through the villages's living, working, civic, and religious spaces, past houses and shops. Women and children look down from the balconies of the houses, and the men run in the streets, which reproduces the traditional gender roles and symbolic spaces. When a town plaza is barricaded off to form a closed "ring" for a taurine fiesta, it is still an integrated space with multiple uses. The only spatial separations are between men and women.

In a corrida de toro, women and men sit together in the bullring, a building dedicated exclusively to this public spectacle. Although political rallies, rock concerts, and operas are now held in some bullrings, they are generally used only a few times a year, standing idle most of the time.

In the contrasts corridas/vaquillas and bullrings/streets, one can see that having and maintaining a bullring is a measure of a town's wealth and, thus, importance. The Ministry of Interior rates bullrings as first, second, or third category rings: "category" translates into size of ring and city. Cities consider their plaza de toros as part of their monumental, or artistic, patrimony. Books trace the histories of bullrings in big cities such as Sevilla, Madrid, and Bilbao. Thus, to have a *plaza de toros* is not only a statement about that town's *afición a los toros*. It is also a statement about the town's sophistication, culture, size, power, and importance with respect to other towns nearby without a plaza de toros, where calves must be run in the street.

A further difference between cows in the streets and bulls in the plaza is that, although the bullring belongs to the municipality, one pays to go to a corrida. This is not so in vaquillas. Money is always an important issue in the bullfighting world. Bullfight tickets are expensive, and many people who would like to go to a corrida say they cannot because they do not have the money; yet vaquillas are always free.

Urban versus Rural

Another consideration about place in los toros is the urban/rural contrast. The corrida is essentially an urban phenomenon. Of the more than 170 localities where corridas took place in 1984–1985, the great

Table 3.3 Afición a los Toros by Size of Town

Population (thousands)	<2	2–10	11–50	51–200	>200
Men	44.4%	52.2%	47.2%	34.8%	32.8%
Women	32.2%	41.0%	32.1%	30.5%	26.1%

Source: Alef, S.A., Gabinete de Estudios Económicos y Sociales 1983.

majority of them were cities or towns of over twenty thousand people: 363 out of 495 corridas. Provincial capitals always celebrated more corridas than other places in the province. The smaller the town, the fewer the number of corridas.

In general, the further one goes down the taurine fiesta hierarchy, the more rural the settings. An official in Madrid told me that "the encierros begin where the asphalt ends," referring to the rural nature of encierros. Vaquillas take place primarily in towns smaller than ten thousand people. Moreover, in a government sponsored survey on bullfighting, those towns (of two thousand to ten thousand inhabitants) had the highest percentage of fans (table 3.3).

Cost may be one determining factor. Many small pueblos would have difficulty affording a corrida de toros. For a population of two thousand people to pay for six toros and three toreros would cause the ticket price to be too expensive for many people. How price influences the category of spectacle chosen is evident in several ways. For example, even where a town prefers to run a toro in its streets, the town's economic situation may preclude buying a bull and require paying for a cow (well documented by Mirá 1976), or even suppressing the taurine fiesta altogether ("Fiestas sin . . ." 1985 : 10).

North versus South

Moving to another level, the opposition between the categories North/ South corresponds to the opposition between vaquilla/corrida. Corridas dominate in the South, while vaquillas dominate in the North. It is well known that the "greatest afición a los toros is in Andalusia," that is, the South. I have heard this expression repeated for fifteen years. However, upon investigation, things are a little more complex.

In Andalusia los toros means only corridas. Since corridas originated in the South, they are the local form. In a 1983 survey, almost 43% of

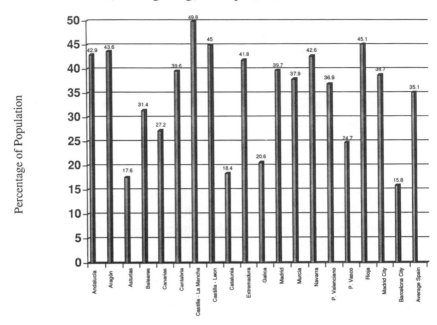

Figure 3.1. Afición a los toros by region in 1983

Andalusia's population said they were aficionados of los toros. However, the survey put three central regions and Aragón above Andalusia
for percentage of fans (figure 3.1). Furthermore, Andalusia comes in
eighth, behind six central regions and Navarra, in attendance at los toros in 1983 (figure 3.2). These regions have a higher percentage of fans,
but their populations are smaller than Andalusia's.

Although more corridas took place in Andalusia than any other region (table 3.4), what happens to Andalusia with respect to the other
taurine fiestas? When one looks at the numbers for *novillada con picador* (calf fights), for example, Andalusia comes in second place with only
forty-five *novilladas* compared to Madrid's sixty-eight.

Sevilla is the most populous province in Andalusia and the symbolic
center of Andalusian values. The bullring in Sevilla is the most important in Andalusia and is claimed to be the "cathedral" of bullrings in
Spain. In table 3.1 one can see that Sevilla has more corridas than
any other kind of taurine spectacles. Informants all over Spain said
that "real" bullfighting fans *(auténtica afición)* come from Sevilla. The
equation "Sevilla = afición a los toros" was ever present.[5]

When I asked in Sevilla about lower-level taurine fiestas, that is, encierros and vaquillas, I was told that "these things were held in the North, not in the South." The numbers are faithful to the collective representations in this case. In 1984, only seven vaquillas were celebrated in Sevilla province.

Spaniards say that vaquillas and encierros are characteristic fiestas of the "North."[6] Official figures confirm this. The category encierro in Navarra, for example, has twenty times as many local-level bull games as the national corridas: 472 encierros and vaquillas to 22 corridas (see table 3.1).

The question thus arises as to why there is a preference for corridas de toros in the "South" and vaquillas and encierros in the "North." Corridas de toros dominate numerically in the South because these fiestas are urban, class-related phenomena, stressing hierarchy rather than equality. Southern Spain is characterized by midsized and large cities, where various antagonistic classes live side by side and social hierarchy is open and blatant (see chapter 2). Anthropological literature describes strained and conflict-ridden class relations in these large southern towns

Figure 3.2. Attendance at los toros in 1983

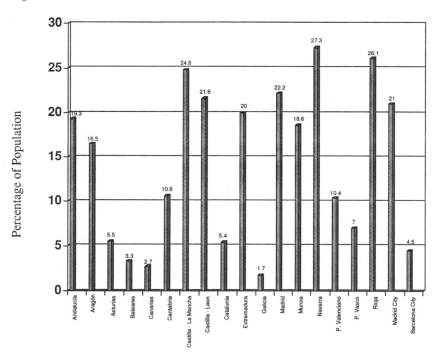

Table 3.4 Corridas de Toros in Spain

	1984	1985	Alef survey afición % of population
Region			
Andalucía	117	123	42.9%
Madrid	67	⸳ 63	39.2%
Castilla – La Mancha	47	46	49.8%
Valencia	43	39	36.9%
Catalonia	34	35	18.4%
País Vasco	21	12	24.7%
Navarra	20	20	42.6%
Aragón	20	15	43.6%
Logroño	17	17	45.1%
Extremadura	16	19	41.8%
Murcia	12	20	37.9%
Baleares	7	6	31.4%
Cantabria	6	7	39.6%
Galicia	4	4	20.6%
Asturias	3	3	16.6%
Provinces of Research			% of Spanish population
Madrid	67	63	12.5%
Sevilla	23	23	4.0%
Navarra	20	20	1.0%
Valencia	13	19	5.0%
Vizcaya	7	7	3.0%

(Brandes 1980; Gilmore 1980; Press 1979). This literature also stresses that town festivals (Carnaval, Feria) reflect this class conflict.

Vaquillas and encierros seem to take place more often in the North because these games, which stress egalitarian participation, take place primarily in small towns. Small towns are characteristic of northern Spain, where villagers themselves are likely to all be owners of the farmed land. Anthropologists who have done work in these northern villages (Aceves

1971; Douglass, W. 1969; Freeman 1970) stress the egalitarianism between families and the sexes that is prevalent there.[7]

Before proceeding, I must deal with the anomaly of Madrid province and the taurine spectacles there. Referring to table 3.1, one notes immediately the very large number of taurine fiestas celebrated throughout the province. In 1984, of the 178 municipalities 158 celebrated some kind of taurine fiesta. The vast majority of the corridas took place in the city of Madrid (43) in 1984, but there were 28 other corridas in the province.[8] The large number of corridas indicates that Madrid is a province of large cities, and indeed, six cities in the province have populations of over one hundred thousand people. However, the largest category of taurine fiestas by far was the encierro (393 in 113 different towns). The large number of encierros supposedly indicates that Madrid is a province of small towns, which it is (there are 121 municipalities with under two thousand inhabitants).

Where to locate Madrid on the North/South opposition would seem problematic. But in its position as Center, it mediates between the North and the South, that is, it is neither, yet both. This is also true of its taurine fiestas. Looking at table 3.1 one sees that Sevilla (South) has many more national format fiestas than local-level fiestas (53 to 7). In Navarra (North) local-level formats clearly dominate (465 to 49). Madrid, however, has 360 national taurine fiestas and 393 local-level fiestas. This relative balance between national and local formats in its taurine fiestas truly makes Madrid the "center" and mediates between the forms of the North and the South.

Town size and kind of taurine fiesta may be connected, but informants do not make this relationship in explaining why one province prefers one form over another (i.e., why there are no encierros in Sevilla or why there are so many *toros embolados* in Valencia). Instead, the answer always has to do with local identity. Sometimes people merely shrugged their shoulders and answered, "Tradition." Others would use history and explain that while the corridas had their origin in the South, encierros and vaquillas had much longer histories in the North, which is true. Therefore, since taurine fiestas are associated with celebrations of community identity, polluting that identity with a nonindigenous taurine fiesta is a contradiction of sorts.[9]

In Navarra, Vizcaya, and Valencia specific taurine fiestas are identified with the regional "personality" (e.g., encierros, *sokamuturra*, and toros embolados, respectively). In each province, since citizens believe that the local taurine form has been practiced there since "time immemorial," the town fiestas always include that form as part of the unchangeable town "character," as part of the communion of corporateness. Usually townspeople emphasize that their fiestas date from at least the fourteenth century, or some earlier century.

Therefore, the overt motivation for preferring a toro embolado over a corrida in most people's minds was simply local identification and history. The North is typified by the forms categorized under vaquillas because those forms arose prior to the corrida, which did not originate until the eighteenth century in the South. The various northern provinces and regions are conceived as existing with their specific personalities long before the end of the Reconquest (1492), and their taurine fiestas manifest the continuance of those "personalities" through time. The South, reincorporated much later into "Spain," readapted the aristocratic bullfighting form into a new spectacle, the corrida. Even after it spread to become the *fiesta nacional,* the corrida remained Andalusia's symbol of local identity.

National versus Local

The final contrast of places for corridas and vaquillas is the "national versus the local" focus. Previous description has implied several times why the corrida and the upper-level fiestas are national spectacles. In 1984 and 1985 every province in Spain (except two in Galicia) had at least one corrida de toro. The rules governing the corrida apply nationally and originate in the central government. Fines to ranchers and toreros and other punishments are decided in Madrid. Each plaza de toros is constructed according to national measurements and specifications. Until recently, permission to hold a corrida has always been granted by central government representatives. The president of the ring has always been a representative of the national government (civil governor or police chief). Corridas always take place at the same time of day, in the afternoon. The toreros fight in all rings, crisscrossing the country almost daily in summer, weaving the threads of their trips into a giant Spanish tapestry. The bulls are also sent by train from one end of Spain to the other. A Ministry of Agriculture publication claims that toros bravos are raised in seven of the nine river basins that traverse Spain (Ministerio de Agricultura 1980:33). Many fiestas are televised on the main national channel.[10] The daily national newspapers all include pages dedicated to corridas de toros in the spring and summer months *(El*

País, ABC, Ya, Diario 16, El Alcázar), with summaries of what happened and criticisms of the performances of the bulls and toreros.

Vaquillas and encierros are local fiestas because neither their form nor their repercussion is national. Rather, they are peculiar to one place. Only the specific towns know the rules and the choreography of these traditional fiestas. They take place in the town streets or plazas. Only villagers know where the dangerous places are. Commonly, these rented animals may be used in other parts of the province but do not usually travel out of their own region. Punishment for a participant's wrongdoing does not come from Madrid but rather from other participants. The time of day varies from place to place, from an early morning encierro (street run) to a midnight toro embolado (burning torches on horns). The toreadores are local boys, and although some boys from nearby villages or towns participate, they do not crisscross the nation like a torero.

The local fiestas receive little attention in the national press. In general, the national media do not report on these events—except the encierros in Pamplona. Even the local newspapers, which perhaps give advance notice of these fiestas, do not report on them after they have happened, unless there were injuries.

Values

By opposing corridas with vaquillas, a fourth category of relationships emerges. This category consists of contrasting values projected by the corridas and vaquillas. These values refer to each other, thus creating a dynamic discourse. This further emphasizes the need to consider los toros in their totality, from corridas to vaquillas.

Slow versus Fast

Change in pace is one of the most striking characteristics when comparing the national versus the local taurine festivals. The corrida's art, culture, order, and control must always be carried out slowly, "with grace and style." All the formalities of the corrida must be done in a stately, rather rigid, controlled style. A perfect pass in a corrida occurs when the torero stands his ground without moving a foot and very slowly passes the bull 180 degrees or more around his body. For the torero to jump or run around is "ugly" *(feo)*. Control must be achieved in a dignified way. After a particularly good series of passes, the bull should look confused and the torero should be able to turn his back and walk slowly away from the bull without the bull charging. Thus dominance has an aristocratic bearing. Grace is slow.

As one moves down the taurine spectacles, the action speeds up. First, the animals are smaller and faster. Even in a *corrida de rejoneo* (horseback), the horses prance and dance constantly, and the pace is generally much quicker. In the lowest-level fiestas movement and action is constant, everything is fast. In an encierro the runners and bulls run or sprint the whole distance of the course. In vaquillas and *capeas*, although not all the participants are in constant motion, when they take their turn, they run and jump and dodge the cows. Compared to a corrida, there is no attempt at grace. No one turns and walks away from a calf or cow in a vaquilla. One always runs at least a short distance away. Movements are jerky. A capea has no "aristocrats."

Hierarchy versus Equality

In the corrida hierarchy is emphasized everywhere. In the seating arrangement, tickets for *Sol* (sun) are less expensive, while tickets for *Sombra* (shade) are more expensive. In the relationships between president-public and president-torero, the ring president makes all final decisions about the bulls: the number of pics a bull must take, the awards and warnings given to a torero. In the relationship between torero and torero, seniority decides position in the opening parade and the order of performance. In the relationship between the torero and his team, the torero "directs" the other members of his team. Most importantly, hierarchy is emphasized in the relationship between the torero and the bull. The torero's objective is to "control" and "dominate" the bull, which is what the public comes to see. The corrida is not a contest, and the public protests vociferously if the torero does not control the bull. The oft-repeated key phrase for the bullfight is *"parar, templar, mandar"* (to stop, to modify, to command). Finally, the bull is killed and the hierarchy between man and beast is made even more manifest.

In the lower-level spectacles, hierarchy is not totally absent. Until recently only males participated, and even now the number of young women is very small. Clearly some young men gain more prestige by their feats than others, and sometimes one part of town competes against another. In some fiestas the participants dominate the bull by extremely violent means, eventually killing it.

However, rather than hierarchy, what is projected in the lower-level taurine fiestas is egalitarianism, or equality, at least within the community. Certainly the relationships among the young men *(cuadrillas,*

peñas) who run together are explicitly egalitarian. Equality is underlined by the fact that anyone can participate (Echeverría 1983:137).
More significantly, especially in encierros, the young men do not want
to "control," or to dominate, the animal, which would be impossible,
but rather they want to identify with it. In Pamplona, one runner, Javier
Hermosilla, told me that he does not like to see the bull killed. "If I
were from Sevilla or Madrid, I probably wouldn't go to a corrida." He
said he loved the bulls, but it was a very pure love *(amor puro)*. He did
not wish to dominate the bull. Even in the many different kinds of vaquillas, the participants do not try to kill the animal, which is done after
the fiesta if at all, but rather they try to touch or slap the cow, grab its
tail, jump over it, or pull its rope without getting hurt or hurting the
animal. Thus, there is overt equality between participants, as well as an
identification between the participants and the bulls.

While "order" is almost an obsession in the corrida and upper-level
fiestas, in the intermediate categories it begins to disappear. These
spectacles involve much more informality and spontaneity. Finally, the
lower-level spectacles project, outwardly at least, "anarchy." This term,
seen repeatedly in the literature, is used by corrida aficionados to describe the local fiestas. Antonio, an ex–merchant marine now living in
Madrid and working in a Japanese company, was showing me his taurine library collection when I asked him about capeas and vaquillas. He
answered, "Capeas? They are anarchy. Barbarism. The boys are drunk.
Total disorder. No, they aren't serious." [11]

Culture versus Folklore

Another difference between corridas and vaquillas is the opposition between "culture" and "folklore." Corridas are consistently assigned to
the realm of culture. In the largest national newspaper, *El País,* bullfighting news is located in the section with theater, film, and book reviews. It is not near the sports section. Defense of the corrida, against
the antibullfighting press, is always done in the name of Spanish culture
(playing on the two meanings of culture), emphasizing that corridas
belong to the history and traditions of Spain. On the other hand, the
lower-level fiestas (vaquillas, encierros, etc.) are said to be part of the
"folklore" of Spain. In the Spanish romantic movement of the second
half of the nineteenth century, capeas and vaquillas, as examples of
romanticized "local color," were common subjects of literature and
painting.

In general, in the comparison of culture and folklore, "culture" is the more valued term. In Spanish terms, *"folklore no es serio"* (folklore is not serious). Similarly, culture belongs to urban society, like corridas, while folklore belongs to rural society, as do vaquillas.

Art versus Barbarism

A further opposition between corridas and vaquillas, often heard among aficionados and others, is that of "art versus barbarism" *(arte* versus *barbarie)* ("Toros: arte o barbarie" 1985). A frequently used expression for the corrida is *"el arte de toreo"* (the art of bullfighting), or *"el arte taurino."* The toreros are referred to regularly as "artists" or "maestros." On the other hand, capeas and vaquillas are often judged as a barbarism (barbarie). Recall the already cited comment by the aficionado Antonio, where in one breath he described capeas as anarchistic and barbarian.

These last two oppositions (culture versus folklore, art versus barbarism) are a bit paradoxical because those against bullfighting, the *antitaurinos,* often take the negative attributes of the lower-level fiestas (i.e., folklore, barbarism) and apply them to the corrida itself. Bullfighting's enemies often accuse the "planet of the bulls" of being merely folkloristic Spain (as opposed to an implied "real," cultural Spain). In the 1986 bullfighting season, several different groups sponsored an antibullfighting campaign. These groups pasted up hundreds of posters before important corridas all over Spain. The posters, which showed a dying bull lanced by the Spanish flag, read, "Neither art nor culture. The national shame." For fans of the corrida, the lower-level taurine spectacles are a barbarie. For people against the bullfight, the corrida itself is a barbarie.

Politics: Left and Right

During the 1980s, different political tendencies were associated with the two different poles of los toros. The corridas were associated with Franco's Spain; the vaquillas and encierros were associated with "democracy" and, more specifically, with the Socialists. These contrasting associations were never produced by one person. Instead, several people would relate the corrida to Franco's Spain. Then, in other conversations and in the press, I would find comments connecting the encierros to democracy, and/or the Socialists. These associations were not based on any abstract inherent characteristics of the respective spectacle. That is, no one associated the corridas with the dictator Franco because corridas projected the values of hierarchy, order, and control. Nor did anyone relate the vaquillas to democracy because they were more democratic, or because they represented the values of equality, anarchy, or identification. These associations were made for more concrete reasons.

One reason the corrida was associated with Franco's Spain (1939– 1975) was because during that time the lower-level fiestas (encierros, *sueltas de vaquillas,* capeas) were prohibited. It is unclear why they were prohibited. The official word from the taurine section of the Ministry of Interior, where I interviewed various officials in 1984 and 1985, was that these fiestas were prohibited to avoid mishap and serious accidents to participants. It should be pointed out, however, that all large gatherings were prohibited during this time. Carnaval and various other potentially subversive fiestas were banned. Clearly, these taurine fiestas were prohibited not merely for safety reasons but for political considerations too.

While Franco prohibited encierros and capeas, the corrida numbers grew. Before Franco, from 1901 until the Spanish Civil War in 1936, there had been an average of 257 corridas per year. Immediately after the beginning of the Civil War, the herds of toros bravos were decimated, and for years corridas were not held. But by 1942 there were again 247 corridas per year.

At the end of the 1950s corrida numbers began to rise above the pre– Civil War averages (see figure 1.2). Between 1965 and 1975 corridas averaged 623 per year. The rise in numbers is totally coincident with the influx of foreign tourists that had just began to invade Spain. Tickets to a bullfight became a must for many foreign visitors. It has been calculated that one in six tourists go to a bullfight (Claramunt 1982:121). Since tourist money quickly became one of the mainstays of the Spanish economy, a whole industry arose that consisted of selling "Spain" to northern European tourists. Since corridas de toros formed part of the images that were "Spain" for northern Europeans (along with flamenco music and dance, ceramics, and, for some reason, Mexican hats), Spanish entrepreneurs obliged and organized more bullfights. During these years many Spaniards expressed this fact by insisting that only the tourists went to the bullfight.

However, tourism was not the only reason for the rising numbers of corridas. The government also actively promoted bullfights. Franco and the "Spain" that won the Civil War, the Nationalists, seemed to value the fiesta nacional in a special way. Although Franco was from Galicia, a region without much of a bullfighting tradition, he was a great aficionado of los toros (Gutiérrez Alarcón 1978). Corridas were included in the bundle of images considered to be *"castiza"* (pure) Spain, which Franco and his Nationalist supporters in general patronized. General Franco was often photographed with popular bullfighters, especially El Cordobés, the most important torero of the 1960s.

Under Franco, the conservative Andalusian landed gentry continued to occupy powerful political positions to an extraordinary degree (de Miguel 1976; Moreno Navarro 1978). The regime subtly associated *toreo* with the landed gentry *(señorio)* (Barquerito 1985:541), as many of these landowners included a bull ranch *(ganadería)* among their properties, much like a status symbol. In 1984 an Andalusian land-owner, who also has a bull ranch, proudly showed me a picture of him-self with Franco and declared that Franco had been like a father to him. Many people still seem to think that these southern landowners are the people who most attend bullfights (in the taurine literature see also Barquerito 1985:541; Villán 1985:35). Thus, the relationship torero-*ganaderos*-Franco linked the corrida to Franco in the minds of many Spaniards.

In fact, had it not been for the Nationalists (the Right) during the Civil War, the toro bravo and the corrida de toros may well have died out completely (Gutiérrez Alarcón 1978). At the outbreak of the Civil War in July 1936, many day workers simply invaded the hated bull ranches, symbols of Andalusia's nonproductivity and the people's pov-erty, and slaughtered the bulls. After the first few weeks the Nationalists established themselves in Andalusia, Salamanca, and northern Castile, where the best ganaderías were located. Thus, in Nationalist territory the bulls and their ranch owners were protected by the army after the first chaotic weeks of the war. The ganaderías in the Republican zone, on the other hand, were decimated by peasants, first in a spirit of social revenge and later out of hunger. The bull breeders pleaded that a mini-mum of stud bulls and cows be saved, but this was not done.[12]

The Republicans and the political left had been against los toros. The further left the party was on the political spectrum, the more opposed it was to los toros. The Anarchists opposed bullfighting totally, calling the corrida a "remnant of medieval cruelty," claiming that it "desensi-tized people to suffering and distracted them from the task of educating themselves" (Mintz 1982:86). People openly wondered if bullfighting would be abolished if the Communists won the 1936 elections (Boado and Cebolla 1976:156). Aficionados thought the Left was against bull-fights because it had been polluted by European ideas. In many ways, these attitudes continue today.

From 1982 to 1996, the Socialists ruled Spain and therefore were in charge of los toros. In general, since political parties were legalized in 1977, none has taken any radical or ideological stand against los toros. Most adopt positions like Sr. García Alonso, cultural advisor of the Region of Madrid. "The fiesta of the bulls is a fundamentally cultural phenomenon, rooted in the most profound part of our culture" (Mocholi 1986:9). Nevertheless many aficionados still believe the Socialists are hostile to the corrida. Aficionados frequently accuse the Socialists of indifference or outright war on the fiesta nacional. Thus, it was a paradox for many people when in the summer of 1985 the vice president of the Socialist government, Alfonso Guerra, professed his long-time ambition to be a torero.

Although the Socialists and other leftist parties have historically been against the corrida, they are now associated with the lower-level taurine fiestas.[13] Beginning with Franco's death in 1975 and democracy's official arrival in 1977, a very conscious recovery of the "local traditions" and folklore was undertaken. This recovery is both a manifestation and a celebration of two activities Franco had repressed: the pueblo's participation in public life and regionalism. Encierros, capeas, and vaquillas reappeared openly in town festivals in many areas of Spain. In 1982, the year the Socialists came to power, a law was passed repealing the Francoist prohibition of these fiestas.[14]

Many towns had never stopped celebrating their taurine fiesta during the Franco years. They had simply called it a livestock fair rather than a bullfight (Mirá 1976). However, many towns had suppressed their fiesta until after 1982. In these places, when I asked how long they had held encierros, I received answers such as "since the arrival of democracy," or "since the Socialists came to power (in the town)," or simply the dates "1978–1979" or "1980."[15] The association of Socialists with encierros was very explicit, although at the same time, many informants insisted that the encierro was an authentic tradition of the pueblo "that had been lost."

Therefore, if one looks at the two extreme poles of the taurine fiestas, corridas and vaquillas, each form has grown in numbers when its associated political groups have been in power. Corridas are associated with Franco's Spain (at least with the "Spain" Franco wanted Spain to be— the "official Spain"), and their numbers doubled during the Franco years, 1936–1975, relative to any earlier records. Meanwhile lower-level taurine fiestas were suppressed. In 1982 the Socialists won the national parliamentary elections and lower-level taurine fiestas were again made legal. Their numbers grew in the years 1977 to 1986 to far out-weigh the corrida, although no political party proposes banishing the corridas.

I do not mean to imply that either political movement (Francoists or Socialists) consciously saw the corridas and vaquillas in opposition and manipulated them as symbolic statements. Many Socialists, especially, are surprised to think of their party ideologically promoting any aspect of los toros. Some Socialists admit to never having had anything to do with los toros until their new political responsibilities required them to deal with los toros. An example is the mayor of Pozuelo de Alarcón (Madrid) who before occupying that job had never gone to los toros. Since he has been mayor, he "hasn't stopped promoting las corridas in a town that formally did not even have a tradition" (Gómez Mardo-nes 1985:33). Many Socialists seem puzzled by their enthusiastic role of promoting traditional fiestas, since the symbols manipulated in these fiestas are often symbols (e.g., toros and Virgin Marys) formerly thought to belong to the previous Francoist regime (Garrigues 1984:76).

Neither do I want to imply that all Francoists, nor all of the political Right, approve of the corrida. I know many individuals who were avid Franco supporters, yet who detest the corrida. Instead, the temporal connection between the corrida and Franco (the Right) and the vaqui-llas and democracy (the Left) is at the level of vague cultural categories that can be riddled with dozens of individual exceptions. However, these categories are used in Spain as social facts.

Polls by the Spanish polling agency Gallup reaffirm the connection of the political Right and the corridas. No such statistical evidence links the Left to the local-level forms. In 1984 and 1985 surveys were made in which the interviewee was asked which political party he/she had voted for in 1982 or would vote for today. Then the interviewee's inter-est in corridas de toros was correlated to political party. As can be seen in table 3.5, voters for the political parties on the right show much more interest in corridas than those on the left. Moreover, all the national parties show more interest in corridas than the regional (Nationalist) parties do, thus, replicating the national/local associations for corridas.

Ethnography: *La Vaquilla*

We are now in a position to discuss and understand the 1985 Spanish film *La Vaquilla,* described at the beginning of the chapter. The story, a comedy about the Civil War, takes place during a long lull in the fight-ing. The two sides, dug in and facing each other, are at a rather casual,

Table 3.5 Toros and Politics

Political Party Voted in 1982	% of Vote	Interest in los Toros			
		Much	Some	None	No Opinion
AP (Right)	13.0	31.8	27.6	37.9	2.6
UDC (Right)	2.7	25.6	37.1	37.3	—
CDS (Right)	2.8	28.4	30.2	41.5	—
PSOE (Center)	50.2	20.3	31.0	48.0	0.7
PCE/PSUC (Left)	3.4	3.6	42.6	53.8	—
Catalan (Nationalist)	4.5	6.6	2.6	87.9	2.9
Basque (Nationalist)	2.5	9.7	28.0	62.3	—
Other (Nationalist)	1.1	20.2	32.6	47.2	—

Source: Gallup Spain 1985.

even intimate, stalemate. Behind the Nationalist lines, a small town decides to celebrate its fiestas with music, feasts, dancing, and a vaquilla. All of this is advertized over loud speakers to the Republican side of the battle lines to demoralize those troops.

The vaquilla, the little cow, becomes the metaphor for the fiesta. She represents the ability to afford a fiesta, in contrast to the poor, miserable Republicans. (The Civil War was often conceived as a conflict between the rich and the poor.) Yet the animal chosen is not a bull. The choice of the vaquilla represents the ruralness of the location, a small village rather than a large city, as well as the relative poverty of Nationalist Spain. All the village could afford was a scrawny little cow.

The Nationalists have somehow found a torero (appropriately from the South, which we know by his accent) to fight the animal in the ring. (This was a war-time inversion, since toreros do not fight female animals.) Yet, since the action takes place in the North, the town also celebrates an encierro with the little cow, running her from a pen outside the town to a ring set up in the main plaza.

Five Republican soldiers with their own torero sneak across the stalemated battle lines to try to steal the vaquilla. The Republican idea was to spoil the Nationalist's party and get meat for their own side. In this sense, the film alludes to the reality that during the war in Republican Spain the toros bravos were killed for meat and for a sense of social revenge, while Nationalist Spain "saved" the bulls for the fiesta.

In this very funny version of the Spanish Civil War not a shot is fired. The war is only fought over the vaquilla, who in the end lies dead, the only victim of this war. The original title of the film was *Fiesta Nacional*, later changed to *La Vaquilla* in an effort, I believe, to underline that the film was not "serious" but a comedy. Despite the protagonism of the little cow, and the title of the film, there is no opposition between toro and vaquilla here. They represent the same thing, as one Spanish film reviewer inadvertently shows us: "Only the bull, metaphor of a Spain that everybody wants to fight over, dies at the end of the film" (Hidalgo 1985:113).

Part 2

MODERNITY: THE BULLS
AND EUROPE

Chapter 4

THE BULL THAT RAVISHED EUROPA

When I arrived in Valencia, a large Mediterranean city surrounded by orange groves, I immediately began to look for the official agency in charge of taurine affairs—the governmental office that gave permission to hold bullfights, kept track of the dates and kinds of fiestas, levied fees, and upheld regulations. I was especially interested to know how many of each taurine format had been held that year in the province.

In Valencia in 1986, these statistics were split between the national government (Gobierno Civil) and the local government (Generalitat). Numbers for the national spectacles such as *corridas, novilladas,* and *becerradas* were in the Ministry of the Interior. The people in this office were very helpful and gave me photocopies of their compiled data sheets for the previous year. They told me that all of the "traditional fiestas," the *encierros, toros embolados,* and *vaquillas,* were handled by the new local government, the Generalitat Valenciana, and its office for taurine affairs, and sent me on my way.

By the time I arrived at the second office, the man in charge had already been alerted that I was coming and what I was looking for. He had consulted his superior, who had given him orders to tell me and give me nothing. All of my explanations were for naught. I would have to get permission to see the numbers from the general director of the interior himself.

It was weeks before I was conceded an interview. The director's office was in a wonderful, old, restored palace. The director himself looked like a modern, young, well-educated, no-nonsense executive, which is typical of the new, younger generation of politicians who have taken over Spain since 1982. I explained to him my study and the reason I was collecting the statistics. He was polite, straightforward, and understood my project. He was also at pains to explain why he did not want to give me the information. He obviously wanted to be open and efficient (the "new" Spain), however, he wanted to avoid problems. He did not want information (names of towns, dates of fiestas) made public. He spoke a lot of the animal protection societies who were causing trouble and mounting campaigns. (Was I one of them?) He wondered about the legality of local bulls of fire (toro embolado). "We are talking about a culture and a tradition with a lot of history," he said. "We'll see what we can give you. I have to study this."

And study he did. Two months went by before I was given access to the statistics on Valencian "traditional bullfighting fiestas." In 1985 alone, there had been over 1200 fiestas in the province of Valencia where bulls, with torches of fire on their horns, had been set free in village and town streets.

Most interesting is the interpretation other Spaniards gave for the director's stalling action. Typical was that of two friends in Barcelona. "Now that we want everyone to see us as 'Europe,' these officials are not interested in publicizing these embarrassing facts about us still having bullfights."

Taurofilos versus Taurofobos, Taurinos versus Antitaurinos

When one talks to a Spaniard anywhere about bullfighting, *before anything else,* the person declares himself or herself to be either "for" or "against" the bulls. This is a statement principally about that person's (and Spain's) place in Europe and in modern life.

Los toros are a polemical phenomenon in Spain. Although bullfights have been referred to for over one hundred years as the *fiesta nacional,* an important part of the population rejects this label. It is not only the label that people often dislike, but also the phenomenon itself.

Sociological surveys on los toros abound. Although regions differ, the averages for all of Spain are quite equal among the many surveys. A 1983 Alef poll found that 50.8% of people interviewed said they do not like los toros (table 4.1). In a 1986 Gallup poll, 50.5% of the interviewees said that they had no interest in the corrida de toros (table 4.1). Percentages favoring los toros/corrida are a bit more complicated. Most of the rest of the population (48.4%) were divided between "much" and "some" interest; 1.1% had no opinion. The Alef poll had 34.6% of interviewees calling themselves "fans," while 14.6% were indifferent (table 4.1).

Gallup surveys for the years 1971–1986 generally say the same thing: that almost half of the Spanish population says it does not like bullfighting. In 1971 only 43% said this, in 1977 54% of the population had no interest, in 1985 and 1986, 50% had no interest (table 4.2).

Table 4.1 Comparison of Spanish Surveys on Bullfighting Interest

Alef December 1983		Gallup April 1986	
Toros		**Interest in corridas**	
aficionado (fan)	34.6%	*mucho* (much)	17.6%
indiferente (indifferent)	14.6%	*algo* (some)	30.8%
no le gusta (don't like)	50.8%	*nada* (none)	50.5%
		n.s./n.c. (no answer/don't know)	1.1%

Sources: Alef S.A., Gabinete de Estudios Económicos y Sociales, "Investigación Cultural," E/724, December 1983; Gallup, Instituto de Investigación, "Tema: Toros," IG 2482, April 1986.

Table 4.2 Bullfighting Surveys over Time

Gallup	1971	1977	1985	1986
Interest in corridas				
much	22%	17%	19%	18%
some	32%	28%	30%	31%
none	43%	54%	50%	51%
no answer/don't know	2%	1%	1%	1%

To say one does not like los toros or is not interested in las corridas may have nothing to do with actual behavior. Furthermore, the confusion between levels also complicates the issue since the primary usage of *los toros* means corrida, while its secondary usage means a local form. (Does a person not like corridas de toros but participate enthusiastically in a toro embolado?) A common fieldwork experience was to hear people reject one category of the bulls and yet identify with another. Recall Javier, the Catalan (chapter 1), who did not go to corridas but was going to Pamplona to run the bulls that summer.

We shall see that to be "for" or "against" the bulls in Spain communicates a message that has to do with more than just the intrinsic values of the spectacle itself. It does not matter if the speaker is referring to the whole phenomenon of the los toros, or to only one category of los toros, because the primary message really has nothing to do with the spectacles themselves. Rather, it is a statement, an affirmation, of identity. In many cases, especially in conversations with other Spaniards, this identification is often regional (see chapters 5–8), or sometimes political (see chapter 3). However, always in conversation with foreigners (e.g., the anthropologist), as well as in the majority of Spanish contexts, to be "against" los toros is to be "European" and "modern," to be "for" the bulls is to be "Spanish" and "traditional." The paradox is that, no matter how modern Spain is, it cannot escape the bulls in its dialogue with modernity. This chapter deals with the semantics of these positions and describes the Spanish definition of the construct "modernity." [1]

The Fifth World Swimming Championships, held in Madrid in August 1986, afford an example of the metaphorical use of los toros in the Spanish dialogue about modernity. Hosting the World Swimming Championships was widely spoken about in terms of convincing the international sporting community that Spain could organize a major event well. It was a trial run for the Olympic Games. (In August 1986, Barcelona had not yet been chosen as the site of the 1992 Olympics, although it was a candidate.) Despite this challenge to Spain's modernity, the mascot chosen for the championships was a bull in a Speedo swimming suit *(Pepe el toro)*. Moreover, the organizers, wanting to give a Spanish tone to the opening ceremony, decided to hold it in Madrid's monumental bullring.[2] The televised ceremony consisted not only of the typical parade of national teams and speakers, but also an exposition of bloodless bullfighting on horseback *(el rejoneo incruento de un toro)*. Instead of stabbing the animal and killing it, the riders aimed their spears and lances at a small pillow tied to the bull's back.

Spanish reaction to the bloodless bullfight was twofold: indignation and dismay. In Bilbao's fiestas a week after the swimming championships, I attended a colloquium held by the bullfighting club, Cocherito. One evening the rejoneo incruento in the swimming championships was discussed publicly. The *aficionados,* who were from all over Spain, criticized vehemently the use of the pillow, claiming it ridiculed the art of rejoneo in an eagerness to please foreigners. This is the purity argument.

The "other" Spain reacted with the Europeanizing argument. Letters to the editor of the newspaper *El País* reveal these sentiments. One person wrote that the opening ceremony produced in her "an impression of ridicule and shame, even taking into account how, as a Spanish citizen, I am used to such surrealistic eccentricities from our institutions and public organisms," and further noted that "the so boasted about modernity, to which our politicians say they are directing us, didn't come off very well" (Roda 1986:7).

Another writer asked that if the pillow was used and the animal was not killed, so as not to wound the sensibilities of the swimmers, why couldn't it be used for the sake of "the battered sensibilities of hundreds of thousands of respectable Spaniards? . . . We demand, as European citizens, that our sensibilities be respected, until [los toros] are eliminated in all of the national territory" (Torres 1986:7).

One person suggested finalizing the ceremonies with a corrida de toros on inner tubes (Roda 1986:7), while another suggested filling the bullring with water and having a frogman-*torero* bullfight a whale (Vázquez Montalbán 1986:32).

Terms of the Debate 1983–1986

"This is ominous because it means los toros are much more deeply rooted than I thought."
Spanish Hispanist upon hearing the number of taurine fiestas that took place in Spain in 1985

Why is it so "ominous" that there are many fiestas de toros in Spain? This Spaniard has many times declared to me his dislike of los toros. For this scholar a large number of fiestas de toros would mean that Spain is not as "modern" as he would like to assert. Furthermore, for those Spaniards who are against los toros, the fiesta is seen as an impediment to Spain's Europeanization (i.e., modernization).

Most *antitaurinos* insist (although my research shows otherwise) that los toros is a dying spectacle. Many informants stated that nobody goes to los toros anymore, just tourists. These antitaurinos call the fiesta a barbarous, non-European, third worldish, primitive anachronism.

Barbarous

The most typical accusation against los toros in 1983–1986 was that the fiesta was barbarous *(bárbara)*. While its supporters maintain that it is an art *(arte)* and part of Spanish culture, its detractors repeatedly call it a barbarism *(barbarie)*. A May 1986 Gallup poll asked if the corrida was "a barbarous spectacle that should disappear" or "an artistic manifestation that should be conserved" ("El Sesenta por ciento . . ." 1986: 46). It is barbarous because it is bloody and cruel. Many detractors are ashamed of the slow, "torturous" death inflicted upon the "innocent" animals.[3]

For Spaniards in animal protection leagues, the primary preoccupation should be the suffering of the animal. Their arguments downplay the risk of life that the torero takes and, in fact, hardly even acknowledge it. They emphasize the one-sidedness of a corrida. Already mentioned were the posters showing a dying bull, lanced by the Spanish flag, that said, "Torture is neither art nor culture. The national shame."

Although many Spaniards clearly identify with the pain of the bull, others think that to promote a "cruel" spectacle is not worthy of a civilized people. Moreover, this only perpetuates the myth of the Spanish as a "cruel" nation.

This argument takes us to the European context. It was "Europe," specifically the English, that spread the Black Legend *(leyenda negra)* about the cruelty of the Spaniards (Hill 1967:28). The Black Legend supposed that Spaniards were somehow more cruel than other European nations, and vast exaggerations abounded about the murderous actions of the Spanish conquistadors in America and the extent and fanatic violence of the Spanish Inquisition, as well as the Spanish affection for other bloody spectacles such as bullfights. These other European countries conveniently forgot about their own witch burnings and other religious and political persecutions. Thus, it is Europe that defines "cruel." Moreover, Spaniards say, it is Europe, and primarily the English, that disapproves of bullfighting, labeling it "cruel."[4] The term *cruel* is socially defined, meaning not only "deliberately inflicting pain and suffering," but also "non-European."

People in Spain do not simply project their arguments against los toros onto "Europe." Some European institutions actively engage in antibullfighting campaigns. The English and their animal protection leagues are perceived by many Spaniards as leading the attack against los toros. In 1985 and 1986 the English Royal Society for the Protection of Cruelty against Animals (RSPCA) and the Eurogroup for the Welfare of Animals, in conjunction with Spanish groups, were gathering information on corridas such as numbers of bullfights celebrated and numbers of people involved. In fact, my own work was hampered because my English appearance and accent almost inevitably led people to connect me with the animal protection leagues when I approached them with the same questions. Government officials and others in charge of statistics and permissions for los toros felt "under siege" by these animal defense leagues. I was often received with suspicion and a stonewalling attitude. One bull rancher actually sent a lackey to "check me out" before he would see me. He later admitted that he had been stung by "bad press" after an earlier interview with someone who turned out to be an antitaurino.

In the spring of 1985, right after the accords for Spain's entry into the EEC had been finalized, but before the formal signing of the treaty

Figure 4.1. The "Spanish debate": the bullring in Madrid in 1992. The graffiti says, "Toreros-Assassins." (Photographed by the author)

in June, a British member of the European Parliament submitted an amendment that would have banned Spain's and Portugal's entry into the EEC until bullfights were prohibited. The amendment, which was backed by English, German, and Italian animal protection societies, was based on the EEC prohibition of degrading treatment and unnecessary cruelty to animals.

This action motivated many people to consider their *afición a los toros.* As usual, los toros were the catalyst for comments about the relations between Europe and Spain. Many people spoke to me of the amendment, and the media was full of commentary. Even the Spanish anthropologist and antitaurino Julio Caro Baroja retorted, "These gentlemen of the North have a puritan attitude about los toros; meanwhile they fill up with steaks and roasts of other animals" (Sánchez Bardón 1985:28). In general, most people I spoke to defended Spain's cultural independence, rather than the corrida per se.

In June 1985 a riot broke out in a soccer stadium in Brussels, Belgium before an international match between Liverpool and Turin. The British fans viciously attacked the Italians, leaving many dead and hundreds wounded and hurt. Several times in the weeks after this incident, when discussing the possible EEC ban of los toros in Spain, informants pointed out that the British were much more violent and beastly than the Spanish (referring to the incident in Brussels) and that they should attend to their own problems before "arrogantly criticizing a fiesta that has centuries of popular roots." As of the summer of 1989, the amendment was still before the parliament but no action had been taken.

Non-European

Barbarous means more than "cruel" and "bloody," it also means the opposite of "cultured." For Spain, the barbarians *(bárbaros)* were the Germanic tribes such as the Goths and Vandals who invaded and destroyed the high culture and civilization of Rome in the fourth and fifth centuries. Compared to Rome, the bárbaros were thought to be without culture. Culture is related to several ideas: enlightened, civilized *(culta),* educated, and rational. All these adjectives, as I will show, add up to "Europe." When los toros are "barbaric," they are "non-European." This is the modernity argument, and "non-European" is the second adjective used against los toros.

When the Gallup polling agency explained why the percentage of antitaurinos had increased between a 1977 poll and a 1986 poll, it used this modernity paradigm. "This evolution could be foreseen in a society that, like the Spanish one, is arriving at indisputable heights of modernity and Western culture: modernity and Western, (adjectives) whose principles clash head on with the definition of *lo taurino*" ("El Sesenta por . . ." 1986:46). It is assumed that the opposition modernity/taurine is self-evident for the reader, and no further explanation is offered.

"Europe" is constantly invoked as the antithesis of los toros. In a humorous spoof on "the world of the bulls" in June 1986, the largest national newspaper, *El País,* summarized the argument in the following way. "Until this spectacle ceases, until the infamous cloak of blood has dried over the Iberian Peninsula, Spain will not really be Europe; it will not accede to the community of civilized nations, and it will remain stained with the indelible stigma of barbarity" (Boffe 1986:2). Others call for the abolition of los toros as "European citizens" (Torres 1986:7). Bullfighting fans, on the other hand, criticize the government's lack of interest in los toros as due to its European slant.

Even the animal defense leagues resort to this image contrast. In June 1985, the ADDA (Asociación para la Defensa de los Derechos del Animal) published the following protest in various Spanish newspapers the week before the fiesta of San Juan, which is traditionally celebrated with fiestas de toros all over Spain. "SOS to the authorities of Extremadura, the Spanish government, all of Spain. A bull, atrociously martyrized to death, by the whole town, with the cutting off of its testicles as trophies, while it is still alive. (This is one of the most brutal and bloody patron saint fiestas in Spain, promoted by the Town Halls.) *Is this European Spain?*"[5] (my emphasis).

Third Worldish

Another frequent criticism is that los toros are a "third-world spectacle," which, again, underlines their non-Europeaness. The third world, after all, is the twentieth century's version of the fourth century barbarians. Critics sound ashamed that they have to be identified as Spaniards with such nonmodern, uncivilized spectacles as los toros. (*Third worldish* is a term regularly used to criticize various aspects of Spanish life, especially perceived inefficiencies. For many Spaniards the ultimate shame of the February 1981 coup d'etat by Colonel Tejero and the Civil Guard was the third-world image of Spain presented to the world.)

Primitive Anachronism

"Europe" equates with modernity. Los toros are the antithesis of modernity, not only because they are not "European," but also because their origins are literally lost in the mists of time. When speaking about the origins of los toros, most informants said that the bull spectacles came from Crete, thus stressing Mediterranean culture and the ancient roots of the phenomenon. Many fans "admit" that los toros are an anachronism, a survival from earlier times. For some, this is all the more reason to maintain and promote these spectacles, for the sense of continuation and connection with the past and for the historical corporateness of "Spain." Others see this anachronism as a reason for los toros to die out, since the spectacle better represents a past historical moment, not the late twentieth century.

Another adjective used to describe los toros is "primitive." Again, this poses the fiestas against "modernity," "civilization," and "Europe." It is not only the format that is primitive, but also the emotions elicited. The themes of life and death are primitive in a primordial way. Furthermore, this controlled celebration of aggression and the bloody rite are more savage (in the evolutionary sense) than civilized, thus more primitive than modern. Some defenders acknowledge these primitive characteristics in the fiesta but maintain that they are a part of human nature that we will never lose.[6]

History of the Polemic

> Take away the bull from here, and we'll see what is left. Would we recognize ourselves without the passion for and against [the bulls]?
>
> Antonio Gala 1985:7, my translation

Although in the 1980s to be "against" los toros has to do with "modernity" and "Europe," this very same argument against los toros has been used for at least two hundred years. Moreover, the *fiestas taurinas* have been polemical since at least the fifteenth century (Cossío [1947] 1965[2]:86). While there is no doubt that los toros provide spectacles for the masses, it is equally possible to say that they have masses of enemies. Furthermore, these enemies have often been important figures in Spanish history. When Gala asks, "If you take away the bull from here . . . will we recognize ourselves without the passion in favor of or against it?" his implication is not only about today but about Spanish history.

José María Cossío dedicated part of *Los toros,* volume 2, to a history of the polemic about los toros. It is a detailed and scholarly account of all the moral discussions about the bulls until the 1940s. But Angeles

Prado (1973:64) notes that the background of the polemic consisted of the concept that people had about the nation *(patria)*. Prado then suggests we bear in mind the "two Spains" and the two different interpretations of Spain "to frame and better understand the differences of opinion about the corrida de toros."

Religion and the Bulls

Before the end of the eighteenth century, the principal arguments used to combat the fiesta de toros were religious motives. When the church lost its grip over society, so did religious arguments against the bulls. Beginning in the fifteenth century, the church's censure of los toros was directed against the fact that a person risked his life in a fiesta de toros. With this moral argument, the church fathers were merely continuing the condemnation from the early centuries of the Christian era of the circus spectacles of combat with wild beasts. The church hierarchy in Rome considered the fiestas taurinas as fights with wild animals, which led two popes to prohibit them (Pio in 1567 and Sixto V in 1586). Excommunication for those who took part in these fiestas and refusal of Christian burial to those who died fighting bulls were the threats that backed up the bans (San Juan de Piedras Albas 1927:44). The Spanish monarch of the time, Felipe II, although not especially a fan of the fiesta de toros (Boado 1976), petitioned Rome to lift its ban for Spain due to the symbolic significance of the fiestas. "Such an old custom, it seemed to be in the blood of the Spanish who could not go without them without great violence" (San Juan de Piedras Albas 1927:53). The church tried to prohibit its clergy from attending los toros, los toros from taking place on religious holidays, and towns and villages from dedicating toros to their virgins and patron saints, but these attempts failed. Although ostensibly the church hierarchy was arguing for the value of human life, the church was also involved in a power struggle with the secular leaders of Spain's world empire.

Others, besides the church hierarchy, were worried about human life in these centuries. Isabel I, after watching a fiesta de toros in Medina del Campo in 1495, was so horrified by the death of several men that she suggested that the bulls' horns be covered so as to protect the men from death (Boado 1976:21).

A second argument, which Cossío ([1947]1965[2]:88) calls the "sensibility position," had also appeared by the fifteenth century. This line of reasoning attacks the fiestas de toros as useless cruelty to the animal. This "sentimental" argument runs through many attacks on los toros. Contemporary animal protection leagues, which were founded at the end of the nineteenth century, reject the taurine games on this basis.

Europe and the Bulls

If the sixteenth century is the height of doctrinal and religious censures against the fiestas de toros, the eighteenth century is characterized by attacks of the civil powers. In the second half of the eighteenth century, reigning monarchs prohibited the fiestas several times. Both the local-level fiestas, such as encierros and vaquillas, and the corrida de toros were affected by these prohibitions. From this point on, one's opinion of los toros would have to do with one's concept of what "Spain" was. Some of these arguments continue to be in use today.

Beginning in the Spanish Enlightenment (1750–1808), "Spain" began to be opposed to "Europe." By the mid-nineteenth century "Europe" had been adopted as the model for progress (López-Morrillas 1981:xvi). Thus, the concerns about what Europe thinks, what Europe thinks of Spain, and whether Spain is Europe are concerns already voiced by an elite but influential group of men in the Spanish Enlightenment. Since the Enlightenment, the fiesta de toros has participated as one of the idioms in this dialogue (sometimes debate). The fiesta was the antithesis of "Europe."

In the second half of the eighteenth century, influenced by Enlightenment thought, the Bourbon monarchs initiated an attempt to modernize Spain. Spain's cultural and economic awkwardness was obvious, and reform was imperative. This reformist zeal included attacks and prohibitions on fiestas de toros by civil authorities. Every monarch between 1750 and 1808 banned and prohibited the fiestas, obviously with little success since the bans had to be repeated.[7] In retrospect, all these reforms and ideas were attributed to French, or European, influence. Significantly, these eighteenth-century reformers came to be known as the *afrancesados*—the Frenchified ones.

In general, the antitaurinos of this period used two arguments. One was the economic harm the fiestas could do in Spain. Raising bulls was an inefficient use of land and was prejudicial to Spanish agriculture. Furthermore, there was the economic waste of all those sacrificed animals. Also, the frequent celebration of these spectacles cut down on the work time and industry of Spanish laborers (see Cossío [1947]1965[2]: 124–50).

These arguments against los toros, although reflective of economic concerns of the epoch, were secondary to the concerns Spaniards had about the European opinions of the bullfight. The bullfight was continuously criticized as not being "European." "What is, then, the opinion of Europe on this point? Rightly or wrongly, they call us barbarians because we maintain and keep the fiestas de toros" (Jovellanos, 1790 letter to Vargas Ponce, in Cossío [1947]1965[2]:143).[8]

"Barbarous" is the adjective most often used by Spanish antitaurinos. It is the adjective that begins to dominate the literature of the eighteenth century and, as seen above, continues in use today. "Barbarous," "blood thirsty," "bloody," "gory," and "cruel" are all adjectives used to describe the bullfight from the Enlightenment on.

The implicit logic in all antitaurino arguments since the Enlightenment has been that something in the fiesta de toros causes the Spanish character to be different from the European character. The antitaurinos have hoped that by eliminating fiestas de toros from Spain, Spain would become more "European." By the nineteenth century, the economic argument of the antitaurinos had almost disappeared. However, the pro and con positions with respect to the fiesta were continuously reinterpreted through the European paradigm. Moreover, almost all detractors were thought to be influenced by European ideas. Especially fervent antitaurinos were the Krausistas, the Institute of Free Education (el Instituto de Enseñaza Libre) and the Generation of 1898— all thought to be Europeanizing movements. Those who defended the fiesta[9] defended it explicitly from foreign criticisms *(censores extranjerizados)*.

Nationalism and National Character

The nineteenth century is characterized in all of Europe by the appearance of nationalism and definitions of national character. Toward the end of the century, during a crisis of doubt and examination provoked by the loss of the last colonies, the Spanish intellectual community tried to define the essence of Spain, the Spanish character, and its "tragic flaw" (Prado 1973). For the Generation of 1898, los toros were intimately concerned with the reason for Spain's failures (vis-à-vis Europe). None of the Generation of 1898 writers, except Valle Inclán, was in favor of los toros (Cambria 1974:48–100).

The mission of all these intellectuals was to "denounce the superficial and frivolous, the 'España de pandereta' (tambourine Spain), so that the true and authentic Spain would emerge" (Cambria 1974:51). For these authors los toros represented frivolous Spain, and it was this group of intellectuals that generated the idea of the "two Spains."

Probably the most prolific antitaurino writer, Eugenio Noel, wrote early in the twentieth century (1912–1931). In newspapers, books, and conferences, Noel lambasted los toros as the consummate symbol of *flamenquismo*. *Flamenquismo* was Noel's term to describe all those characteristics that made Spain scientifically, intellectually, and morally backward (Cambria 1974:187). Flamenquismo was especially associated with Andalusia and the Andalusian cultural complex.[10] Although the target of Noels's criticism was flamenquismo, his implicit and explicit standard of measure was "civilized countries" and "Europe" (Noel 1912:27–28). "I aspire for the representative man of Spain not to be a torero, who is, in substance, a man of total ignorance, with few morals, and not at all appropriate to give Europe days of glory" (Noel 1912:24).

With more or less interest, the debate about los toros continues up to the present, employing the same terms of discourse established in the Enlightenment: the toros represent the essence of "Spain," and thus the question is whether to "Europeanize" Spain or not. In the background one can hear the definitions of the "two Spains" echoed in this debate.

Throughout these centuries, the significant characteristic of the taurine debate has been the extent to which it has engaged Spain's citizens. The Spanish Gallup polling agency states that perhaps the most noteworthy characteristic about its many polls on los toros from 1971 to 1986 is the rate of answers obtained among the people interviewed: only 1% of the population gave no answer or "did not know." "There are very few subjects that merit the social attention of the totality of the population, as occurs in this case" ("El Sesenta por . . ." 1986:46; table 4.2).

The Relation to "Europe"

Fotografía Española
  Spanish Photograph

Encampanada en su terreno
  Encamped in his territory
para que no la pise nadie.
  so that no one will step on it.
Las aguas, banderilleando
  The waters, like banderillas
los ibéricos costillares . . .
  on the Iberian ribs . . .

Apoyada en Africa, es una
   Standing on Africa, it is a
embestida que se prolonga.
   charge which is prolonged.
Toro creciéndose al castigo
   Bull growing under the punishment
bajo el gran caballo de Europa.
   Below the great horse of Europe.

Javier de Bengoechea in Roldán 1970:270, my translation

History of the Separation from Europe

In the cited verses of the above poem, the bull (as Spain) is situated between Africa and Europe. Although the bull is standing on Africa, it is facing and charging toward Europe (the horse) and the punishing lance.

Geographically, the Iberian Peninsula is part of the continent of Europe. But in 1846 the romantic French writer Alexandre Dumas published a book about his travels in Spain in which he made the infamous comment that "Africa begins on the other side of the Pyrenees." Many Spaniards think this represents Europe's opinion of Spain. It has been repeated to me many times, and there are endless references to it in print. If Europe has represented the first world and civilization, and Africa has represented the third world and barbarity in the Western view of things, Spain's position in this scheme has been debated. The Spanish preoccupation with "Europe" has to do with cultural identity.

At the risk of repeating the chronology of the previous section, I believe it is important to review the history of "Spain" with respect to Europe, as portrayed in Spanish collective representations. Otherwise it will be difficult to understand the importance of this relationship.

In the sixteenth century, after the discovery of the Americas, Spain became the ruler of a world empire. In that century, Spain is said to have first rejected northern Europe with the Spanish stance against Erasmusian religious reform. The idea of Spanish isolation from Europe originates here.[11] Foreign books were prohibited, and no Spanish student was allowed to leave Spain to study in a foreign university. Spain was closed off to "harmful" outside influences. Spaniards point back to this century when they explain what made Spain miss the "train of modernity" and thus be "different" from the rest of Europe.[12]

By the seventeenth century Spain was losing control over the trade with the American colonies. The loss of this source of wealth had

long-term disastrous consequences for the Spanish economy and corresponded to a slow shift in global power from Spain to other countries
in northern Europe.

By the eighteenth century Spanish decadence was obvious to the
Spanish and visitors alike. The new French monarchy established on
the throne of Spain (the House of Bourbon) attempted to modernize the country but was largely unsuccessful. The Enlightenment figures
were in Spain in the second half of the eighteenth century, but in retrospect it was seen as a movement of an elite minority that did not penetrate deeply into Spanish life. These northern European ideas failed to
take hold in Spain at that time (Domínguez Ortiz 1976).

The nineteenth century began with an attempt to put European Enlightenment ideals into practice with a liberal constitution (the 1812
Constitution of Cádiz). But Spain had been invaded by the French
(1808) and was fighting a war of independence, as well as a civil war.
Consequently, the constitution had no chance. In 1814, at the end of
the war, the country was in ruins and a despotic monarch, Fernando
VII, returned to the throne. What almost every Spanish schoolchild
knows is that Fernando VII closed the universities and opened the first
bullfighting school in Sevilla. Fernando's despotic rule, it is said, de-
layed the advent of the modern world in Spain. Many of Spain's intellectuals were forced into exile in northern Europe during Fernando
VII's reign and did not return until his death in 1833.

The rest of the nineteenth century until the Civil War in 1936 is described as politically unstable. The "old regime" had ended, and debate
concerned what to substitute in its place. This period is characterized
by several civil wars, military coups, monarchical restoration, constitutional republics, and dictatorships. At the same time, a slow but progressive imposition of liberal economic views and centralization of the
state began. Parts of Spain began to industrialize. Spain arrived at the
social forms and content of the Industrial Revolution at the very same
time that the rest of Europe was beginning to question the effects of
industrialization and the values of the bourgeoisie.

The European romantic movement, a literary and philosophical
movement that took place in the first half of the nineteenth century, was
a response to the disillusionment with the Industrial Revolution and the
idea of progress. More specifically, according to H. G. Schenk (1966:
3–14), romanticism was a reaction against rationalism. It was the erup-
tion of the irrational.[13]

Except in theater, Spain did not experience much of a romantic movement (usually located in the years 1833–1843). Yet romantic authors from all over Europe visited Spain in the first half of the nineteenth century. Significantly, the Romantics, reacting against rationalism, left northern Europe and went to Spain and other southern European countries, where they hoped to find the irrational. As will be seen below, the terms *rational* and *irrational* have become adjectives used to refer to "Europe" and "Spain" respectively in current Spanish speech.

The visions that the nineteenth-century romantic poets and authors created of Spain established the definition of the Spanish character for the rest of Europe that has persisted until today. Most of the authors (e.g., Theophile Gautier, Washington Irving, Rimsky-Korsakov, Hans C. Andersen, Alexandre Dumas, and Prosper Merimée) visited and wrote of southern Spain, specifically Andalusia. During this period the romantic writers and other travellers wrote of the romantic and passionate figures of the gypsies, the bandit, the mystic, Carmen, and most important of all, the bullfighter. The torero was a typical romantic hero: arrogant, individualistic, and often tragic. Spain, because of its primitiveness (i.e., nonindustrialization), represented a romantic paradise.

Spain as Andalusia and the Spaniard as torero were, thus, first European inventions. (Fifty years later, with the Generation of 1898, Spaniards would define "Spain" with reference to Castile rather than Andalusia.) Later European travelers, often having read the earlier authors, merely reconfirmed the stereotypes. Most travelers had to include a bullfight on their itinerary. By the second half of the century, when the division between agricultural (rural) and industrial Spain was beginning to be evident, Europe was calling all Spaniards toreros. "Stereotypical Spain" *(España tópica)* had been born. Some Spaniards may have identified with this characterization. Many others were mortified by it. How could Spain be modern if the Spanish were toreros? [14]

Even in the 1980s tourists are often criticized for arriving in Spain with their heads full of Spanish stereotypes (established by the Romantics in the nineteenth century) and refusing to see or look for any other Spain except "topical Spain." In interview after interview, tourists are criticized for not seeing the "real" Spain and perpetuating the myth that Spaniards "are toreros and dance flamenco." "Either we do not know how to explain ourselves or foreigners are more stupid than we had supposed" (Vázquez Montalbán 1986:32).

The affirmation among bullfight detractors that "only the tourists go to the bullfight" is common, as noted earlier. It means, of course, that the "real" Spain is modern now and does not do these third-world things. Ironically, these tourists are primarily from Europe (80% of Spanish tourism is European, 15% is American).

An example of the perpetuation of, and paradoxes in, the "Spaniards are toreros" myth follows. In April 1985, a conference was held in Madrid in which correspondents from foreign newspapers participated in a round-table discussion on the images of Spain abroad and the influence of the press. Correspondents were present from *The New York Times, Newsweek, Le Pont,* and *La Libre Belgique.* A Spanish university professor complained that "the press exports an image of Spain that does not correspond to reality, perhaps because the reporters feel impotent to speak about our country if they don't use the stereotypes: los toros, el flamenco, sun, paella, and sangria." The foreign reporters explained that although for them Spain is no different than any other country, the readers of their newspapers still believe the *tópico* that "Spain is different." Tom Burns of *Newsweek* explained rather lamely how hard it was to write about modern Spain for a public with set ideas. "We tried to do it, but out comes Rafael de Paula and destroys everything."

Rafael de Paula is a well-known gypsy bullfighter, admired by many for his cape work. On March 19, 1985, he was arrested after a bullfight in Santa Maria del Puerto. The police took him away in his bullfighting suit. Paula had been accused of arranging for two men to beat up and stab his wife's purported lover. (Paula's wife, also a gypsy, was not living with him at the time, and it had been rumored that she had been seeing an ex–soccer player.) Paula was detained in jail for two weeks before he was freed on bond, right before Easter. He immediately went to his home town of Jerez and did penance by participating anonymously in the Easter Week processions. On Easter Sunday he fought in Sevilla's important bullring, the Maestranza, on the opening day of its bullfighting season. According to some, there "Sevilla pardoned Paula" ("Sevilla perdonó . . ." 1985:128). Several weeks later he appeared in his native Jerez and killed all six bulls himself in a kind of symbolic statement about his control of bulls (if not of his wife).

The case was front page news in the five provinces I studied. News stories were carried for several weeks. National magazines printed many stories about the torero. In the newspaper *Navarra Hoy,* there appeared a cartoon of a bullring with a bullfight poster announcing the next bullfight: "The wife of Rafael de Paula against 36 million Spaniards." Allusions were made in print in several places to the story's similarity to the myth of Carmen, "like a page that escaped from the nineteenth century" ("España desde fuera . . ." 1985:14; de Salas 1985:5).

Most certainly, as Tim Burns, the *Newsweek* correspondent, implied, this news article did appear in foreign newspapers. I saw it in the Charlottesville, Virginia newspaper with a photograph. It was a phenomenon in Spain that generated much discussion and brought out again the national argument over los toros.

In 1898 Spain lost the last of its colonies in the Spanish American War, and the literary Generation of 1898 began to deal with "the problem of Spain." What had happened to Spain? How had it fallen from the pinnacle of world power in the sixteenth and seventeenth centuries to the status of a second-rate nation at the end of the nineteenth century? Spain, as compared to its European neighbors, was poor and backward. One answer was that Spain had to "Europeanize" *(europeizarse)*. Spain had rejected the values of Europe and had missed out on the Industrial Revolution and a "modern" way of life. The solution to Spain's many social, political, cultural, and industrial problems was to copy Europe.

Those who wanted to import European solutions to Spanish problems became known as Europeanizers *(europeizantes)*. For other Spaniards, that a great nation should copy ideas from elsewhere was insulting. Furthermore, they found the crass materialism of the Protestant north repugnant. These conservative purists called the Europeanizers the "anti-Spain," and Spain thus continued to be opposed to "Europe."

The 1936–1939 Civil War was fought over these two visions of Spain's future. When General Franco and the Rebels won the war, it seemed that Spain would not Europeanize. During this time Spain isolated itself further when Franco elected to keep Spain neutral and not participate in World War II. Later this isolation continued when the victorious Allies decided to boycott and withhold diplomatic relations from fascist Spain. Franco's reaction to the diplomatic and economic boycott was to reject and vilify even further "Europe" and the European influences of "masons, Jews, liberals, reds, and heretics." Spain would preserve her moral purity and again close herself off from harmful outside influences.

The Cold War, however, convinced the Allies to recognize Spain again and to invest in Spain's primitive, but non-Communist, economy. Franco relented. By the end of the 1950s the industrialization and urbanization of Spain was in progress. By the mid-1970s Spain had become the tenth most industrialized nation in the world.

Thus, economically, Spain had officially become "like Europe." The government wanted recognition of that fact in 1960, when it formally applied for membership in the EEC (the Common Market). Europe, however, used this economic organization to make a cultural comment. Spain was still "different." Spain was denied EEC membership until democracy might be reestablished.

On March 29, 1985, ten years after Franco's death, Spain was accepted into the Common Market. Newspaper headlines in my research provinces declared: "Something more than a market" ("Algo más . . ." 1985:21); "Today, finally, we are less different" (Marco-Gardoqui 1985:35); "The international inferiority complex is overcome" (Méndez 1985:26). The separation from Europe was finally over. A newspaper correspondent wrote, "The Pyrenees, the beginning of Africa according to Alejandro Dumas, have been definitively knocked down and Spain is now irremissibly open to the modernization that comes from the North, (open) to Europe" (Papell 1985:39).

Not everyone had an inferiority complex; there was some ambivalence. On June 12, 1985, the various ministers and representatives convened in Madrid to sign the treaty under which Spain would formally join the EEC. Each of the seventeen people who signed the treaty received an original pen and ink drawing by Salvador Dalí, who was considered a kind of legendary national monument in Spain. Each drawing is a sequence of the Greek myth "El rapto de Europa" (The Rape of Europe),[15] where Zeus, in the form of a bull, ravished and carried away the beautiful Europa to Crete where the first European civilization was born. Dalí explained the choice of his themes: "It seems like a paradox to me. It is Europe that has to ingress into Spain. It was the Iberian toro that held onto Europe. The only one who has understood this myth is Salvador Dalí! The bull, which is Spain, did not take away Europe, he held on to her with his determination, with all his bravery, and kept her where she is. Europe owes to Spain her very being. We are the bull that ravished Europe for ourselves" (Santa Celia 1985: 30, my translation).

"The Meaning of Europe"

In the opposition Spain/Europe, "Europe" does not simply include the rest of the European continent. As the historian Sánchez-Albornoz (1956:593) points out, "Europe" means the countries included in the old Carolingian Empire at its greatest expansion: France, Germany, the Netherlands, Switzerland, and England. Although in the 1970s and 1980s "Europe" often meant the countries of the EEC, usually Italy and Greece were not included. Nor were the countries of Eastern Europe. In general, "Europe" meant northern Europe and France: industrialized, productive, Protestant (except France), cold, wet, non-Mediterranean, and rational Europe. But "Europe" means more than just a place on the map. Before 1985, when many Spaniards were affirming that Spain must rejoin "Europe," the term was a symbol of a culture and a system of values.

The word that best sums up the description of "Europe" is modernity *(modernidad)*. The formal entry into the EEC was constantly described in the press as a challenge of modernity *(un desafío a la modernidad)* (Ibañez 1985:30). "Europe" represents economic, political, and cultural "modernity," clearly a value-laden word. Objectively it means different economic, political, and social *forms* than those perceived to be used in Spain at the time.

Economically, "Europe" was the free market, as opposed to Spain's protected market. One commentator wrote that since "commerce had always been considered as something vile and plebeian," the conversion to the competition of commerce must be making "our ancestors turn over in their graves" (Jiménez Lozano 1985:10). Politically, "Europe" was "the synonym of liberty" and "the synonym of democracy when democracy was only a dream" (Onega 1985:4). Furthermore, for Spain, which had suffered three civil wars in 150 years due to opposing ideologies about the nature of the state, "Europe" was "living together in peace" *(convivencia)* (Gomis 1985:4). Culturally, "Europe" has meant "social progress" ("La adhesión de España . . ." 1985:18). Spain had become "Europe" in order "to enter into progress, into sociocultural development or else stay in third-world indigence" (Papell 1985:39).

An attribute consistently applied to "Europe" and which seems to sum up economic, political, and cultural modernity is the adjective "rational." In contrast, "Spain" is characterized by irrationality (Ninyoles 1979:93–100). The Spanish historian Sánchez-Albornoz (1956:593) summarizes, "(Europe) has incessantly launched new and fertile, creative ideas, legitimate children of reason; (Spain) has only given birth to ideals, bastard secretions of passion." The opposition of "rational" and "irrational" (and thus, implicitly "Europe" and "Spain") appears in the language of those who defend los toros.

Rationality and the Bulls: "Modern Fans"

"Rational" and "rationality" were two of the most important descriptions of "Europe." For many Spaniards, Spanish history was "irrational," and their model for the future is for Spanish life to be more "rational." I propose that these terms are really euphemisms for two worldviews and that "Europe" and "Spain/los toros" also correspond to "rational" and "irrational," respectively.

From Bilbao to Sevilla, I was repeatedly told by fans that "the bulls are not something rational." These were not criticisms by antitaurinos, rather these were fans, usually modern business executives, university-educated professionals, and scholars. What they were saying to me was that I could not expect rational ("European") justifications from them about los toros because they themselves suspended their rationality when they went to los toros.

Oftentimes people admitted that los toros were cruel, barbaric spectacles. Some even admitted feeling a bit perverse. In Valencia, a doctor accompanied me to a corrida during the 1984 Las Fallas fiestas. She was clearly excited to participate in this part of the Fallas, which she had not done in a long time. (She even insisted on drinking a few glasses of wine beforehand in a bar, a typical part of the ritual of going to los toros.) Afterward, discussing the corrida, she admitted that she liked the bulls and that as a girl she had had a crush on a torero. But several years earlier, when she had gone to a corrida with an American male friend, she had been so embarrassed for Spain that she refused to go again. She said that when she watched the spectacle "through her friend's eyes" she hadn't known how to explain los toros to him. Perhaps she was trying to explain an "irrational" event with "rational" terms.

What do these people mean when they tell me the bulls are not something rational? It is all the more strange because most often fans describe the corrida as the confrontation of the forces of rationality with the forces of mere animal brute strength, or irrationality: mind over matter, order versus chaos. Several authors have pointed out that the corrida's final organization and codification at the end of the eighteenth century were almost surely a response to the criticisms of the Enlightenment figures. An emphasis on the geometry and rationality of the corrida is evident in all analyses by aficionados.[16]

How can these two points of view be reconciled? Recall that those who told me that going to the bulls was not a rational act were all people who identify with "modern Spain." It was as if they had no argument to justify going to the bulls. As one journalist said, "Many defenders of tauromachy suffer from a bad conscience" (Villán 1985:35).

One justification is to affirm that los toros is an art. Villán defends los toros as artistic creation, saying "all art implies a considerable dose of disarrangements, irrationalities, and contradictions, and that the victim is in the constant presence of the stellar moments of humanity" (Villán 1985:35).

Furthermore, these people say the corrida is a fiesta, and as a fiesta it is a moment when norms and rationality are suspended, a "ludic parenthesis," as the mayor of Valencia called his fiestas. In the summer of 1986, people used the word *ludic* several times to describe the fiestas, and specifically fiestas de toros. This meaning of fiesta gives one permission to switch into a mode of being different from that of everyday rationality.

However, I suggest that in saying one likes los toros but qualifying that "it is not a rational thing," one is giving value (almost nostalgically) to a premodern, or at least romantic, worldview. At the same time, they are unconsciously, even stubbornly, maintaining one's "Spanishness" in the face of the Europeanization of Spain. In the dialogue Europe/ Spain, "Europe" represents rationality and modernity, while "Spain" represents irrationality and tradition. In the language of "Europe," the word *irrational* has a negative connotation, but in the language of "Spain" it implies a better quality of life.

Until joining the EEC in June 1985, many Spaniards had longed to be formally recognized as "Europeans." Nevertheless, it was evident in many conversations that people thought Spain possesses a quality of life that is not characteristic of northern Europe. Many times Spaniards expressed to me that the risk of "Europeanization" was to lose the positive values and qualities of "Spanish" life. Thus, despite their desire for the European material progress and the desire to be taken "seriously" by the northern Europeans, Spaniards sometimes complained that the Europeans do not know "how to live." [17] Two worldviews or "mentalities" are envisioned as confronting each other: quantity versus quality, modernity versus tradition. The European model is "rational" in that it has made capitalistic, economic choices to produce, while the Mediterranean or Spanish model has concentrated on a better quality of life.[18]

Many Spaniards often told me that they thought Spanish people spent more time socializing with friends, drinking in bars, and eating in restaurants than the northern Europeans. Furthermore, people constantly told me that Spaniards knew how to have a fiesta better than northern Europe, where everyone is always "serious and working." Especially in the South, there was a feeling expressed that Europe (and the north of Spain) took work and production too seriously. Obviously, it would be difficult to measure if Spaniards spend more time socializing, but the collective representation exists as a differentiating element between "Europe" and "Spain."

In the mid- to late-nineteenth century some northern Europeans began to describe the two mentalities of quantity and quality in formulas that implied progression through time (modernity versus tradition). H. S. Maine wrote of the movement of status to contract, Marx wrote of the change from the production of use value to exchange value, Tönnes wrote of the switch from Gemeinschaft to Geschellschaft, and Durkheim wrote of mechanical and organic solidarity. All these writers were trying to express, albeit in historical terms, their recognition of the new worldview generated by the Industrial Revolution and capitalism. When northern Europe was beginning to express this tension between the values of quantity and quality of life, Spain had only just started on the road to industrialization. These tensions have been expressed in Spain, not only in historical formats, but typically in geographical or spatial formats. One formula to express tension between the worldviews of quantity versus quality has been to compare the North and the South or the Center and the Periphery of Spain. Another format has been to oppose "Europe" (rational production) to "Spain" (irrational consumption).

Therefore when a Europeanized Spaniard assures me that he likes los toros but that los toros are not a rational thing, he is reaffirming the value of "irrationality" and the value of the symbolic category "Spain" in the dialogue "Europe-Spain." Even in the north of Spain in Bilbao, which is usually considered European in the Center/Periphery dialogue, the following editorial appeared when negotiations for the EEC treaty seemed about to break down. It says more about the writer's point of view than anything else: "The Europeans without us, the Spanish and Spain, feel lame, armless *(manco),* or one-eyed. They need the soul and the bull of the myth. The soul of Spain, which is something more than a club and a bull's hide[19] has not yet seduced and ravished Europe" (Armas Marcelo 1985:49, my translation). For this writer, "Europe" without "Spain" is missing a soul. Many "modern" Spaniards want to integrate the "Spanish soul" into their "European" being. It is as if now that Spain is officially Europe (through joining the EEC), Europeanized Spaniards can return to being "Spanish."[20] To go to los toros is to accept "Spain."

Quite eloquently, Antonio Gala, a writer, newspaper columnist, and

representative of liberal Spain under Franco, summarizes the categories
expounded in this chapter:

> I am not able to defend los toros. I can't defend (la fiesta) nor attack it.
> I carry los toros deep in my blood. Every time the infinite silence that
> propitiates and awaits a good series of passes takes over in the bullring,
> a windmill turns in my stomach. It isn't necessary to make exaggerated
> shows of apology. It might be—and maybe it is—lack of culture and
> underdevelopment. We might be a third-world country. Maybe we
> aren't yet civilized. But, what characterizes us is the fiesta
> de los toros and everything that leads up to it and is implied by it.
> Who decides what civilization is? And above all, who decides what our
> civilization is? (Because if we are bloody and crazy and crude, it isn't
> because of los toros; on the contrary, los toros make the violence
> delicate, golden and silky; they make it mystical and magical.) I don't
> understand much about los toros . . . nevertheless, their fiesta runs
> through my veins, it forms part of me and I part of it. . . . It is because
> of what it has that is not learned that I consider the fiesta culture. A
> country with so many contrasting and even opposite aspects is allied
> in the background by the corrida, the lidia, the capea, the encierro:
> Barcelona, Bilbao, Pamplona, Sevilla, Caceres, Valencia. I cannot
> defend it nor attack it. In an Andalusian capital, an affected lady,
> president of the Animal Protection Society, got ready to leave the bar
> where she had invited me to a coffee because she was also a town
> councilor and she was going to preside a corrida. I understood. I
> myself am the honorary president of various animal protection societies
> and yet I can't seem to wiggle myself out of the bulls. Because I am in
> their hide—the hide of Spain—because the bull is not an animal for
> us; it is much more: a symbol, a totem, an aspiration, a eucharist with
> those around us and our forefathers. The bull: we adorn him, we feed
> him, we sacralize him, we lance him, we put bandarillas in him, we kill
> him, we applaud or boo him after his death, we cut him up, we eat him,
> and we make poems about him and we paint pictures of him and we
> write music for him. Take away the bull from here, and we'll see what
> is left. Will we recognize ourselves without the passion of the pro and
> con of los toros? . . . The same thing happens to me with the bull as I
> have written that happened to Abdherraman with Azahara, "I love
> her simply because I can't do any other thing but love her. If I could
> control my love, perhaps I would not love her. But my power is not
> that great." You understand me. And if you don't understand me, you
> forgive me.
>
>   Antonio Gala 1985:7, my translation

Finally, I cite the well-known unapologetic comment of a political essayist at the beginning of the century: "If I were dictator of Spain, I would suppress the corridas de toros with one swoop of the pen. But until then, as long as there are (corridas) I will continue to attend" (Pérez de Ayala 1963:810, my translation).

Significantly, as "Spain" has arrived closer to its "European" ideal, the number of fiestas taurinas has again risen. According to Gallup, in the 1970s afición and the actual numbers of taurine fiestas went down, supposedly an indication of Spain's modernization (see table 1.5). The bullfight was dying. In the 1980s fiestas taurinas, as well as all other fiestas, experienced a comeback and rise in numbers. In the summer of 1985, the treaty with the EEC was signed. It was also described as a Golden Age of bullfighting, with 493 corridas. In 1988, twenty-three million people attended bullfights in Spain, three million more than in 1987, and the number of corridas rose 11% over 1987 to 509, the highest number in the past decade.

Part 3

TRADITION: THE BULLS AND REGIONAL IDENTITY

Chapter 5

THE FIESTA CYCLE

The fiesta (bullfights) leaves winter along the Levante; it tries out its
April showers in Sevilla; on San Isidro's day it urges Madrid's spring
blooms to show their colors; it becomes nobly brave in the fiestas of
San Fermín and in August it is enthroned with praises to Our Lady, in
our villages, cities, and towns. . . . It is as though the bull's hide shape
of Spain is moved annually, and without decree, with the celebration
of the bull, of the bulls.

—Amon n.d., my translation

As introduced in chapter 1, the almost exclusive context of bullfights
are the *fiestas mayores,* which are usually the patron saint festivals, of the
many villages, towns, and cities throughout Spain. Los toros are one of
the many elements that compose these fiestas and are thus intimately
bound to perceptions and projections of local and regional identity. In
this and the following chapter, I show how the many taurine games are
used and manipulated in this discourse about local and national identity. In contrast to the Spanish desire for modernity, identity is still connected to having many "traditions."

In the first part of this chapter I define fiestas in Spain. I show how
"identity" is expressed through fiestas and the place of the bulls in the
expression of this identity. Finally I describe the cycle of bullfights that
ties the many parts of "Spain" together, while at the same time talking
about difference.

Fiestas: Identity and the Bulls

The abundance of fiestas celebrated at the community level in Spain has
often been noted (Bennasser 1979; Velasco 1982b). In the past, these
fiestas were usually coordinated with the Christian calendar and cycles
of agricultural work at intervals of forty days (Roma 1980). Not all fiestas were "celebrated," nor could they be, since fiestas interrupt the
various economic activities. But fiestas did mark off and separate the
succession of agricultural tasks such as planting, harvesting, and storage.

Labor time was antithetical to festive time, a characteristic that remains today. In contrast to material production, fiestas celebrate and produce social relationships.

Since the 1960s, the fiestas have undergone two changes. The first is a reduction in number, especially of religious fiestas, in the name of economic productivity. The second change has been the expansion of fiestas mayores, from a single day to many, including the eve of the fiesta plus the day or days following the fiesta.[1]

Although towns celebrate a variety of fiestas, there is only one patron saint per town, and its fiesta is celebrated only once a year. This fiesta (*fiesta patronal*) is usually the most important community celebration in the whole year. It is frequently called the major fiesta (fiesta mayor), or the big fiesta (*fiesta grande*), to distinguish it from other minor fiestas (*fiestas menores* or *fiestas chicas*).[2] Another term for fiesta mayor is *feria* (fair). *Feria* indicates that the fiesta once included a livestock fair and market.

The patron saint festivals have flourished in these years of industrialization and modernization. The majority (60%) take place in summer, between June 24 (San Juan) and October 7 (Virgen de Rosario). August 15 is the day with the greatest number of patron saint celebrations (Virgin of August, the Feast of the Assumption). There is a relative absence of patron saint festivities during the months November–December and February–March. Traditionally summer was the time of great agricultural activity, and therefore the patron saint festivities interrupted task-oriented duties. Today, however, many of these expanded celebrations closely coincide with the traditional month-long summer vacation of Spanish workers in August.

According to Spanish anthropologist Honorio M. Velasco (1982b: 19), the fiesta mayor is distinguished from all other fiestas by the following characteristics: an important religious authority, or authorities, is present in the religious rites; the religious images are dressed in their most luxurious robes, jewels, and crowns; los toros are usually present; there are more and bigger performances, shows, and other attractions than during other fiestas (often there are small amusement parks with rides set up); special foods and an abundance of food are offered and eaten; special clothes are bought for the main festival events; the more money spent, both on a public and private level, the bigger and better the fiesta is considered to be (the money runs *[el dinero corre]* in a potlatch of consumption); and the fiesta mayor lasts longer than any other fiesta (usually four days to a week in the 1980s). Most importantly, the fiesta is "major" because it congregates more people than other fiestas and implicates in greater measure the various social entities that make up the community.[3]

Identity

Anthropologists have underlined the importance of one (or more) fiesta in a town or village as a symbolic moment when the community condenses into one time and space its "attitudes about its ecological, historical, expressive, aesthetic, religious, economic, social, and political relationships" (Prat Canos 1982:158).

Following Leach, Turner, and Geertz, there is a consensus that the fiesta is a reflection of the society and its culture, a reflection that can be real or symbolic. In other words, in Geertz's terms it is a *model of* or *model for* society, or both at the same time. No author doubts that the fiestas can be either a faithful reflection of the social structure or the symbolic negation of the same social reality (i.e., a reflection of what the society would like to be but is not). Nevertheless the fiesta mayor "creates the illusion of community" (Velasco 1982b:7).

Paralleling the anthropological interest has been a revitalized popular interest in fiestas since the death of Franco in 1975. Although most fiestas probably never ceased being celebrated, the dictatorship suppressed many (e.g., Carnaval) and others fell into disuse. Since 1975 there has been a revival of fiestas in many towns and an expansion and elaboration of others, especially the fiesta mayor.

Fiestas have to do with a real or longed for identity, and identity has to do with keeping "traditions" alive. In all fiestas in the 1980s informants emphasized the following ideas: *lo autóctono y propio* (what is autochthonous and one's own), *volver a ser sí mismos* (to be oneself again), *buscar las propias esencias* (to look for one's very own essence), and *lo más típico de antaño y hogaño* (the most typical of past and present). These expressions were heard and seen repeatedly. Towns wanted to connect to the past, as well as reconstruct the present in a familiar way. While they wanted to differentiate themselves from neighboring towns, emphasizing a unique identity, they also wanted to identify themselves as members of a particular region, *nacionalidad*, or culture, thus emphasizing a shared identity.

Some towns merely continued celebrating, more vigorously, traditional fiestas that had never disappeared. Other towns added elements considered to be "authentic" to the town or regional culture. For example, in Pamplona's fiestas of San Fermín, it was not until 1985 that the calf dodging contest *(recortadores)* was added to the program and advertised as the "original form of taurine game in Navarra." Other towns had to start from scratch, instituting totally new fiestas and choosing the elements that would become "traditional." The Autonomous Community of Castilla–La Mancha, created in 1978, celebrated its fiesta in Guadalajara in 1985 with parades of groups in regional dress, dancing, regional music, *encierros,* a *corrida,* bike races, and a dance. This arbitrary social construction of "culture" is always done in the name of "historical essence"—for towns "to be themselves again."

Los Toros

Los toros are one of the many elements that comprise a fiesta mayor in the five provinces I studied, but in other provinces this is not the case. Informants talk as if los toros were included or reincluded in fiestas for historical reasons. They were called an essence of the fiesta.

In the mid-1970s, when Franco had banned many of the local forms, for most people *los toros* probably meant the corrida. The corridas at that time were often full of foreign tourists, and their numbers had expanded beyond their traditional fiesta mayor framework. Moreover, they were strongly identified with Franco, the political Right, and non-European Spain (see chapters 3 and 4). Horn-shaving and underweight animals only added to the third-world image of los toros for many Spaniards. The phenomenon did not seem representative of twentieth-century, modern Spain.

After 1975, with the return of democracy, the old problem of how to politically construct "Spain" resurfaced. "Modernization" was now taken for granted by many Spaniards, and the question became how to define one's place within modern Spain. The search for local identity was on. When towns researched their fiesta mayor, in many cases they discovered that los toros had been a part of their fiesta for "time immemorial," or at least since the Middle Ages.[4] But the tradition did not need to be anchored so far back in time. Probably more persuasive were memories, often related by informants, of going to los toros with a father or grandfather. In this context, los toros did not just mean the corrida; instead the phrase referred to a "unique" local form. Each local tradition of los toros became a "differentiating element," a form shared regionally, yet with some unique aspect.

Most of the local taurine forms had never truly died out. They had continued under other names, such as "livestock fair." Other local forms had become quite marginal and had almost disappeared due to lack of

community participation. Since 1982, some towns that had been celebrating a corrida during their fiesta mayor added an encierro, *becerrada,*
or *suelta de vaquillas.* Other towns reconstituted their defunct fiestas
totally after 1982, ignoring corridas (national format) and choosing vaquillas (local format).

These lower-level forms of los toros are not spectacles like corridas
but are fiestas of participation. Thus, they serve as metaphors for the
fiesta mayor itself, one of whose characteristics is participation by all
town citizens. Only in Sevilla, said to be the home of the "true" *afición
a los toros,* were the lower forms not added to the fiesta mayor programs.
The paradox is that in Sevilla the local form *is* the corrida. Therefore,
only upper-level spectacles are usually included in ferias in Sevilla, and
the people are condemned by their "identity" to be spectators, not
participants.[5]

However, the corrida also represents a "fiesta" in a very basic way.
Although not a metaphor for participation, the corrida is a metaphor
for consumption, in the sense of immolation or sacrifice. One of the
characteristics of a fiesta is that it is the antithesis of labor and material
production. Some foreign residents in Sevilla complained to me about
the energies Sevillanos spent on Feria and how it was such a "waste"
because it "wasn't producing anything for Spain." Furthermore, vast
amounts of money, both on the municipal and individual level, disappear in the fiesta. In Sevilla people have special savings accounts in banks
just for Feria, and many Sevillanos told me they were totally "cleaned
out" after the fiesta *(nos deja fritos).* Much of this money is spent on
the consumption of large amounts of expensive food and drink and the
invitation of others to join. In Pamplona the youth clubs collect money
and save all year for the food and drink they will consume and offer to
the public during the fiestas. In Valencia each neighborhood is in charge
of building the neighborhood *falla* (a gigantic wood and papier-mâché
structure). Everyone works and raises money throughout the year to
pay for the falla, which will hopefully turn into a glorious bonfire as it
burns at the height of the fiesta, at midnight on March 19.

Each fiesta is, of course, the result of much labor, which is sacrificed
during the week of fiestas in an orgy of general consumption, each city
vying with the next for glory in its willingness to potlatch for the sake
of its reputation. Valencia's burning of its fallas is only the most obvious
example of the ephemeral nature of the consumptive rituals. In the afternoon of March 19, Valencianos walk around admiring the structures
that will burn that evening, which is the main event of the whole fiesta.

Comments like, "How beautiful! What a pity it has to burn!" are heard repeatedly. In all the fiestas mayores I visited there was regret at the end, during the consumption of the fiesta. People literally had tears in their eyes. The essence of the fiesta is that it must be destroyed, sacrificed, used up. One newspaper correspondent, writing of Sevilla's Feria, called the history of the Feria a "feriofagia."

Just as Valencianos walk around admiring the sacrificial fallas, in every city the bulls for the corridas are put on view for the public. They come to inspect, admire, and judge the worthiness of the bulls that will be killed in the ring during the fiestas. Exclamations such as *"¡Que bonito!"* (How beautiful!) are heard at these corrals, as well as when the bull enters the ring for the last time. One of the complaints against the *fiesta nacional* is that thousands of bulls are killed "for no reason," although their meat is always sold and eaten. The corrida, like the fiesta in general, is a celebration of consumption. A virgin bull is meticulously cared for and fed for four years to be sent to the ring for twenty minutes of glory and immolation. What better metaphor for the fiesta nacional!

Los Toros: Nationalism versus Regional Separation

Anthropologist John Cole (1985) has suggested that in the Mediterranean lands of Italy and Spain, since the countryside had been culturally, as well as politically and economically, subordinate to the city, the traditions selected in the nineteenth century as the symbols of nationalism were derived from an urban-elite tradition. In contrast, the proponents for regional separation in Spain had to draw upon symbols derived from rural life. Therefore, the category of los toros chosen to "represent" the town in its fiesta mayor will have to do with the extent to which that town identifies itself with and participates in "Spanish" national culture, or instead, defines itself as a separate culture. The upper-level national formats of los toros, represented by la corrida, are urban phenomena and represent national culture.[6] The lower-level local formats, represented by *vaquillas,* are for the most part rural phenomena and therefore represent regional culture. Corridas unite the provinces as like entities, that is, they share "Spanishness." Vaquillas, of which each form is different, define the provinces as different from each other.

Using the collective representations of "Spain," one can say that there are vaquillas in the North and corridas in the South: there are cows in the North and bulls in the South.[7] The use of the sexes of the animal to make a symbolic analysis of "Spain" immediately changes North/South (relations of equality) to Center/Periphery (relations of hierarchy), since bull is to cow as Center is to Periphery. Furthermore, it is a way of stating that there is separatism (vaquillas) in the North and nationalism (corridas) in the South.

Another author has talked about "Spain" through the emotions that the North and the South feel toward the bull. According to contemporary novelist Fernando Sánchez-Dragó, the bull is the totemic animal of Spain (North and South), even though the animal is loved in the South, home of the corrida, and hated in the North, where "they trap him, they tie him up, they chase him, they put ropes around him" (García 1985:11). If the bull is the totem of Spain, then according to Sánchez-Dragó the South loves "Spain" and the North hates "Spain," a typical interpretation of the North's strong sense of regionalism. Sánchez-Dragó is wrong, of course; the North loves its forms of los toros and the animal itself as much as the South loves its form.[8]

Although all five capitals I studied celebrate the corrida in their fiestas mayores, Madrid and Sevilla celebrate only corridas, while the three capitals of Vizcaya, Navarra, and Valencia bring the rural form into the city and celebrate a form of vaquillas as well as corridas. In other words, although these latter cities participate in a national culture represented by the corrida, they also emphasize separateness, which is represented by a form of vaquillas.

Corridas

The capitals of Vizcaya, Navarra, Valencia, and Sevilla each celebrate eight corridas during their fiestas. Madrid, literally the center and fount of Spanish nationalism, celebrates *twenty-four* corridas during its fiestas, three times the number found anywhere else. This exaggeration of the national symbol corresponds to Madrid's perceived role in creating and insisting upon some form of "Spanish" nationalism. In fact, the entire province of Madrid celebrates far more corridas than any other province. It is the one province where even relatively small-sized towns celebrate their fiesta mayor with a corrida.

In the nineteenth century the corrida de toros was an excellent vehicle to convey the growing sense of nationalism of the new urban bourgeoisie classes, those who could afford to go to corridas. Born in the cities of Andalusia, the corridas' popularity spread between the late-eighteenth century and the mid-nineteenth century to cities all over Spain. By 1860 the railroad was being used to transport bulls (and *toreros*) from one part of Spain to another, thus weaving together the many parts of the country. Although there were not any truly national rules for the corrida until 1930, by 1868 Madrid and Sevilla were using similar rules (Cossío [1943]1980[1]:807), and the public in the large cities began to expect to see the same spectacle in other cities. From 1880–1920, monumental bullrings were built in most cities. Newspapers began to carry accounts of corridas throughout Spain. After 1845, hundreds of magazines appeared, dedicated exclusively to the corrida (Cossío [1943]1980[1]:544). Corridas were celebrated during big city fiestas, and the public must have been aware it was participating in a "Spanish national" phenomenon.

Vaquillas

If Madrid emphasizes corridas, Vizcaya and Navarra emphasize local forms, vaquillas. In Bilbao (Vizcaya's capital), during its week of fiestas there is a corrida every afternoon. Each morning, however, two local taurine fiestas are also celebrated: *sokamuturra* (cows on ropes) and vaquillas (cows freed in the ring). Moreover, near midnight two *toros de fuego* (firecracker "bulls") appear among the festive crowds: one for children and one for adults. In Pamplona (Navarra's capital), during its fiestas a corrida is also held every afternoon. However, every morning at 8 : 00 A.M., there is an encierro of those bulls. After the running of the bulls, the Pamplonicas celebrate a suelta de vaquillas (cows freed in the ring). Pamplona also has a toro de fuego *(zezensusko)* every evening at 9 : 30 P.M.

In both Bilbao and Pamplona, to have bulls and cows running around on paved streets emphasizes the juxtaposition of rural and urban forms. Both cities are preserving and exalting these rural forms in an attempt to distinguish themselves from the national culture.

Valencia is an interesting example where a rural form of the bulls is brought into the city because of its association with "Valencian identity." While Pamplona's encierros date from the late-nineteenth century and Bilbao's sokamuturra dates from the beginning of this century (Caro Baroja 1984:20), in Valencia the rural taurine fiestas were not introduced into the capital city until 1985 and 1986. Separatist movements in Valencia were never as strong as in Catalonia or the Basque Country. Although the rural population of Valencia had distinctive traditions, occupations, dress, and architecture and in general spoke Valencian (a dialect of Catalan), the inhabitants of the capital did not speak Valencian. Since the arrival of democracy, the Autonomous Community of Valencia has set about promoting the use of Valencian and reestablishing a stronger sense of Valencian identity.

Although in 1985 in Valencia province there were more than 1,199 *toros embolados* (bulls with burning torches on their horns) and vaquillas (cows freed in the ring), neither of these forms had ever been held in the capital city. In 1985 it was decided that during the week of Fallas, Valencia's fiestas, there would be a suelta de vaquillas in the morning (before the afternoon corrida) and a toro embolado one night, though the events were rained out. But the next year during Fallas they were offered in the bullring.

Some people were scandalized by the mixing of categories. One government official in charge of taurine affairs said these lower forms were not "dignified enough for the great, important bullring of Valencia." They only cheapened the fiesta. However, planners had included these forms in an attempt to build afición because they supposedly had more to do with "Valencian identity" than the national corrida.

Cycles

The fiesta mayor in a town or city is merely one of several fiestas celebrated. The other fiestas, called minor (menores, chicas), implicate fewer (often only one) of the social entities or corporate groups that make up the community. These are the fiestas of individual church parishes, neighborhoods, different guilds or craftsmen, age groups (e.g., all young men from 18 to 25), or gender. These social entities are defined and opposed in rituals stressing mechanical solidarity, rather than the organic solidarity attained in fiestas mayores. The minor fiestas celebrate the internal homogeneity of a sector of a town, while the major fiesta synthesizes and celebrates the community's heterogeneity. All town fiestas are in a hierarchical relationship, however, and it is the fiesta mayor that orients the rest. The importance of the fiesta mayor results from the social integration that it establishes and reaffirms, which explains the use of the patron saint of the whole town or city for these community rituals. Nevertheless, Velasco (1982b:22) has suggested that the unit of study should be not one fiesta but the relationship of all the fiestas together, which he calls a cycle.

While one can speak about the cycle of fiestas within a village, town, or city, it is also possible to speak of a cycle of fiestas in a larger context. Velasco (1982b:17) refers to the cycle of fiestas at the level of the *comarca* (administrative district, county) in Castile. Aguilera (1978:141) produced a study of the fiesta cycle in a "multicommunity" of sixteen small villages and one small town in southwestern Spain. In this case the cycle consists of the fiestas mayores of all the towns. Although each town competes for splendor with the others through its fiesta mayor, a recognized hierarchy acknowledges one town's moral importance and size. As in the example of Almonaster and the sixteen small villages, the patroness of Almonaster, Santa Eulalia, and the fiesta mayor of Almonaster become the unifying symbol of community identity and cooperation for all villages involved. Rodríquez Becerra (1985) implies that this also happens at the level of the province in Spain: Sevilla's Feria is the model for the many other ferias in the area and yet is recognized as the most important, drawing participation from the whole area (and not vice versa); Valencia's Fallas serves as the model for many of the smaller towns in the province. Prat Canos (1982:163) and Rodríquez Becerra suggest that this happens on a regional (or ethnic) level also: the Romería del Rocío would be the culminating fiesta for lower Andalusia.

A cycle of fiestas, marking the boundaries of a "community," has three fundamental characteristics. First, it supposes that the participants in the fiestas are aware of and familiar with the symbols evoked and the rituals used (Rodríquez Becerra 1982:32). Aguilera (1978:14) speaks of "communication" and social intercourse within the boundaries of the community.[9]

Second, a cycle of fiestas is characterized by the noncoincidence of dates for the fiestas. Instead, the fiestas are spread throughout the festive calendar. Fernandez and Fernandez (1976) show this for the *romerías* (pilgrimages) in Asturias; Velasco (1982b) notes this for the Alcalá area in the province of Madrid. The noncoincidence of dates allows people from other towns to attend and participate in the fiestas. The presence of outsiders is important because the fiesta mayor needs to be witnessed by others for purposes of definition.

Finally, a cycle of fiestas functions to define and identify the corporate groups that make up the cycle, but one fiesta in the cycle will "create the illusion of community" and unity, like the fiesta mayor in a single town. This most important fiesta will exteriorize the perception the "community" has of its hierarchical relationships and relations of opposition or of complementarity.

Using the above definitions, I propose to take the notion of a fiesta cycle to an even higher level than that of the city or region. I propose that a fiesta cycle exists at the level of the nation (or nation-state) in Spain. This cycle consists principally of six fiestas: Fallas (Valencia), March 15–19; Feria de Abril (Sevilla), April 21–28 in 1986; San Isidro (Madrid), May 15–22; San Fermín (Pamplona), July 7–14; Semana Grande (Bilbao), August 17–24 in 1986; and Pilar (Zaragoza), October 9–12 (map 5.1). Each of these fiestas marks the corporate boundary

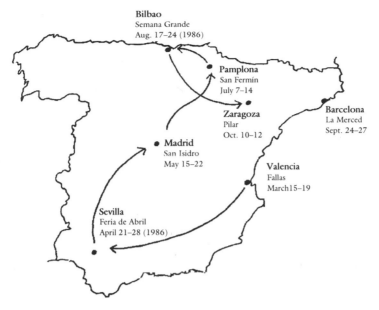

Map 5.1. The fiesta cycle of Spain.

of a city as well as a geographical region of Spain.[10] These fiestas run from March to October at intervals of about thirty to forty days. Los toros is one of the elements common to all six fiestas, but the members of the six communities are familiar with and aware of the other symbols activated in each fiesta. People from all over Spain attend these fiestas. One fiesta, San Fermín in Pamplona, although it encompasses all of the structural oppositions inherent in the community being defined ("Spain"), also creates the illusion of unity of "Spain" (see chapter 8). The existence of the community of "Spain" is, as I have explained in chapter 2, often put into doubt. Although not all Spaniards participate or identify with this community, I believe that the annual functioning of the "Spanish" ritual cycle proves it exists. Some citizens may even participate fully in the cycle and yet still take the political position that they are not "Spain." I maintain that the mere fact that they use and understand the symbols of the whole cycle underscores the working of the community for at least some Spaniards.[11]

The Bullfighting Cycle

I discovered the fiesta cycle that evokes the community of "Spain" through the study of los toros. It was clear that at the top of the hierarchy of los toros, a series of corridas, each in different cities, was perceived as a kind of cycle.[12] People spoke of the "taurine calendar" or "bullfighting season." The "season" has a beginning and an end. Expressions such as "it winds its way through Spain" or "it travels up and down the Spanish geography" were used. The season (cycle) moves in a clockwise direction around Spain, starting on the Mediterranean coast and going South to North. In the literature the taurine cycle is often described in poetic terms, as a thread that weaves together the many disparate parts of Spain *(las Españas)* (Bonifaz 1980 : 142–55).

Although avid bullfighting fans usually include more points along the cycle, most people were aware of the three to five most important fiestas in the bullfighting season. Even people against los toros could refer to the most important fiestas and knew where the season begins and ends. If just three fiestas were named, they were Sevilla, Madrid, and Bilbao, in that order. If more were named, they were Valencia, Sevilla, Madrid, Pamplona, and Bilbao (and people in Valencia and Pamplona always named the five). Zaragoza was always given as the end of the cycle. These fiestas were also constantly referred to in the bullfighting literature as the most important fiestas. Joaquin Vidal, a bullfight critic, describes the "classic ferias of the taurine season. . . . For the universal fans, the fair of Valencia gives an indication of the artistic moment of the figures; Sevilla is happiness and the test-tube of the profiles of art; Madrid, an exam in front of the wise and uncompromising tribunal; Pamplona, the test of bravery; Bilbao, seriousness and the bull" (Vidal 1985 : 25, my translation).

These important corridas coincide with, and are embedded within, the context of each city's fiesta mayor (Bonifaz 1980 : 144). These sets of corridas are named after the fiesta mayor of each city: Fallas (Valencia), Feria (Sevilla), San Isidro (Madrid), los sanfermines (Pamplona), and Pilar (Zaragoza). Only Bilbao's corridas are not referred to by the title of its fiesta mayor, called la Semana Grande.

The Cycle of "Spain"

Since the larger context of the taurine cycle was the fiestas mayores, I probed to see if a "cycle" was recognized at this level also. When I asked what the most important and typical fiestas in Spain were, three were always given: Fallas (Valencia), Feria (Sevilla), and San Fermín (Pamplona), in that order. Madrid's San Isidro was often a distant fourth choice. I include Bilbao's and Zaragoza's fiestas in the cycle because of their prominent position in the bullfighting cycle.

In retrospect, it seems logical that these six fiestas form a cycle that

defines "Spain." Imperial Spain had been described as the coexistence
and interdependence of ethnicities, or cultures (i.e., the various *reinos*).
The monarchy mediated between the various interests of the many
Spains. After the mid-nineteenth century and the rise of the nation-
state, what had been "parallel traditionalism" became "competing definitions for the essence" of Spain (from Geertz 1973:45). The problem
of integrating the "many Spains" into "one Spain" then appeared. The
fiesta cycle deals with this competition and integration. Five of the cities
are among the largest cities in Spain: Madrid (1), Valencia (3), Bilbao
(4), Sevilla (5), and Zaragoza (6) (Barcelona is the second largest) and
have been so since the mid-nineteenth century (Mitchell, B. R. 1981).
Four of the cities represent the four most important geographical categories in Spain: North (Bilbao), Center (Madrid), South (Sevilla), and
Levante (Valencia) (see chapter 2). They also represent the various parts
of the division of labor in the national economy, which was established
in the mid-nineteenth century: Bilbao (heavy industry), Valencia (light
industry), Madrid (administrative services), and Sevilla (agriculture and
extra labor [migrants]). Zaragoza is an important military and religious
center. Pamplona's inclusion in the fiesta cycle is justified, as I show in
chapter 8, by its role as the symbolic synthesis of "Spain."

At least four fiestas (Fallas, Feria, San Isidro, and San Fermín) command national news attention. Spanish television covers them extensively, as do the national newspapers, often on the front pages. People
from all over Spain attend these fiestas: a boatload of four hundred
Catalans arrived in Sevilla for Feria 1986; special trains are set up to
leave Madrid for Valencia's Fallas and Pamplona's San Fermín. These
travelers are often migrants returning home, but they are also people
from all parts of Spain. For example, at Feria I met a couple from Alicante and a man from Bilbao; at Fallas I met a woman and her friends
from Jerez; recall Javier, the Catalan, who wanted to go to San Fermín
to run with the bulls (see map 5.1). Some people go specifically for the
corridas and also enjoy the larger fiesta; others go just to the larger fiesta
and hardly pay attention to the corridas in the background.[13] Usually
the cities' populations swell to overflowing during the fiestas and hotel
rooms are difficult to find. Private homeowners rent rooms to out-of-
town guests.

Thus, two things happen at the same time in each of these fiestas
mayores. First, there is the fiesta itself, of which the corridas are a necessary ingredient. The fiesta seems to be speaking about the local identity and personality and celebrating the history and corporateness of the

city. Second, there are the corridas, which are compared and contrasted with the corridas of other cities. Each corrida denotes a point in a cycle that depends on corridas in other cities for its completion.

Although local-level taurine fiestas are also celebrated in some cities, these do not tie the cities together (except with the bull as protagonist) as explicitly as the corridas do. In fact, the lower-level taurine fiestas separate the cities. However, by the mere fact that the cities' fiestas ma-yores share a defining characteristic (i.e., the corrida cycle), the cities themselves are brought into a relationship. No matter what the extent of the role of los toros in each fiesta, they provide the vocabulary for a shared discourse. Moreover, while it is possible to say that corridas make these highly differentiated cities equal (e.g., in theory, no bullring is more important than another), each city attributes a specific behavior and personality to its "bullring." These behaviors and personalities dif-ferentiate each city from the others in the cycle. So, what started out the same (a spectacle with a national format) becomes different as it relates to others. We are back to local identity.

More than just los toros are shared in these fiestas mayores. In fact, the cities constantly make reference to each other during their fiestas. In Valencia in 1985, there was talk of the "San Ferminization" of one of the rituals in Fallas *(mascletá)* ("San ferminización . . ." 1985:24). Fireworks always brought comments about Valencia (fire and firecrack-ers are the essence of Fallas). In Sevilla I was told that the fireworks marking the end of Feria "were something from Valencia, not original to Sevilla," and were therefore peripheral to the essence of Feria. How-ever, fireworks have been part of Feria since the turn of the century (Collantes de Terán Delorme 1981). The fireworks shot off each night along the river in Bilbao's fiestas were also advertised as organized by different Valencian companies. During Bilbao's fiestas one of the im-portant upper-class locales (Hotel Ercilla) set up a *caseta andaluza* (An-dalusian tent), a replica of one used in Sevilla's Feria. There people met to drink and to eat typical Andalusian dishes and talk about the corridas. In Sevilla's Feria one of the *casetas* (tents) was patronized by Asturians from the north of Spain. Along the walls were painted scenes contrast-ing the Andalusian and Asturian dance styles, musical instruments, drink, work, and dress. However, without a doubt, it is in reference to the bulls that people most talk of other cities.

The components that make up the fiesta mayor in Spain are part of a general European tradition (Pitt-Rivers 1984:27). What belongs to each region, and different cities within a region, is not the content of the fiesta (e.g., music, dance, costumes, religious ceremonies and icons, and food) but rather the style (format) of the fiesta or the peculiar way of dealing with each element (Pitt-Rivers 1984:27). Similarly, the use of the bulls in these cities' fiestas is part of a general Iberian tradition and, even though the corrida is a national format (and symbolizes the "nation"), each city has a peculiar way or style of dealing with it.

I plan, therefore, to treat the bulls not only as a metonym of the fiesta, as one of the important elements that compose a fiesta, but also as a metaphor of the fiesta and its meaning. Although the prominence of the bulls varies from city to city, the shared collective representations about the bulls talk about "Spain."

Differentiation among the Corridas

The public of each bullring has its own "personality," that is, it behaves differently and appreciates a different kind of bull and torero. *Aficionados* insist that the standards in their city are much higher than anywhere else. However, the public's behavior in Pamplona scandalizes Sevilla's aficionados, and the size of the bull in Sevilla is ridiculed by aficionados in Pamplona.

The Bull

Each ring "wants" a different kind of bull. Veterinarians at each ring are in charge of inspecting the bulls and rejecting the ones that are "unsuitable" for their city. Size and shape of the head and horns are the primary attributes looked at, as well as tameness, eyesight, and lameness. These attributes contribute to the animal's appearance *(presencia)*.[14] Many animals are rejected by the veterinarians. Once in the ring, the animal's essence *(esencia)* comes out.[15] Is it noble or tame? Does it enjoy the fight or flee from it? It is well known that Sevilla likes small graceful bulls, while Bilbao and Pamplona want enormous bulls with wide horns (large animals are slower than smaller ones). Madrid wants a large but attractive animal. Valencia wants something between Madrid and Sevilla. Ranchers pick the bull to send to the various fiestas according to the animal's physical characteristics. It is typical to see 400 kilogram bulls in Sevilla and 700 kilogram bulls in Pamplona. Pamplona's aficionados assured me that the toreros were "afraid" to come there because of their huge bulls. Supposedly Madrid's public is the most demanding of "perfection" in a bull. Certainly, I saw the public boo and reject more bulls for aesthetic imperfections in Madrid than anywhere else.[16]

The desired bulls correspond to stereotypes about the physique of each region's people. The South's small graceful bull equates with the supposed physique and style of the Andalusian. The North's big bulls correspond to the image of the big, thick-necked Basque peasants. Madrid, as usual, mediates between the two styles.

Although most bulls come from ranches in the Center and South, originally there were three different lines of Spanish bulls: from Navarra, Castile, and Andalusia. Even now, each region shows a certain allegiance to its bulls. The original line of bulls from Navarra has died out, and now all first-category bulls trace ancestry back to three or four ranches in Andalusia. Nevertheless, cows are raised in Navarra for local fiestas, and Navarrans say that the terrain toughens the cows and makes them more suitable for the local fiestas than Andalusian animals.

Torero

Each ring appreciates a different kind of torero. Valencia's bullring has the reputation of liking flamboyant bullfighters *(toreros-tremendistas)*. These toreros do all kinds of spectacular things with the bull, for example, bite his horn, lean an elbow on the animal's face, or kneel down to receive the bull for the kill. The rest of the bullfighting world criticizes these "tricks." Sevilla, on the other hand, looks for the artistic bullfighter *(torero-artista)*. It is not so important that the torero be consistent as it is that he have the potential for moments of ecstasy. The Sevillanos look for a relationship with the bull that can be likened to a dance, a ballet. Grace, slowness, and art are combined in a series of passes in which the torero stands motionless. Madrid wants a torero who is serious, almost solemn. Some of the toreros who are popular in Sevilla are booed in Madrid because they are not consistent or fail at the "moment of truth." In Madrid the kill is as important as the passes. The North wants a torero who physically dominates the bull. Every city develops a special relationship with toreros from that city or region (e.g., Valencia, El Soro; Sevilla, Curro Romero; Madrid, Antoñete).

Again, the torero's style corresponds to the stereotypical "personality" of each city. Valencianos are portrayed as gay and sensual; Sevillanos are artistic; the Madrileños, as Castilians, are traditionally severe and serious; Basques are a bit brutish, lacking in grace.

Ring

Some bullrings have their own name (Sevilla, La Maestranza; Madrid, Las Ventas; Bilbao, Vista Alegre), and although each is officially owned by the city, different cities have different traditions of managing them. Sevilla's ring is run by a private organization; Valencia's City Council recently took over management of its ring; a private businessman runs Madrid's ring, but the city earns part of the profit; Pamplona's ring is managed by a religious charity organization; Bilbao has always managed its own ring strictly for charity. Although the dimensions are the same, in some cases the architecture of the ring is distinctive. Valencia's ring is built in a mozarab style, typical of the area. Sevilla's is the oldest ring, built in 1767. Madrid's is the biggest ring, built in a neo-Arabesque style with twenty-four thousand seats.

The sand in most of the rings is usually yellow, but Bilbao has sand that is a dark grey color and called "black." The yellow sand in many rings combines with the red color of the wooden fence surrounding the sand ring to replicate the colors of the Spanish flag, red and yellow, which have been in use since the eighteenth century, except during the Republic. However, whether or not the Spanish national flag is flown depends on the bullring. In Madrid the Spanish flag is flown and used all around the ring as banners. The red fence even has a yellow stripe painted on it, repeating the theme. In Sevilla the Spanish flag is also flown. However, in Bilbao, Pamplona, and Valencia the Spanish flag is nowhere to be seen, although regional flags and banners are everywhere.

Although throughout Spain the public seating is divided up in the same way and labeled similarly, in each ring there is usually a section of *Sol* (sun) that is traditionally occupied by the older lower-class bullfight aficionados. These fervent fans lead the criticism of the plaza president, the bulls, and the toreros. In Sevilla this section is known as *tendido* 11; in Madrid they are *andanas* 7 and 8.

Music

Each plaza has a band in the stands that plays music to liven up the spectacle, but what and when the band plays vary by ring. The *paso doble* (march), of which there are many written just for corridas, is one kind of music always present. In Pamplona, after the sixth bull the band always plays a lively *jota,* music typical of the region.

Each plaza has its own rules about when music may be played. In Sevilla, the band plays during the entry of the toreros, when the torero places the *bandarillas,* when a torero takes a lap of honor around the ring, and when the dead bull is taken out of the ring by the mules. The band can also play if the public thinks a torero is performing well with the bulls. In this case, the public will signal the band to play. Music during the performance in Sevilla emphasizes the idea of a dance between the torero and bull. In Madrid, there are only three moments when the band will play: the entry parade, during a lap of honor, and when the bull is dragged out. Madrid, as usual, emphasizes its nonfrivolous nature in its sparse use of music.

There is more music than just the official band, however. In Valencia, Pamplona, and Bilbao the regional hymns are also sung before the parade of toreros and their *cuadrillas*. In Pamplona and Bilbao there are youth groups *(peñas)* that attend the corridas together, each of which has its own five to ten member band. Especially in Pamplona, with fifteen clubs, a cacophony of bands often competes during the toreros' performances.

Public

Each ring is also known for its public's composition and behavior. The youth clubs, whose members attend los toros together, characterize Spain north of Madrid. Often these peñas are the center around which the whole fiesta revolves.[17] Peña members dress alike and are thus recognizable as a block in the ring. Of these five provinces, only Pamplona and Bilbao have peñas (in Bilbao they are called *comparsas*).

In the North and along the Periphery, eating in the bullring is a tradition. After the third bull in Valencia, Pamplona, and Bilbao a kind of unacknowledged intermission takes place (during which the sand in the ring is cleaned and smoothed) when everyone eats a meal brought from home.

The behavior of each ring's public also has a reputation. In Sevilla the public is very serious, which is evident in the total silences at points during the corrida. Then, at the end of a series of particularly good passes, the public erupts as one voice in the exclamation "*¡Olé!*" In Madrid, the public is known as complaining, severe, and critical. Bulls and toreros hardly ever please the public in Madrid, a public that sees itself as demanding perfection and thus protecting the purity of *toreo*. In contrast, in Pamplona and Bilbao the boys' clubs dance and sing, often ignoring what is happening in the ring, making noise and acting up even during the "moment of truth," the kill. Pamplona's clubs throw food and fruit at every *picador*.

Structural Considerations

The bullfight cycle is composed of several fiestas that are repeated in the same order every year. The preceding sections describe how each point

Table 5.1 Bullring Differences

	Valencia	Sevilla	Madrid	Pamplona	Bilbao
Bull	medium sized	small, agile	big, but agile	enormous, wide horns	enormous
Torero	tremendista, flashy, tricks	artist	serious, solemn, consistent	dominance, no fear	dominance, no fear
Ring					
managed by	city	Maestranza	empresario	religious organization	city
seating	17,000	13,000 (oldest)	24,000 (biggest)	13,000	19,000
banners	regional flag	Spanish & regional flag	Spanish & regional flag	regional flag	regional flag
Music	regional hymn	—	no music during torero's performance	regional hymn, jota, peña band	regional hymn, peña band
Public					
food	eat merienda	—	—	eat merienda	eat merienda
activities	—	long silences, ¡Olé!	severe critics	dancing, singing, fiesta	dancing, singing, fiesta
Local-level toros	toro embolado, vaquillas	—	—	encierros, vaquillas	sokamuturra, vaquillas

(city) around the cycle differs as to the kind of bull, bullfighter, ring music, and public identified with it (table 5.1). Thus, the corrida, despite its national format and national rules, nevertheless differentiates the cities from one another. The varying characteristics of the corrida in each of these cities are metaphors for the "individual personalities" of these important cities. Recall that one characteristic of a fiesta cycle was to "define and identify the corporate groups that make up the cycle." The striking differences between the corridas in each city certainly parallel other differences between them.

The Spaniards talk about each regions' different personalities, cultures, or histories that separate them from each other.[18] The fiesta cycle, or the coincident corrida cycle, puts these "personalities" in relationship. All the cities' fiestas must be included to complete the cycle; they are complementary. Thus, the cycle itself is a metaphor for "the Spains."

Discussions of the bullfighting cycle lead to several other conclusions. First, the six important fiestas are often collapsed into just three: Sevilla, Madrid, and Bilbao. Second, these three fiestas quite often represent the three geographic categories of the South, Center, and North. Third, although there is a level in which all three places are considered equal and complementary, the primacy of the Center is also acknowledged.

Equal complementarity is conveyed in the expression *"Sevilla lanza, Madrid consagra, Bilbao asegura"* (Sevilla launches, Madrid consecrates, Bilbao guarantees). One torero, Paco Camino, put it this way: "You have to fight in Sevilla, but above all you have to triumph in Madrid, and ratify the triumph in Bilbao. After passing Bilbao you can rest" (Irizar 1985). These comments stress the importance of all three bullrings or geographical areas. In fact, triumph in all three is equally important for a torero's "season," and for the idea of the "whole." He must gain the approval of each different audience. Each part of the country contributes an important aspect to the whole phenomenon of the corrida cycle. The South is said to be the original source of the corrida; the Center is the source of the rules; the North is the source of toreo (the early forms of games with bulls).

At times this complementarity of differences is reduced even further, from three areas (Sevilla, Madrid, and Bilbao) to just two (North and South). North and South are considered to be essentially quite different but, implicitly, equally necessary for the whole phenomenon of toreo (i.e., Spain). The North wants a fiesta, the South wants art. The North eats in the ring and wets down its snack with lots of wine; the South only wets down the dust in the ring. The afición in the North is *torista* (focuses on the bull), while the afición in the South is *torerista* (focuses on the bullfighter).[19] The South wants the torero to establish a beautiful, graceful relationship of dominance with the bull, while the North is not interested in the aesthetic qualities of the relationship as much as the test, the challenge of confronting an equal opponent. Another way to say this is that the North focuses on the physical appearance (presencia) of the animal, while the South bypasses the presencia and looks for the personality or "nobility" of the animal (esencia). These oppositions parallel the "two Spains" of hierarchy and equality, or the tradition of aristocratic Spain versus democratic Spain.

The bullfighting cycle seems to offer two models of how to integrate the different parts of Spain. On the one hand, the nonhierarchical paradigm of North/South is used and equal complementarity is emphasized. It seems as if a ritual of hierarchy (the corrida) is used to make equal the many highly differentiated regions of Spain.

However, competing with this egalitarian model is its contradiction: a blunt statement of hierarchy. Recall that Madrid's fiesta consists of twenty-four corridas, three times anywhere else. Its bullring is called the "first" *(primera)* ring in Spain. It is also a well-known maxim that a torero is not really a "torero" until he "fights the bulls in Madrid" *(hay que torear en Madrid)*. Supposedly, Madrid's fans are the most demanding, and a torero's first appearance in Madrid's bullring begins his real career as a bullfighter.[20] The maxim replicates the wider reality of power politics in Spain, and in fact, the expression "hay que torear en Madrid" is often used as a metaphor in political life (i.e., success in politics at the local level does not guarantee success at the national level).

Madrid's position as Center also assures its "weight" in the cycle. Although Madrid is identified with the South in many aspects of the bullfight cycle (it has no peñas, no food), other typical characteristics of the bullring seem to synthesize the qualities and characteristics associated with both North and South. The bull for Madrid must have a combination of presencia (North: size/form) and esencia (South: relationship); the torero must dominate, but artistically. Thus, in spite of Madrid's real asymmetric dominance in the cycle (twenty-four corridas instead of just eight, as elsewhere), its dominance is in several ways due to its role as synthesizer.

Two competing models of "Spain" exist simultaneously in the bull-fighting cycle. One model treats all the parts as theoretically equal and necessary. This represents a plural model, "the Spains." The other model implies that Madrid is the most important and dominating point on the cycle, which represents the singular "one Spain" view of nationality. Although Madrid's role as synthesizer is stressed, it is difficult for this role to be salient given the other political associations with Madrid (as Center, dominating the Periphery). Thus, Madrid's fiestas do not serve as "illusions of community" in the cycle.

In the following chapters, I discuss the place of the bulls in three important fiestas, in Bilbao and Sevilla, which seem to be polar opposites of each other, and in Pamplona, which synthesizes, with the use of bulls, the many oppositions in "Spain" and creates an "illusion of community."

Chapter 6

THE NORTH: SEMANA GRANDE IN BILBAO

The "Big Week" (Semana Grande) in Bilbao includes a huge wooden statue of a peasant sitting in the square that "eats" children and later "poops" them out; a tall, puppetlike doll in the form of a disheveled, old woman that "dances" in the streets; young cows on long ropes that lunge at boys only to be jerked away just in the nick of time; and parades of people from two different parts of the city that converge upon the bullring.

Vizcaya

Bilbao is located in the western part of Vizcaya, which is one of three Spanish provinces that make up the Basque Country (País Vasco or Euskadi in Basque). Historically, the Basque provinces were differentiated from the other areas of Spain by the use of the Basque language *(euskera)* and the existence of special *fueros* (rights) that were not lost until the nineteenth century.

The Basque nationalist movement was founded in 1895 by Sabino Arana and gained momentum in response to the rapid capital industrialization of the Spanish state. Although the movement was founded in Bilbao, the center of Basque nationalism today is the nonindustrialized parts of Guipuzcoa and northern Navarra. The eastern part of Vizcaya is well integrated into the Basque Country, but western Vizcaya belongs to the culture area of Cantabria and Asturias (Caro Baroja 1972:377). However, Basque nationalism has increased since the 1970s, while the industry of the entire Basque Country has entered into crisis. Both of these phenomena have led to social strife, political tensions, and a general lowering of the standard of living.

Bilbao, capital of Vizcaya, had more than 433,000 inhabitants in 1981. More than one million people live in the Greater Bilbao metropolitan area, the largest urban concentration in the Basque Country

(48% of the Autonomous Community of Euskadi, 87% of Vizcaya) (Instituto Nacional de Estadística 1985:67, 487). However, Bilbao does not occupy the expected position of influence and leadership "either in the Basque economy, or above all in the social and cultural life of the Basque Country" (Linz 1986:447). Linz calls Bilbao the "periphery of the periphery" (1986:369).

In 1900, at the beginning of industrialization, Bilbao had 83,000 inhabitants. By 1930 the population had grown to 306,500 inhabitants and by 1981 to over one million. This growth was due principally to immigrants: non-Basque workers and employees from central and northern Spain (Linz 1986:448). These immigrant groups did not assimilate easily into the Basque culture, with its non-Indoeuropean language and ethnocentrism.

However, there is also a second segment of Bilbao society that is not strongly identified with Basque nationalist sentiment and that occupies a central position in Bilbao. The Basque Left calls this group the "oligarchy." The oligarchy is Bilbao's capitalist bourgeoisie (businessmen and bankers). This elite has strong family, economic, and political ties to the Spanish national elite and has played a key role in the economic structure in Spain for the last fifty years (Tamames 1986). In a sense, Bilbao is more important economically, socially, and culturally to "Spain" than to the Basque Country.

The Basque nationalist movement originally described the Basque society as made up of independent rural peasants and owners of small and midsize businesses in the many small cities and towns of Euskadi. Thus, the two dominant classes in the Bilbao area (immigrants and the oligarchy) are "peripheral to the ideal image of Basque society" (Linz 1986:449). A middle class exists in Bilbao, but it is not demographically dominant.

Bilbao is situated seventeen kilometers inland on the Nervion River. Both sides of the river are lined with heavy industry such as shipyards and steel factories. The three social groups are associated with different spaces within the Bilbao area. The immigrants crowd into the outlying cities and in Bilbao on the left side of the Nervion. The oligarchy lives on the right side near the bay, while the middle class lives in old Bilbao, also on the right side of the river, and in neighborhoods extending into the northeast.

Bilbao is surrounded by emerald green, alpine-type mountains, which are visible from all parts of the city. The rural countryside is very important in Basque regional symbolism. Mechanization of farming is difficult due to the small plots of land and mountainous terrain. Traditional forms of agricultural life, although changing, are still visible and celebrated. It is in mainly rural Vizcaya that the Basque language is spoken.

Bilbao's Fiestas

The week-long fiestas of Semana Grande (Aste Nagusia in Basque) always begin on the first Sunday after August 15, the fiesta of the Virgin of Begoña, Bilbao's patron saint. These fiestas have less of a continuous tradition than those of other areas. The forty-year Franco dictatorship caused many of the fiesta's more popular "Basque" street manifestations to disappear. According to newspaper reports in the 1960s, the only festivities celebrated then were los toros and theatrical presentations.

In 1978, three years after the death of Franco, the city government reorganized the Semana Grande fiestas. The goal was to make them more "popular," with more participation, and to make them more reflective of "folk" culture. The fiestas in their present form, then, are relatively new. However, Bilbainos are convinced that these new fiestas merely revive old, authentic traditions of their Basque and urban culture. In 1985 Bilbao's mayor proclaimed, "We are ourselves. And we have to show it. Our own identity and personality (folklore, food, rural sports, *corridas de toros,* Basque customs and the recovery of ancestral festivities of the purest accent)" (Robles 1985:25, my translation). A couple of elements have persisted in these fiestas since the beginning of the century: los toros and Gargantúa, a large papier-mâché and wood child-eating monster in the form of a Basque peasant. The other elements chosen, or reconstituted, to compose the Semana Grande are significant indicators of Bilbaino identity.

There are actually two different celebrations in Semana Grande in two very different locales. One celebration, the dominant, Town Hall–sponsored, and most popular one, revolves around Basque rural games, sports, dress, and other Basque traditions of music, dance, and food. A smaller celebration (in number of participants but not press coverage) involves privately sponsored activities that revolve around the corrida de toros. The first activities celebrate "typical" aspects of predominantly rural, preindustrial Basque life. The second activities celebrate sophisticated urban culture, upper-class relationships, and "Spanish" national relationships. Although the official program contains only the first activities, the press covers both sets of activities. Historically it was the second set, having to do with los toros, that never disappeared during the Franco regime. Both celebrations make up Bilbao's fiestas.

Locations

As stated above, the different sides of the Nervion River, which runs through the center of Bilbao, are identified with two different social groups. The right bank is the location of the old city center. Extending north along this bank are the homes of the "native" Basque middle classes and, further north, the bourgeois class. The left bank, which has a much larger population, is associated with Bilbao's expansion at industrialization from the 1880s on and is the home of many immigrant workers from other parts of Spain. Thus, the right and left banks of the Nervion River are used to talk about an inherent conflict in Bilbao: the relationship between a Basque (native) minority and a Spanish (foreign) majority. They also speak about the difference between old versus new Bilbao, preindustrial versus industrial Bilbao, and the middle class versus the workers (i.e., lower classes). Thus, there is a moral asymmetry where the "right bank" comes to mean "pure, authentic" and "left bank" means "polluted, unauthentic." In 1986, a definite pro-Basque "official" atmosphere dominated the city. Any pro-Spanish sentiments were literally hushed. Non-Basque residents would look around and lower their voices if they were speaking to me about anything considered anti-Basque, for example, complaining about their children having to learn the Basque language in school.[1]

Semana Grande takes place on both sides of the river. The city-sponsored activities take place in the old, original, preindustrial part of the city on the right bank. This part of the city was constructed between 1310 and 1830. Narrow, winding streets characterize this area, and the city's sixteenth-century cathedral of Santiago and the Basilica of Begoña are located there. During the Semana Grande many fiesta activities happen at the same time. These activities take place in the several small plazas in this part of the city.

The principal fiesta site, however, is the Arenal. This plaza, called the "neurological-sentimental center," borders the river. At one end of the Arenal is the church of Saint Nicolás and at the other end is the monumental Arriaga theater and opera house. The oldest bank in the city, the Bank of Bilbao, has its oldest building on this square. A bridge crosses to the other side of the river from this square. During the fiestas it is in this huge plaza, which is mostly a wide promenade along the river, that the youth clubs *(comparsas)* set up their booths *(txoznas)*, where Marijaia resides during the week of fiestas, where Gargantúa is located, where the *sokamuturra* (calves on ropes) take place and the *toro de fuego* (firecracker bull) appears, where the mules *(mulillas)* set off toward the bullring in the afternoon, and where one watches the midnight fire-cracker displays. Thus, the center of the popular fiestas is located on the Basque side of the river but not buried deep within the old city center, where the Basque folk dances and sports take place. Rather, the Arenal is located at a bridge that unites the right and left bank.

Two of the "traditional" activities associated with the Semana Grande are theater performances and los toros, the only two activities offered during the Franco years. These two very different types of ac-tivities have many things in common with respect to the fiestas. Both the bullfighting fans and the theater fans offer their respective spec-tacles during Semana Grande. Bilbao's eight corridas are offered only during this week, and theater owners say that people go to the the-ater only during the fifteen days around Semana Grande. In los toros, bulls and *toreros* from all over Spain converge upon Bilbao during this week, while in theater, actors, actresses, directors, and playwrights from throughout Spain arrive in Bilbao to put on their plays. In other words, both these activities have obvious references to the rest of the "Spanish state." Therefore, it is appropriate that the sites for these activities are located on the left side of the river. To get to the bullring and the thea-ters, one must cross the bridge from the Arenal and go to the new part of Bilbao.

The street that begins at the bridge of the Arenal turns into the most important boulevard, Gran Vía, on the left bank. Renamed Gran Vía de Diego de Haro (the founder of Bilbao) after 1975, this grand boulevard crosses the left bank from one side to the other. It is the commercial and social center of the left bank. Some important government build-ings, large department stores, cafes, theaters, banks, and hotels are lo-cated on this wide street. It is near this street that the smaller, privately sponsored fiestas take place.

Two four-star hotels in Bilbao hold a series of activities having to do with los toros and the theater. The Hotel Carlton is located exactly in the center of the Gran Vía. The Hotel Ercilla, site of even more activity and where most of the toreros stay, is located two blocks from the Gran Vía. The hotels hold seminars and colloquia on the bulls and theater. Los toros dominate the activities, however.

In 1986 the Hotel Carlton offered a painting exhibition of taurine themes, while the Hotel Ercilla had an exhibition of taurine sculpture. The Ercilla was where the Club Cocherito, Bilbao's well-known bullfighting club, held daily panels on bullfighting topics. From these hotels various organizations awarded prizes to the toreros, ranchers, and *pica-dores* for the best performance in the previous year's corridas. Several national radio stations sponsored reviews and critiques of the day's co-rrida in the hotels. The toreros who have performed in the corrida spoke and answered questions at these colloquia. They also made their rather dramatic exits to the bullring, dressed in their "suit of lights," from the lobby of the Hotel Ercilla and returned with their teams (e.g., picador and *bandilleros*) still dressed to accept the adulation of triumph or the humiliation of defeat.

In 1986 Hotel Ercilla had set up a temporary restaurant called the Taberna del Toro. In the lobby of the Ercilla was a *caseta andaluza* as a bar for drinking and visiting with friends. Every time I was in the Hotel Ercilla, the lobby was packed with elegantly dressed people, as well as members of the national and Basque newspapers, radio, and television stations busily interviewing many of these people.

Thus, the center of the private fiestas takes place on the left side of the Nervion and illustrates Bilbao's ties to the rest of Spain. These ties are symbolized by the hotels' guests from all over Spain, as well as by the emphasis on the corrida. Furthermore, those Bilbainos who fre-quent such elegant, four-star hotels are probably the upper classes with traditional economic and social ties to the same classes all over the Span-ish state. The activities in these hotels represent not only the relation-ships with Spain, but also are symbols of sophisticated, upper-class, ur-ban culture such as exhibitions, theater, restaurants, and fine clothes.

Hotels versus Txoznas

Another symbolic contrast between these two fiestas involves the build-ings around which each is oriented. The left bank fiestas take place in luxury hotels, with services such as doormen, chamber maids, barmen, and modern conveniences. The focus of the right bank fiestas is the streets and plazas, which are always a symbol of the pueblo, or common people. Set up in the plaza of the Arenal are the txoznas, kiosks, or bars put up by the youth clubs (comparsas).

Traditionally these comparsas were organizations of young men who attended los toros together, parading to and from the bullring as a group. When the comparsas, which correspond roughly to neighbor-hoods, were reconstituted in 1978, several declared themselves to be nontaurine comparsas, that is, they were not interested in going to, or supporting, los toros. Instead, these are purely social groups that cele-brate the fiesta together. All the comparsas have Basque names.

The Town Hall gives each comparsa space for its txozna along the river wharf in the Arenal. Each txozna is set up side by side with the next. Basically a txozna has a wall in the back and three sides that are a bar, across which drinks and food are sold and served. Inside the bar area the kitchen area is covered by a roof, but customers at the txozna are not under the roof. Each txozna has a specialty, such as *chorizo* sausage boiled in cider or porkloin sandwiches with pimento, but mostly beer and cider are sold. Different rock music blares out of each txozna from tape decks starting about 9:00 P.M. Since the txoznas are side by side, one tape melds into the next along the line.

Txozna (in Basque; *choza* in Castilian) means "hut" or sometimes "hovel or shanty." Compared to the four-star hotels on the other side of the city, the txoznas are hovels. By the second day of the festivities, the area and sidewalks around the txoznas are strewn with trash, spilled beer, and vomit. In the hotels the middle-aged people are elegantly dressed; the young people that crowd in front of the txoznas at night are dressed in jeans and T-shirts. While the hotel patrons drink whiskey and maintain control, the crowds at the txoznas drink beer and lose control. The hotel and txoznas summarize the two faces of the Semana Grande fiestas.

I describe the existence of two parallel fiestas that only coincide briefly at the plaza de toros. However, the fiestas patronized by the city government, which published the fiesta program in the daily newspapers, and by the vast majority of Bilbao's population are only the activities that take place in the *casco viejo* (old town) and the Arenal. Guide books describe these activities as "typical" (i.e., Basque) of Bilbao's fiestas (Sánchez 1982:153). The radio, television, and newspapers covered and advertised the events in the hotels but did not include them in the fiesta program.

The two simultaneous messages of the right bank fiestas are "equality" and "Basqueness." The symbols of equality glorify the common man (el pueblo). The symbols of Basqueness consist of activities that define fiestas in all Basque towns; many of these activities refer to pre-industrial, rural life.

Casco Viejo: Equality and Basqueness

Equality

The figure of Marijaia was called the "anthropomorphic symbol of the fiesta" ("La llegada de . . ." 1985:5). Created in 1978 to represent the people of Bilbao, Marijaia's appearance marks the beginning of the fiestas and the burning of Marijaia on Sunday night marks the end. Marijaia's creator, Mari Puri Herrero, explained that she wanted to create a representation of someone who had been waiting a long time to have a fiesta, a clear reference to the disappearance of the "popular fiestas" during Franco's reign and their reappearance in 1978.

Marijaia is a fifteen-foot tall figure of an older, rather plain-looking woman with a goofy smile and arms outstretched in the air as if she were celebrating or dancing (figure 6.1).[2] She is dressed in peasant clothes: a scarf, white billowing blouse, a sash around her waist, and a long skirt down to the ground (the man carrying her "hides" under this skirt). Her blonde hair differentiates her from the stereotypical dark-haired women of southern Spain. Marijaia represents all the "oppressed" categories of people in Spain, especially under the dictatorship: old, rural, female, and lower class. In this sense, she represents the pueblo. She is also a good symbol of the oppressed Periphery. In Bilbao's fiestas, the normal order of things is turned upside-down and Marijaia becomes the supreme authority ("La llegada de . . ." 1985:5).

The fiestas begin at the Basilica of Begoña, which is on a hill overlooking the old, original center of the city. On Saturday at 6:00 P.M., a firecracker is set off and Marijaia appears (reappears) amidst the crowds of people. Assembled are the mayor and the representatives of the various political parties in city government, as well as the members of the twenty comparsas dressed in various outrageous costumes such as Charlot, butterflies, and devils. The Giants and Big Heads (see below) are also present. In 1985 the members of the Fiesta Planning Committee appeared in top hats, white shirts, bow ties, and their undershorts. Accompanied by the city band and other musical groups of *txistularis* (a Basque horn), the officials form a parade *(bajada)* that goes down the hill to the Arenal. All along the way, comparsa members shoot water pistols at the public and throw bags of talcum powder. From the balconies of the houses, people throw buckets of water on the marchers. When they arrive at the plaza of the Arenal, full of people, there is another small official ceremony, more firecrackers are set off, and the *pregonero* (town crier) reads a salute to the fiestas. Marijaia is then taken around to all the txoznas, as if giving her blessing to each one.

During the week of fiestas the comparsas take turns caring for Marijaia. Each part of the day she accompanies one comparsa or another. At 5:00 P.M. every day she joins the *subida* (the parade of comparsas up to the bullring) and enters the bullring. Afterwards, she parades with the

Figure 6.1. Marijaia. The hand on the left side of the picture is toasting her with a *bota,* a wine bag. (Newspaper photograph courtesy of *Deia,* Aug. 20, 1986; photographed by Arambalza)

comparsas from the bullring back down to the Arenal. At various times during the week, she is the object of an attempted abduction by the "forces of evil" (groups of actors or other "figures"). These abductions are unsuccessful, since of course, nothing can interrupt Bilbao's fiestas, which she represents.

On the last day of the fiestas at 10:00 P.M. Marijaia participates in the funeral march—for herself. The comparsas parade through the streets to the music of funeral dirges, carrying a coffin and mourning the end of the fiestas. Again, there are attempted abductions of Marijaia, but this time to save her from her fate. Always she is found and the funeral march continues. At 11:00 P.M. Marijaia is burned in the Arenal and her ashes swept up and deposited in the river, until she is resurrected the following year. For now, the fiesta is over. "Only 360 days till the happiness and joyfulness again take over the hearts of the citizens of the town!" ("Agur . . ." 1985:5).

Marijaia not only represents the pueblo, she belongs to the pueblo. There is no formality about Marijaia. She "moves" in a casual, dancing way. When she is not being carried, she is leaned up against a building or a txozna. The press constantly reported how her nose had been bashed in or her dress had been ripped. She is held in affection but not in awe.

In many ways the comparsas also represent the pueblo. Since 1978 the comparsas have been composed of both men and women. Although most members are in their late teens and twenties, older member participate in parades to and from the bullring. The dress for the comparsas is usually unisexual, and all members wear the same costume: baggy pants; white shirt; vest; long, blouselike work shirt; sash at the waist; kerchief at the neck; and a beret or hat of some sort. If the girls wear skirts, they are midcalf with large work-shirt type blouses. In other words, there is no emphasis on male/female difference in dress. In fact, in most cases, as far as dress was concerned, difference was denied.

The general population wears no particular costume at all, with casual summer dress being the norm. In 1986 some comparsas tried to get people to wear a blue scarf around their neck. Every once in a while, I saw small children dressed as "Basque peasants" *(campesinos vascos)*. In most cases these were young girls wearing a dark blue denim dress with a kerchief over their heads and laced up espadrilles on their feet. I only saw one or two little boys dressed in "peasant" dress: white shirt and pants, vest, handkerchief around the neck, white espadrilles, and a beret, though these were very isolated cases.

Every morning around 11:00 A.M., the day begins with the parade of Giants and Big Heads. In much of Spain, Giants are tall (twelve feet), papier-mâché figures that are usually dressed like royalty. These figures are paraded through the streets during patron saint festivals and other fiestas. In Bilbao, as in other parts of the North, the Giants are not royalty. Rather, they are dressed like simple Basque countrymen and countrywomen. The female Giants wear long skirts, or housecoats, with aprons over them. Over their shoulders they wear shawls or vests and on their heads they wear work scarves. The male Giants wear work pants, saggy old jackets, and caps or berets on their heads. These Giants make quite a contrast to the jewel-bedecked kings and queens in other cities. The Big Heads (Cabezudos) are smaller, human-sized figures with enormous heads. These characters function as tricksters. They carry foam-rubber spiked sticks that they use to hit children over the head. Thus, an age hierarchy is emphasized in the parade of Giants (adults) and Big Heads (children); although by their dress, the Giants are identified with and made equal to the pueblo (instead of contrasted with them).[3] The Giants and Big Heads are billed as entertainment for children and programmed early in the day.

Also around 11:00 A.M. Gargantúa's Breakfasts begin. At this time two enormous oxen arrive at the Arenal pulling a cart carrying Gargantúa. Gargantúa, also named Julén, is a huge twenty-foot high figure of a plump, Basque peasant seated at a table, with both hands on the table in front of him and a knife sticking up from the figure's right hand. Julén is at the table ready to eat. What Julén eats are the children of Bilbao (figure 6.2). The children wait in line to climb the stairs up to Julén's table, where two "chefs" then stuff the child into the mouth of the figure. The chefs close Julén's mouth, and the child soon reappears out Julén's backside. There are always long lines of children (accompanied by their parents) waiting to be swallowed by Julén. Supposedly, whole Bilbaina families have been swallowed up over time by Julén.

Gargantúa, copied from the Rabelais character, is now clearly identified with Bilbao's fiestas. There have been six Gargantúa figures in the history of Bilbao, dating from the mid-nineteenth century ("El sexto Gargantúa . . ." 1986:2). (In a poster from 1900 announcing the fiestas of Bilbao, Gargantúa was drawn in the background as one of the symbols of the fiesta.) Thus, the figure predates the industrialization of Bilbao. For the 1986 fiestas a new Gargantúa was built with a much more gentle, much less scary face than the previous figures. Supposedly the previous child-devouring monsters often caused much fear among the children, and some children had been served up to the monster with

Figure 6.2. Gargantúa, or Julén, "eating" children during Bilbao's fiestas.
(Newspaper photograph courtesy of *Correo Español–Pueblo Vasco*, Aug. 18, 1986)

much resistance and crying. (In 1986 the children I watched went quite willingly.) The figure was inaugurated by a priest who declared, "Let the little children come unto me" ("Dejad que . . ." 1986:23).

The "sacrifice" of the children is not only a rite of passage to Bilbaina identity and adulthood, but possibly also originally represents the sacrifice of the children to rural life and toil. The giant peasant (the land) consumes each new generation. At any rate, today in Bilbao it is not the land that consumes rural children, but rather the many heavy industries and factories belonging to the capitalists that consume the children of the urban proletariat. Perhaps the 1986 version of Julén, with his kinder face, represents the idea that salvation ("let the little children come unto me") is to be found in the image of the rural peasant in contrast to urban reality. This is the Basque separatist movement's message.

Nevertheless, Gargantúa represents el pueblo. He sits in the Arenal and is accessible to all children. Gargantúa arrives every morning pulled by oxen, typical beasts of burden in the traditional rural Basque countryside. (Oxen are also the protagonists in Basque sports [see below].) His presence serves as a material link between the generations, as parents also slid down his throat when they were children.

The symbolism of Marijaia, the membership of the comparsas and their costumes, the attire of the Giants, and Gargantúa all stress identification with the pueblo. Unlike the fiestas on the other side of the river, these symbols celebrate equality and ignore most hierarchal aspects of the society, with the exception of age.[4] Not only class differences but also sex differences are denied or downplayed.

A final symbol of equality and the pueblo is the ethos about drinking in the Arenal. In stark contrast to the whiskey-drinking *oligarquía* in the hotels, the txoznas in the Arenal serve beer, the working man's drink, and alcoholic cider, a symbol of Northern identity. Furthermore, the goal of drinking, especially for the young, is to become drunk. Older couples and families with children do not manifest this behavior, nor do they congregate around the txoznas, which again, establishes an age distinction. The atmosphere around the txoznas is one of youthful exuberance with music, dancing, drinking, and joyful drunkenness. The young people drink so much that they often collapse and sleep it off on a bench, or simply on the grass or in the middle of a sidewalk. Walking across the Arenal late at night, one steps over many sleeping youths. This behavior of the pueblo is the antithesis of the upper classes' drinking behavior, where drunkenness is the ultimate disorder.

The drinking behavior underlies another general ethos of the fiestas in the Arenal, that of public foolishness. An air of gaiety and play pervades many of the activities in the Arenal. The sokamuturra (cows on ropes), Marijaia, and Gargantúa are the opposite of solemnity. Marijaia and Gargantúa even look like cartoon figures. In the mornings and afternoons in many of the plazas there are clown acts, magic acts, and humorous puppet shows for children. Performances of street theater take place in many parts of the city. Also, recall the various attempts to abduct Marijaia during the day, which is another example of street theater. The members of the comparsas have license to act up and be goofy. Not only do the comparsa members often look silly in their costumes, but they also act silly in the various parades in which they participate. The Bajada from Begoña is just one example of the comparsas acting foolish: firing water pistols and tossing flour bags at the crowd and parading in their underwear. They also offer silly acts of entertainment during the day at their txoznas. This willingness "to make a fool of oneself" contrasts to the always "dignified" behavior of the hotel of the fiestas.

Basqueness

As elaborated in the twentieth century, the concept of Basqueness celebrates not only an ideal of democratic equality (as symbolized by the ancient fueros [rights]), but also includes the preindustrial virtues of rustic peasant life (Azcona 1984). The rise of Bilbao as one of the first centers of Spanish industrialism at the end of the nineteenth century coincided with the creation of the Basque nationalist movement. Bilbao, however, with its industrialization, economic ties to Madrid, and large immigrant (non-Basque) population, is the antithesis of Basqueness. Nevertheless, Basqueness is stressed in Bilbao's fiestas. Despite the fact that heavy industry provided jobs and one of the highest standards of living in the whole Spanish state, this aspect of Bilbao is ignored in the fiestas in the Arenal. Instead, rural lifestyles are stressed.

Most of the activities on the program during the day are activities typical of fiestas in other Basque towns. The day begins with reveille, played on Basque musical instruments, firecrackers, and the sokamuturra (cows on ropes). Later in the morning the exhibitions and contests of Basque sports *(herri kirolak)* begin. In other plazas there are Basque dances and music. At 1:30 P.M. spontaneous poetry recitals in Basque *(bertsolaris)* take place. Later at night the toros de fuego (firecracker bulls) appear among the crowds, and at the end of the week there are cooking contests.

The exhibitions of Basque sports take place in one of the plazas inside the old town. These contests occur all over the Basque Country during the summer, with men traveling from town to town to participate. There are two types of competition. One pits two men against each other, the other opposes two animals or two teams of animals. Among the men there are contests of weight-lifting *(pulsolaris)* and log cutting *(aizkolaris)*. In weight-lifting a man raises stone and lead weights of 100 kilograms, 200 kilograms, or more over his head, up to his head, or up to his shoulders as many times as possible in a limited amount of time, for instance, three minutes. The men wear rural clothes, wrap a scarf around their waist as a girdle, and protect their legs with a leather apron. In the log cutting contest, two teams of men race to cut in half sixteen logs (from 1.25 meters to 1.50 meters in circumference). The participants usually come from small towns and have other jobs. They are also huge, enormously strong men. It is from these rural sportsmen that the Basque physical stereotype developed. (Again, the bull for the Basque Country repeats this stereotype: it should be huge with large horns.) The animal contests include oxen and draft horses pulling stone weights and battles between rams. All of these exhibitions stress strength.

The Basque music and dances also have an important role in the fiesta program. Basque music uses characteristic instruments, especially the *txistu* (a kind of horn). Basque music is always sung in a chorus, and

Basques are well known for their singing, especially during fiestas. The choreography of Basque dances has been well studied (Caro Baroja 1968 : 183). The dances, as contrasted with the songs, are so difficult and complicated that people do not join in. Instead, audiences watch a group of perhaps twenty costumed dancers perform these dances on stage. Some dances use sticks and others employ ribbons. Rather than gracefulness, athletic skills and dancing in unison are emphasized: the group projects solidarity. All the dancers are dressed alike, in white pants and shirt, beret, and kerchief at the neck. Traditionally only men perform these dances.

On the last three days of the fiesta there are cooking and recipe contests in the Arenal, a celebration of the renowned cooking abilities of the Basques. Throughout the Basque Country, men gather to cook for each other and socialize at all-male dinner clubs, which are always cited as something uniquely Basque. Basque "specialties" are recognized all over Spain and often consist of fish in sauce. In the cook-offs in the Arenal most of the chefs are men, although in 1985 a woman won first prize for her recipe of *bacalao a la vizcaina* (codfish). There were other recipes for tuna, hake, and even a prize for bull's tail stew.

Two further activities characterize fiestas mayores in the Basque Country: the two taurine categories of sokamuturra (cows on ropes) and *zezensusko* (toro de fuego, firecracker bull). Both of these activities frame the day. The sokamuturra begins at 7 : 00 A.M., and the zezensusko appears at midnight. Both activities take place in the Arenal, and both are considered "Basque" taurine fiestas. The press emphasizes that the cows in the sokamuturra come from the neighboring Basque provinces of Guipuzcoa, which is considered the center of Basqueness. One morning when I was watching a sokamuturra, I asked an approximately forty-year-old man if he had participated in these events in his youth. His answer was, "No. I'm from Castile (Toledo). There we have capings *(tentaderos),* but not this." To celebrate and participate in sokamuturras is to be Basque.

Schedule

One daily activity underlines the character of the fiesta as ritualistic inversion. Several mornings in 1986, the city fire trucks arrived at the Arenal and the firemen used their hoses to fill half the plaza with white foam. Young children gleefully jumped and danced around in what the newspapers called "snow in August." Otherwise, however, daily schedules are not especially altered in the fiestas of Bilbao. Although every day is structured basically the same way, Thursday is called the "equator," the midpoint of the fiesta. Friday is considered the day of most participation. It is also the day the corrida is traditionally sold out. Starting on Friday, visitors from other Basque provinces arrive in Bilbao to participate in the festivities.

Los Toros

The various taurine activities in the Semana Grande signify "fiestas" much more than the corridas in the Feria de Sevilla (see chapter 7). This is ironic, since many people think the South has the most afición a los toros. Yet, in Bilbao the toros are more integrated into the fiestas, and each different taurine activity represents a different ethnic aspect of Bilbao. Nevertheless, the corrida unites Bilbao's different social entities.

On the Thursday before the fiestas begin, some of the youth clubs celebrate a *becerrada* (*zekorketa* in Basque) in Bilbao's bullring. In a becerrada members of the public get to cape the two-year-old calf before it is killed. In Bilbao cows (vaquillas) are used and, as usual, they are not killed. The zekorketa in Bilbao is a humorous spectacle that the comparsas put on to make money for charity.

In 1985, eight comparsas participated in the zekorketa, and each comparsa prepared a skit with a cow: one group tried to mount and ride wild ponies while a cow was running around the ring; another group set up a swimming pool in the middle of the ring to jump into if the cow got too close; another group tried to play soccer while the cows were running after them; another skit depicted a honeymoon couple in a big brass bed in the middle of the ring with a vaquilla (Marugán 1985:5). Although the zekorketa seems to be making fun of the seriousness of the los toros, which is typical of Bilbao's fiestas, it also shows that it is impossible to carry out an activity in Spain and ignore the bulls. They are there in the ring and impose themselves no matter what.

As stated above, the sokamuturras (cows on ropes) and the zezensusko (fire bulls) frame the days of the rest of the fiestas. Both these activities are Basque identity markers. The sokamuturras take place in the Arenal, where short iron fences mark off an oblong space. Cows with thick ropes around their horns are set loose from a truck. They dash at the boys in the ring before the herder jerks them away. There are many more participants than spectators.

After the sokamuturras are over, the next taurine activity begins: a *suelta de vaquillas* (freeing the cows in the ring to run after the youths). This activity is an intermediate activity between the early morning sokamuturra and the afternoon corrida. If the sokamuturra represents "Basque" culture and the corrida represents the "Spanish" culture, the vaquillas represent something in between. Although vaquillas represent local culture, their extension is much more national than the Basque sokamuturras. Vaquillas are typical of all the Periphery (Vizcaya, Navarra, and Valencia in my study). Thus, when vaquillas are compared to sokamuturras they are a "Spanish" form of los toros. When vaquillas are compared to the corrida they are a Peripheral form. The vaquillas represent the lower classes in contrast to the corrida's upper classes, but again, they also represent the national "Spanish" culture in contrast to the sokamuturra's "Basqueness." As such, the vaquillas represent the ambiguous nature of Bilbao's disparate population and the demographic dominance of the non-Basque working class.

The suelta de vaquillas (freeing cows in a ring) does not take place in the Arenal but rather in the bullring on the left side of the river.[5] This marks the vaquillas as a non-Basque activity. The suelta de vaquillas begins at 9:00 A.M., which is early, considering that the people have been dancing in the Arenal until 5:00 or 6:00 A.M. Nevertheless, the thirteen thousand bullring seats are totally full every day. I arrived at 8:45 A.M. one day and had to sit at the very top of the stands. The ring itself was packed with young men and some young women, all dressed in jeans and T-shirts.

A master of ceremonies spoke over a microphone, making humorous remarks about each cow and her success or failure at catching people with her horns and throwing them in the air. Basque music was played on loud speakers between cows. The majority of the public was in a gay, laughing mood. Occasionally, a young man would take his jacket, or an old red cape *(muleta)*, and try to pass the cow. The other participants allowed him to do this for one or two minutes. Then the cow would again belong to all the participants.

Despite the important mediating of the role of the *vaquillas,* the corrida is the most important taurine activity. Moreover, it is the total structural opposite of the Basque sokamuturra and is opposed at every level (table 6.1). Yet the corrida is always where the two separate fiestas of the Semana Grande, the hotel fiestas and the popular fiestas, come together and form an encompassing Bilbaina identity.[6] The corrida begins at 6:00 P.M., and at 5:00 P.M. the team of mules that drag the dead bulls out of the bullring appears at the Arenal. They are decorated with red and white (Bilbao's colors) flags and led by men also dressed in peasants' clothes. The mules are led across the bridge to the left bank

Table 6.1 Structural Comparison
of Sokamuturra and Corrida

Sokamuturra	Corrida
old town	new town
right bank	left bank
popular	upper classes
participatory	spectacle
Basque	Spanish
morning	afternoon

and up the hill to the bullring. Many of the comparsas, including Mari-jaia, fall behind and form a parade. Spectators line the streets watching those who are going to the corrida.

As the mules leave the Arenal, crowds begin to congregate around the Ercilla Hotel, where the toreros are staying. Perhaps a comparsa and its band appear to wish their favorite torero good luck. After the toreros have made their exits from the hotel, groups of elegantly dressed people also leave the hotel walking toward the bullring.

Thus, from the different points of the city, two different parades of people make their way to the bullring. Police stop the traffic for the mules, comparsas, and other people marching up the streets to the ring. At the ring these two groups merge and now form *la afición de Bilbao*. Thus, the bullring spatially mediates the two themes of Bilbao's fiestas, hierarchy and equality.

Although Bilbao's afición is united about the kind of bull and torero they like, there is the typical *Sol* (sun) and *Sombra* (shade) class division in the ring. Traditionally, the people who sat in Sombra were the bourgeoisie and their guests. Factory owners used to give away corrida tickets to people they wanted to please or influence. Although I was told this practice has been dying out since the mid-1970s, the people I sat with in Sol described those in Sombra as "the upper-class bourgeoisie."

At the beginning of the week the corrida is not completely full, but on Thursday and Friday the corridas are sold out. These two days correspond to the best cartel (best bulls and toreros). However, Thursday is also the "equator" of the fiestas and Friday the day of the most general participation.

At the end of the corrida the comparsas again form outside the ring and begin another parade back down to the Arenal. Again, all the traffic stops and spectators line the streets. The arrival of the comparsas at the Arenal corresponds to the opening of the kiosk bars. On the other hand, the hotel guests walk back to the hotels to await the arrival of the toreros and the beginning of the many conferences and symposiums on the day's corrida, which go on until 1:00 and 2:00 A.M.

Analysis

In 1985 and 1986, Friday was the only day that the three flags of Vizcaya, the Basque Country, and Spain were raised in front of the Town Hall. In 1983 and again in 1984, in various towns all over the Basque Country, several incidents occurred during town fiestas over the Spanish flag. Members of the various political parties bickered over whether the flag should fly during the fiestas. In some places the Civil Guard, or police, were called to "protect" the Spanish flag. Violence erupted, and in 1983 some people were killed. Since then the issue has been a delicate one.

Bilbao's solution was not to fly any flags except on Friday. Since the fiesta mayor is trying to create an "illusion of community," in Bilbao the fiestas strive to remain nonpolitical. This explains the emphasis on community and living together in peace. In 1985 the mayor opened the fiesta saying, "We are ready, far from the everyday problems of the rest of the year, for the happiness of the fiestas, crowned by harmony and peace" (Robles 1985:25).

More than class, more than gender, what divides Bilbao are questions of national loyalties. The political parties in Bilbao reflect national, ethnic loyalties, not simply class. Moreover, theses divisions are always lurking just beneath the surface of the fiestas. In 1985, the Socialist (a pan-Spanish political party) members of the city council refused to participate in the Bajada from the Basilica of Begoña, which initiates the fiestas, because of the presence of demonstrators chanting support for ETA (the Basque terrorist, separatist organization). That same year two of the comparsas refused to attend the mayor's reception for them at Town Hall on the first day of the fiestas because the invitations had not been written in Basque. In general, the structural solution to these problems has been to emphasize "Basqueness" in the "popular" fiestas, emphasize "Spanishness" in the upper-class fiestas, and locate these two fiestas in different parts of the city. The bullring is the only place where the two groups momentarily coincide.

Nevertheless, it must again be noted that the fiestas in the hotel are

not "officially" recognized. They do not form part of the fiesta program. Municipal money is used to organize only the fiesta in the Arenal,
thus establishing a Bilbao identity based on Basqueness, the common
man (el pueblo), and equality. However, some of the Basque elements
in the fiestas, specifically the sokamuturra and the toros de fuego, relate
the Basques with other peoples in the Spanish state that use bulls in
their fiestas.

Chapter 7

THE SOUTH: FERIA DE ABRIL IN SEVILLA

Feria de Abril means music, *sevillana* music everywhere, accompanied by hand clapping; couples dancing, arms gracefully raised, with sensuous but controlled body movements, as they move provocatively in front of each other and then twirl, pass, and change places; women dressed in polka-dot, bodice-clinging dresses with layer upon layer of ruffles falling to the ground, hair pulled up in a bun, flowers pinned behind the ear, riding behind men outfitted like Spanish country gentlemen on horses that prance and dance and throw their heads in proud and nervous excitement. These couples ride up and down dirt packed streets lined with green and white striped tents where people visit, watch, dance, and elegantly drink small glasses of strong white wine. At night this striking scene is lit by millions of lanterns strung along these streets, creating a fairy-tale fiesta of gaiety and light.

Sevilla

Sevilla is one of the eight provinces that make up the Autonomous Community of Andalusia. The city of Sevilla is capital of the province, as well as capital of the region. Sevilla plays an important role in the mental construction of "Spain."

The city of Sevilla is situated in the valley of the Guadalquivir River. Although Sevilla is seventy-five kilometers from the sea, the river is navigable, and thus, the city is considered a seaport. Called Hispalis by the Iberians or Phoenicians, the Romans conquered Sevilla in 205 B.C. and renamed it Betis. It was an important city in Roman Spain (producing two Roman emperors: Trajan and Hadrian). Under Arab domination, Sevilla became one of the most beautiful cities in Andalusia. In 1248 Sevilla was reconquered by the Christian troops of Fernando III of Castile, who established his court there. The rest of the Reconquest was directed from Sevilla. In the sixteenth century, Sevilla became administrative headquarters for the New World, regulating all traffic with the

Americas until the mid-eighteenth century, when Spain lost its monopoly of trade with those lands. The remains of Christopher Columbus are kept in the cathedral, the third largest in Christendom. The wealth of the Americas flowing through Sevilla made it a city of splendor and art for more than two centuries.

As Spain slowly lost political and economic control of the colonies, Sevilla, and Spain, lost its former glory. In the nineteenth century, the lands in Andalusia passed from the mortmain of the nobility and church to the private ownership of the bourgeoisie who had the money to buy them. Once in possession of the large latifundios *(cortijos),* this new landed gentry *(terratenientes)* settled back to live off rents from their lands and copy the lifestyle of the southern aristocracy. Most of these landowners (often referred to as *señoritos*) lived in the capital city of Sevilla rather than permanently on the land. The great masses of rural folk, now without access to common lands or church lands, were reduced to selling their labor to the landowners. While the landowners created an elegant and graceful lifestyle, the rural masses barely subsisted. By the end of the century there was great antagonism between the landed gentry and the rural proletariat. Banditry was rife, and the political ideology of anarchism had taken hold among the rural poor.

This social structure continued until the outbreak of the Spanish Civil War in 1936. Historians commonly list the "agrarian problem" of the South as one of the numerous causes of the Civil War. At the outbreak of the war, many landless peasants took bloody revenge upon the upper classes and their supporters, especially in the church, but Sevilla was nevertheless quickly retaken by the Nationalist rebel troops. During the Franco regime, the powerful terratenientes played an important role as pillars of the regime and became symbols of "official Spain."

Although by Franco's death in 1975 the agrarian problem had been partly remedied by emigration (to North Spain and Europe), much was still to be addressed. Andalusia is one of the poorest regions per capita in Spain, although the city of Sevilla itself is prosperous. Having ignored the industrial revolution, Sevilla did not begin urban expansion across the Guadalquivir River until the 1960s. Although Sevilla's population grew rapidly during this decade, the immigrants were primarily from Andalusia, rather than from elsewhere.

The gypsies, a small and poor social group, have historically lived in Andalusia and continue to be associated with Andalusia and Sevilla. Given their connections with the Southern symbols of flamenco music and dancing, dress, and bullfighting, the gypsies' symbolic importance is much greater than their numbers indicate.

The province of Sevilla is divided between rich farmland of rolling plains and pasture *(dehesa)*, where horses and toros bravos are raised. The rich cultivated lands produce cereals, olives, and grapes for wine. There is hardly any industry in the province, and even olive oil is refined elsewhere.

Sevilla capital, with over six hundred thousand inhabitants, is an administrative service city still associated with the traditional lifestyle of the terratenientes. The rest of the province is characterized by agrocities and a relative absence of small villages.

In the early to mid-nineteenth century, many European romantic writers visited Sevilla and Andalusia. Thus, Sevilla often serves as the archetype of a Spanish city for foreigners. Merimée's novel, *Carmen,* which Bizet immortalized in his opera, takes place in Sevilla. Beaumarchais and Rossini located the opera *Barber of Seville* there. Furthermore, one of the most popular Spanish dramas, *Don Juan Tenorio,* with its internationally well-known character of Don Juan, has Sevilla as its backdrop. Mozart's opera *Don Giovanni* helped take Don Juan to Europe. In many ways, these images of "Spain" as Sevilla have been as influential in Spain as in Europe.

A sense of regionalism, which blames Andalusia's underdevelopment on Madrid's traditional benign neglect, has grown since 1975, along with pride in the South's cultural distinctiveness. However, in the last century and a half this cultural distinctiveness has manifested itself not as a desired separatism from Spain but as a claim to be the most Spanish of the Spanish regions.[1] Recall that in the Spain/Europe debate, the South represents "Spain." And in the semantics of los toros, the *corrida,* said to be a product of Andalusian culture, is present in *fiestas mayores* all over the peninsula, while the northern taurine forms are not incorporated into the southern fiestas.

La Feria de Abril de Sevilla

Sevilla's Feria is one of Spain's most well-known fiestas. Movie stars, celebrities, and politicians from all over the country attend. One of the first things a visitor reacts to in Feria is that all the social classes in Sevilla are so blatantly celebrating hierarchy and class (Prat Canos 1982).

Feria is set to begin two weeks after Easter Sunday, thus the date varies.[2] Feria was established in 1847 as an agricultural and livestock fair, in the hope that it would stimulate the region's crisis-ridden economy. Ironically, the idea for Feria, the most typical of Sevillana fiestas, belonged to two Catalan and Basque businessmen living in Sevilla. Originally the Feria lasted only three days and later was expanded to six. By the second year the first *casetas* (little houses, or tents) had appeared (Collantes de Terán Delorme 1981). These small, provisional tents gave the ranch owners *(ganaderos)* who came to the fair a private place to relax in the shade and entertain guests. These casetas and the rituals of Andalusian hospitality soon became the hallmarks of Feria. From the very beginning, the Feria has also represented the role of the countryside in the life of upper-class Sevilla. In Feria a series of upper-class country artifacts has been frozen in time and is still celebrated: the dress for men, the use and trappings of the horse, and carriages, as cars are still not allowed on the fairgrounds.[3] Still today, to be seen wearing these clothes and riding in these carriages confers status.

Although the trading, buying, and selling of livestock played an important role for many years, by 1890 the role of livestock began to diminish. About this time the role of the "fiesta" (hospitality, food, drink, and entertainment) took over and became the essence of the Feria (Collantes de Terán Delorme 1981 : 37). The outer forms of the Feria remained (the dress, the caseta, the horse and carriage, the corrida), but the market and its role effectively disappeared.[4] From the very beginning, a corrida de toros was celebrated during the Feria; later there were four corridas, and then eight.

Location

In keeping with its role as a synthesis between city and country, Feria takes place totally on a fairground (*el Real de la Feria,* the Royal [Land] of the Fair), which is three hundred thousand square meters in size. El Real is on the literal periphery of the city, a liminal site touching both city and countryside. Feria has had three sites during its 140-year history, all on the periphery of Sevilla. In 1986 one side of the Real de Feria bordered tall apartment buildings, while the other side bordered grazing lands. The site is not used for any other purpose but Feria, and the day after, the site is empty. Eleven months later it is overgrown with grass and full of trash.

This peripheral site for such an important fiesta is in stark contrast to every other area of Spain, where the old, "original" city center is the location of the festivities, which corresponds to the general valuation of the "center" as authentic, pure, and original. It is especially startling in Andalusia, where anthropological work stresses the preference of city (social) life over country (nonsocial) life and the preference to live in the city center over the outskirts (Corbin and Corbin 1984; Driessen 1981; Gilmore 1980; Marvin 1982). With the location of its Feria, Sevilla emphasizes the role of the "countryside" in its "culture."

Just as Feria is a "ludic parenthesis" in time, the location of the Feria is a "spatial parenthesis." Sevillanos simply relocate their "center" to the area between city and country. On the fairground, another provisional city—of canvas—is constructed. Both the countryside and the city empty out and pour into this new "city," the Feria. On Friday of Feria 1986, one million people were estimated to have been in the Real, while the population of Sevilla is only six hundred thousand. During Feria week Sevilla's center is "empty," there is simply no activity going on. In fact, if you arrived in Sevilla without knowing Feria was in progress, it would be difficult to find out. The city itself is not decorated in any way, and there is very little advertising for the fiesta. In the center, where the historical monuments, restaurants, and stores are located, there is nothing to tell you that one million people are drinking and dancing outside of town.

The "city" that is constructed (and reconstructed every year) is composed of two parts. The main part is a grid of wide dirt streets with dirt sidewalks marked off, all parallel and perpendicular to each other. All the streets are named after well-known *toreros* from Sevilla—thus, los toros literally underlie the Feria. Strung above the sidewalks are ten rows of red and white paper lanterns with light bulbs inside. Across the streets at about twenty-foot intervals are strung four rows of white light bulbs. At each intersection, a large pole is placed in the center with twenty or thirty strings of lights running from the pole to all sides of the plaza, thus forming a canopy of lights at every intersection. Along the thirteen streets are the more than one thousand canvas casetas. Dotting the street corners are popcorn and nut stands. Surrounding the fairground are wooden kiosks, which sell candy and souvenirs.

The secondary part of the "city" is the site of the amusement park, which is immediately adjacent to the caseta area. This park, called the Street of Hell, entertains the children during much of the day and in this way helps introduce them to the Feria.

Casetas

The casetas are the focus of the fiesta. It is inside or in front of the casetas that the singing, dancing, eating, and socializing take place. The casetas (little houses) are supposed to represent the "traditional" Sevillano home, but they are "traditional" in the sense of decoration, rather than architecture or floor plan.

Architecturally, the caseta consists of a rectangular metal framework with a pointed roof that is draped with canvas over the sides and back (figure 7.1). The canvas is always red and white striped, or green and

Figure 7.1. A couple riding on a horse in front of a caseta in Feria.
(Photographed by the author)

white striped (the colors of Andalusia's flag). Most of the casetas are the same size and are completely contiguous with each other. The front consists of a gaudily painted tympanum with scroll and floral designs in primary colors. The rest is usually totally open, with the tent flaps tied back.

The floor plan of a caseta is always the same and consists of two parts or rooms: the caseta and the *trastienda*. The caseta is the front part, open to the streets and the eyes of people who are walking on the "side-walks." It is separated from the street by a short iron railing that runs along three quarters of the front of the caseta. Between the end of the railing and the side is the "entry way." The floor is wooden. This front part is where guests are received and entertained, dancing and singing takes place, and people sit along the sides and railing to watch what is happening in the caseta, as well as in the street. It is also where the owners of the caseta eat the midday meal, with the front canvas closed.

Separating the caseta from the trastienda is some kind of opaque "wall" or curtain, which blocks the public eye from this part of the little house. The trastienda hides all the service parts; usually there is a bar, behind which is kept the food, drink, and food preparation utensils such as a gas stove, small refrigerator, knives, and glasses. Each caseta has a caretaker, who helps set it up and take it down, guards it at night, and helps cook and serve the food. This person works and sleeps at night in the trastienda. There is often a small toilet and closet that can be locked for storing valuables. Thus, the public/private division, typical of Andalusian life, is condensed in the caseta's spatial divisions.

Sevillanos decorate the caseta to produce an "Andalusian" style, its most significant aspect. In fact, several awards are given to the casetas with the "most typical" decorations and plaques are set up on the outside of the caseta to display the prize. The decoration does not in any way look like the interior of the homes in modern apartment buildings in Sevilla. Rather, it is supposed to represent a "traditional house," as in the old neighborhoods of Sevilla (San Bernardo, or even Santa Cruz). A "false ceiling" is created by altering the rows of puffy, paper lanterns and paper flowers or yards of cotton lace curtains that cover the ceiling and drape down the walls. Although each caseta is decorated slightly differently and no one caseta contains all the "typical" symbolic features, some elements are used repeatedly: the walls are often lined with five-foot high paper that imitates the ceramic tile decoration in "traditional" houses, antique portraits and paintings in elaborate baroque frames hang on the walls, and pictures are painted on the canvas wall.

These paintings are of "typical" Sevillano subjects: the cathedral, the Torre de Oro, flamenco dancers, Easter Week processions, guitars, wine glasses, statues of the Virgin Mary, bullfighters, bulls, and horsemen in the fields with bulls. Other decoration on the walls includes huge antique mirrors, flower pots with real or fake geraniums, guitars and *castañuelas,* bullfight posters, and bulls' heads. The wooden floors are usually bare, but in some larger casetas parts of the floor are covered with hemp rugs. Small wooden tables line the sides of the casetas, and the typical chair is high backed and wooden with a woven seat. The wooden back slats of these chairs are painted red or green with floral decorations.

Historically, the casetas belonged to single families who invited their friends to visit, dance, and eat. It was only the very wealthy upper classes who could afford to pay the costs of a caseta and entertainment. Later, several families would join together in setting up a caseta, but lack of space at the original site kept the number of casetas down and restricted to the upper-class families. The city allotted space in the Feria Real and charged a reservation fee. By the 1940s there began to be talk of changing the site of the Feria to gain space and add more casetas. By the 1960s the pressure was intense. In 1973 the site of the Feria was moved across the river to the outskirts of Sevilla beside a new middle-class neighborhood.

The tremendous gain in space allowed for many more casetas. These new casetas belong to people of the middle and lower classes. Many of the families joined together to be able to afford a caseta. More significantly, larger groups have joined together and set up casetas: groups of coworkers, professional fraternities, neighborhood associations, religious brotherhoods, businesses or factories, sports clubs, bullfighting clubs, cultural clubs, big department stores, and political parties. This trend has brought about what Sevillanos refer to as the "popularization" of the Feria. As one middle-class informant told me, "To have a caseta was a privilege. Now we all participate in things." I was always told that before the 1960s there was no real middle class in Sevilla. With the growth of the middle classes came the pressure for participation in all aspects of Sevillano life—even in the *señorial* Feria. After the restoration of democracy, even the workers demanded their right to be present in Feria. In fact, one of the biggest casetas belongs to the Communist party.

While the family caseta is quite small, the casetas that belong to the big institutions and groups are quite large and usually located on the corners of the street blocks. Also, whereas the family caseta has no name, just a number, the group caseta is often given a funny name, which is painted on the outside of the tent. Furthermore, although theoretically all casetas are public, the larger group casetas are much more receptive than private casetas to strangers. Although someone usually "guards" the gate, at a public caseta it is enough to ask to enter (the guard will ask how many of you there are and then wave you in). The political party casetas do not even have a guard. These casetas, in contrast to the family casetas (see below), allow a person to buy food and drink at the bar in their trastienda. Consequently, I always ate lunch and dinner in one of these casetas when I was not invited to a family caseta. Groups of friends and families who could not afford a caseta may get together in one of these casetas to have dinner and spend an evening.

Drink and Food

Guests and friends who drop by to visit a caseta are immediately offered something to drink, with a *tapa* (hors d'oeuvre) to accompany the drink. In many ways the Feria can be considered a fiesta of fortified wine, or sherry. Since the 1940s the typical sherry drunk in Feria is what the Sevillanos call *fino* (pale and dry). Although fino refers to a kind of sherry, as an adjective fino means "fine, of high quality, refined." This sherry is produced in towns near Sevilla: Jerez, Condado, and Sanlucar de la Berremeda. It represents an Andalusian product. It is always drunk in a specially shaped, small glass. Some other alcoholic drinks are also available; in fact, some Sevillanos advise starting in the morning with a beer or sweet sherry to line the stomach. Then one can continue the rest of the day with fino or switch at night in some casetas to whiskey and other hard liquor. (I saw no sodas or colas.) At any rate, the most prevalent and typical drink is fino, and once you start with one brand you should continue all day with the same brand, if possible.

Along with not mixing kinds of fino, one should always eat something (a tapa) with every glass of wine. I was constantly being urged to accompany my wine with food. The objective of Feria was to drink but *not* to get drunk. Considering the amazing amounts of wine and other alcoholic beverages consumed all day and night, I was surprised that I saw only one person who was obviously drunk. On Friday, the high point of Feria 1986, the Red Cross booth reported dealing with only four hundred cases of drinking "problems." The ethos is to drink to be "gay" *(alegre)* but definitely not to lose control, or much less, to become ill. There is no loud talking, no back slapping, no spilling drinks or falling down. One tries to maintain one's "aristocratic bearing." The drink does, of course, function to loosen one's inhibitions and make people more accessible. (One of my hosts, a pediatrician, explained to me, "People change. A man who is serious and never drinks, laughs and gets a little drunk during Feria.") The resulting communitas still stresses grace and self-control, the Sevillano style, as well as the style associated with that of *toreo* in the bullring.

The tapas offered with the drink are, for the most part, typical of those found everywhere in Spain: cured ham, *chorizo,* potato omelette, olives, cheese, bread with tuna, or small sweet pastries. Andalusian specialties were also offered, such as fried fish or snails. The tapas were more elaborate in the casetas of the upper classes, where I was told fresh shrimp is offered. In the upper-class caseta I visited, I was offered small pastries with roquefort cheese spread, which was more sophisticated (and French) than the potato chips and olives I ate in the public caseta.

In the "private" caseta no money is ever used. The host serves. Supposedly, anyone can enter a caseta, and my hosts said that they would never make a scene kicking anyone out, except for gypsies.[5] But only those who are invited and served by a host can eat and drink in a private caseta.

Men serve in the caseta. It was the male hosts who offered me food and brought it to me, sometimes upon the prompting of their wives. With the front flaps down, the host families and perhaps some out-of-town guests may share a midday meal in the privacy of the caseta. Although the wives may have cooked the meal at home, the men set up the tables and serve the food in the caseta. This inverts the normal order of the male/female division of labor, but as one informant assured me, "this only happens during Feria."

Music and Dance

If the caseta and fino are two important elements of Feria, a third is the music of the sevillanas. Sevillana music, both sung and danced, dominates Feria. A development of the flamenco style from the eighteenth century, the sevillanas are a genre of *seguidillas,* with a very quick rhythm. Although they may simply be sung, often they are accompanied by a guitar, cello, drums, percussion, and even piano. Each sevillana is composed of four stanzas, or verses. There are literally thousands of them written or made up on the spot. Individual performers sing sevillanas, in thick Andalusian accents, and no one joins in. In their sung form they are a spectacle, not a participatory rite.

People also dance to sevillanas, but only as couples, usually a man and a woman or a boy and girl. However, it is very frequent to see two women dancing as a couple, but in this case one woman must take the "male" role. Couples form a straight line on the dance floor down the middle of the caseta, men on one side, women on the other. A couple always dances all four verses of the sevillana before sitting down. No matter what the lyrics are, when the sevillanas are played for dancing, the sevillana becomes a stereotyped relationship between men and women, where in four sequences the woman "conquers" the man. The four stanzas correspond to falling in love, the fight, reconciliation, and sublime perfection. The couples never touch, but the whole impression of the dance is of great sensuality and corresponds to the Andalusian concept of male and female. The female seduces with her body, undulating arms above her head and swaying her waist and hips (figure 7.2). Although some younger boys dance more freely and sensually than the older men, the male in general is much less demonstrative, holding his hands in front of him and sedately clapping in time with the music while dancing the four sequences. Between each stanza, there is a slight musical pause before the beginning of the last stanza; timing is important. Those who are standing around watching the dancers accompany the music with *palmas* (short, fast claps with cupped hands in time to the music). Palmas become part of the performance.

Sevillana music begins playing when people start reappearing in the Real each new day, around noon. In 1986 every caseta had a tape deck playing sevillanas at full volume from noon until 5:00 or 6:00 A.M. Walking down the streets of casetas, one walks from one sevillana to another. At least one evening or more, the upper classes must bring in a performance group to sing sevillanas live for their friends in their caseta. The group only stays in each caseta an hour or two. When it leaves, the tape deck is turned back on. Although some of the larger casetas may have a band on one or more nights during a formal dinner, the band always plays dance music: rumbas or sevillanas. Rock music is not heard in Feria.

Schedule and Dress

Feria totally reorients the city of Sevilla. Although businesses do not completely close, offices are usually open only from 10:00 A.M. to 1:00 or 2:00 P.M. The terms *morning, noon,* and *night* take on new referential meaning. "Morning" *(mañana)* begins around noon and goes till 6:00 or 7:00 P.M. (the end of the corrida). "Afternoon" *(tarde)* runs

Figure 7.2. Dancing sevillanas in Feria. (Photographed by the author)

from 7:00 P.M. until midnight. "Night" *(noche)* begins at midnight and goes until 5:00 or 6:00 A.M. Although the program is essentially the same every day of the week, the agenda for the three parts of the day varies.

The "morning" is the most upper-class (señorial) part of the day, characterized by the presence of horses,[6] which are without a doubt the fourth important element of the Feria. During the "morning" the streets of the Real are full of horses, riders, horse-drawn carriages, and passengers. Horses and carriages are signs of wealth. Those without horses stand or stroll along the sidewalks, watching the horses go by. The horses should be owned by those who ride them. Likewise the carriages and tack should belong to the passengers who ride in them. However, many informants told me, and I saw allusions in the press to the fact, that many people merely "rented" a horse or carriage for a couple of hours on one of the days of the Feria. No one I met admitted to doing that, however. Some members of these upper classes devote themselves almost entirely to agricultural pursuits, often they are bull ranchers owning truly immense tracts of land with stables of horses and barns full of carriages. Others, however, now devote themselves to professions in the city. These city people still own land in the country, which is an important status symbol in Andalusia. On their land they may keep a couple of horses and a carriage strictly for Feria. An agricultural businessman commented, "Horses? I don't have any more horses, except the guardian's horse. So when Feria comes around, I take the horse from him. And I ride in Feria" (Burgos 1972:29, my translation).

Those who ride horses must wear specific clothes, further setting them apart from the pedestrian middle and lower classes. Men and women riders use a wide-brimmed hat and wear a "short suit" *(traje corto)* or "country suit" *(traje campero)*. This suit is characterized by the short, waist-length jacket, three-quarter-length wide pants folded up at the bottom, tool-worked chaps, and rough-out boots. This is exactly the outfit worn by the *rejoneadores de toros* (those who fight a bull from horseback). There are other details in this costume, such as a ruffled and tucked white cotton blouse (like toreros wear in their "suit of lights"), a silk cummerbund girdle, silver dangling trim to tie up the pants, and spurs. The horses also must have the appropriate tack: a Spanish saddle on a lamb's wool pad; a blanket tied to the front of the saddle; and a leather bridle with long, floppy leather bangs cut across the horse's forehead. The horse's mane is often braided with two colored ribbons, usually red and yellow (the Spanish national colors).

Some of the women, rather than riding astride, ride side-saddle, in which case they substitute a skirt for the pants. Many women ride with both legs to one side behind a male rider, on the rump of a horse. The rider is dressed as above, but in this case, the woman is dressed in flamenco or "gypsy" dress *(traje de gitana)*. This dress is worn by all women in Feria at night: a brightly colored dress with a skirt of several layers on the sleeve. Young children, in the appropriate dress, are carried on the saddle in front of their father.

In the carriages both men and women wear Sunday street clothes, but women also wear a comb *(peineta)* and *mantilla* on their heads, long dangling earrings, and pearls around their necks. Coachmen are dressed in various stylized variations of the "short suit" with hats from the eighteenth and nineteenth centuries.

While some inappropriately dressed riders, carriage drivers, and horses appeared on the streets of Feria in 1986, there were very few and they were clearly of the lower-middle classes. In general, the middle-class participants would never subject themselves to public ridicule and scorn for trespassing unspoken rules. Although I was a guest in a very hospitable, well-off caseta, whose members rode horses and carriages, I was never asked to ride in a carriage or behind anyone on a horse. One man suggested that I buy a gypsy dress and then he would take me around on his horse. Obviously my street clothes were inappropriate.

Riders and carriage passengers want to be seen. Up and down the streets of Feria they ride in groups, back straight, head up, with arrogant and solemn faces. The only way to describe it is "a pose." The agricultural businessman who spoke of riding a horse in Feria continued explaining why, "up and down, back and forth with the horse. Don't you see? If I don't ride, the directors of the banks don't see me, and if they don't see me, they won't know me, and they won't give me credit when I want to buy a new harvester" (Burgos 1972:29, my translation). On Thursday and Friday one of the central streets of Feria (Joselito el Gallo) got so full of equestrian traffic and carriages that all movement came to a standstill, while some of the outside streets were relatively empty. Occasionally a group of riders or a carriage pulls up to a caseta, where someone is usually expecting them. The riders stay on their horses and are served fino and a tapa. After visiting for a while, off the group goes to visit another caseta.

During the "morning" there is a strict division between streets and sidewalks. Only horses and carriages are on the streets; only pedestrians are on the sidewalks. The casetas become classified with the sidewalks.

People stand outside their caseta talking to visiting riders on their horses. Although, originally, having a caseta probably coincided with owning and riding horses in Feria, since the 1960s, many people can afford to set up a caseta but cannot afford, or do not have the pretensions to the status of, a horse and carriage. In the middle-class caseta where I also was a guest, owned by the families of five professional men, no one rode horses, and one wife told me that was for the well-off people *("¡Gente bien, pero bien!")*.

The "morning" ends with the corrida, which is held in the old center of Sevilla, on the other side of the river. The carriages carry their well-to-do passengers back across town to the bullring. Police regulate the carriage traffic. These passengers descend from their carriages and take up their seats in the *Sombra* (shade) section. Ticket holders for the *Sol* (sun) section walk to the ring.

After the bullfight is over at about 8:00 P.M., carriages and horses disappear until the next "morning." "Afternoon" has begun. People have finished their midday meal and their siestas. Although sevillana music has been playing all morning, people were too busy watching the horses to dance. "Afternoon" is when people really begin to dance to sevillanas, though in the "morning" and early evening children do much of the dancing. Pedestrians now take over the streets. Children were present in the "morning," but now whole families begin to appear. If a caseta is going to have live entertainment, it begins at 9:30 or 10:00 P.M. in the "afternoon." Often a special tapa will be brought out and offered to guests around 10:00 or 11:00 P.M. People returning from the corrida discuss the bulls; young people stroll from caseta to caseta visiting friends; dancing gets delirious; families and couples without casetas stroll the streets, looking in at the socializing inside the casetas; parents buy popcorn or nuts for their children. By 9:00 P.M. in the "afternoon" the lights and lanterns of the Feria come on.

"Afternoon" and "night" are known as the more democratic parts of Feria, although a division between the haves (those with casetas) and the have-nots (those who must walk the streets looking in) still prevails. This situation has been much ameliorated since 1973 with the addition of many public casetas, thus providing everyone at least a place to drink fino. In a sense, the "haves" and the "have-nots" are now confined to certain days of the week and are represented by the Sevillanos (urban haves) and the non-Sevillanos (rural have-nots). On Friday and Saturday people come from the outlying pueblos, swelling the population of the Feria. It is these people who often have no caseta to visit.

Dress in the "afternoon" and "night" is the same for everyone, even the upper classes. Men dress in a suit with shirt unbuttoned and no tie. Typically some men wear the señorito's wide-brimmed hat and put a carnation in their lapel. In general, this unauthentic use of one element of the señorito's outfit is considered a little tacky, and usually only lower-middle or lower class men wear this hat. Little boys under eight, no matter what class, are dressed in the traje corto of the señorito. The dress for women is the gypsy dress. Although young girls and adolescents wear their traje de gitana all day long, married and middle-aged women wear a gypsy dress at least one or two times at night during the Feria. Only grandmothers do not wear this flashy dress.

Many women spend much money on their dress for Feria every year. In the past all dresses were probably individually made. Even now, women who can afford them want an individually made, unique dress, but they are now mass produced and found in every department store in Sevilla. If one focuses on the details, social status can be detected in this dress, but the overall impression is that everyone is wearing the same dress. I saw a disabled, poor woman in a wheelchair wearing a traje de gitana. Even Carmen Romero (President Felipe Gonzalez's wife), who is from Sevilla, attended Feria in a traje de gitana.

The gypsy dress is another symbol of Andalusia, as are the gypsies themselves. Closely associated with Andalusian folklore, the gypsy plays an inordinately large role in the Andalusian collective representations: the gypsy bullfighter; the gypsy flamenco dancer; the dark, sensuous gypsy woman, Carmen; the untrustworthy gypsy horse trader and petty thief. These images represent Andalusia to the rest of Spain. The gypsies, however, are the lowest social group in Sevilla. Their community, always a tightly closed culture, is marginal to and rejected by Andalusian urban culture, at the same time as it represents that culture. People associate gypsies with Andalusian song, dance, and a style of bullfighting. However, the intimate relationship of the gypsies with the Andalusian upper classes is well known (Pitt-Rivers 1971:187). Traditionally, gypsies were the flamenco and bullfighting entertainment at the señoritos' parties.

This ambiguous social valuation of the gypsies is mirrored in Feria. The gypsies themselves are certainly present, but they do not wear "gypsy dresses." Gypsy women, dressed in cotton blouses and plaid skirts, and their children sell carnations in the Real. The children enter the casetas pushing carnations on customers and are usually chased out by the hosts. People constantly warned me about the gypsies who are "notorious pickpockets." Thus, all the collective representations about gypsies are present in Feria: petty thief, flamenco dancer, horse trader (Feria was originally a stock fair), bullfighter, and finally, dark, sensuous woman. The juxtaposition, however, between the Sevillana women dressed as gypsies and the real gypsies, who were dirty, poor, and working, could not be more obvious.

At night all the women in Sevilla dress like those at the bottom of the social status (gypsy women) and walk arm in arm with men dressed like those at the top (señoritos). This couple creates a kind of social compromise, or synthesis, while it replicates the traditional relationship between the landed gentry and gypsies—two of the most important symbols of Andalusian identity.

Around midnight children are taken home, usually by their grandparents; often they are already asleep in their strollers. But the Feria continues. On Saturday night of Feria 1986 I went home exhausted at midnight. I could hardly walk back down the streets due to the masses of people still arriving. Bus loads of people, already singing sevillanas and doing palmas, were also inching their way down the streets toward the Real. The fiesta continued: light conversation, palmas, more fino, whiskey, watching a group perform flamenco or sevillanas, visiting the caseta of a friend. Around 2:00 or 3:00 A.M. the lights in the street go off, but the lights, music, and drinking inside the caseta continue until 4:00, 5:00, or 6:00 A.M. Finally, at the crack of dawn, everyone goes home and the clean-up crews appear.

The schedule of "morning," "afternoon," and "night" activities gets repeated for six days during Feria, but there is another unofficial schedule that Feria seems to follow: the fiesta's rise and fall. As mentioned before, Thursday is called the "equator," the midpoint. Friday the ambiance grows, and Saturday is the day of maximum participation. On these days the streets were most crowded with horses. On Friday "morning" from 1:00 to 3:00 P.M., six purebred studs of the Hispano-arab breed were paraded around the fairground. They stopped for twenty minutes at a time in front of various casetas, like upper-class riders do. These six horses from Andalusia are part of the patrimony of the state, which is trying to protect and preserve their purity. Thus, these symbols of "purity," of the upper classes, and of Andalusia were the centerpiece of the Feria in the center of the week.

Although Friday night and Saturday often register the largest attendance, Feria has already begun its "decline." The increase in attendance is due to the influx of rural people from surrounding pueblos, but the upper classes have begun to leave. The tone of the Feria has changed. Ironically the rural pueblo cheapens, or pollutes, the Feria, which encourages the upper-class flight to the country, where they spend the weekend in their country estates or at the beach.

By Sunday night, a sense of despair has settled over the Feria. People sit gloomily around the casetas without dancing. After the fireworks at midnight, the casetas are taken down. Everyone stressed that soon the fairgrounds would be unrecognizable. Monday is also an official holiday in Sevilla, called "Monday of the hangover." On Tuesday, normal life begins again.

Los Toros

The role of the corrida is not especially evident in Feria, and the bullring in Sevilla is totally separate from the fairgrounds. Although many people insisted upon the centrality and importance of the corridas during the Feria, my experience was that Sevillanos, in contrast to people in other parts of Spain, did not feel they *had* to go to the corrida to experience their fiesta. In the two casetas where I was a guest, no one went to a corrida. (However, one of my hosts took me to a bullfight on horseback [*rejoneo*].) One had to have a caseta, drink fino, dress in the appropriate clothes, dance sevillanas, but the corridas did not define Feria in a participatory way.

Even if it was not necessary to attend the corrida, its role was pivotal in Feria. It acts as the transition point between the señorial and democratic parts of the day. It divides "morning" from "afternoon." The arrival at the bullring of the carriages full of upper-class señoritos is the last time the carriages will be on the streets until the following day and is a spectacle unto itself.

Sevilla's bullring seats thirteen thousand people, but it gives a great sense of intimacy. The seating is all low and quite near the ring. The typical hierarchy represented by Sol (sun) and Sombra (shade) is emphasized during Feria when the Sombra ticket holders arrive in their carriages—symbols of wealth and status. Nevertheless, the architecture of the ring and the "typical behavior" of the fans in Sevilla create a kind of moral unity among the public. This moral unity is reinforced by the contrasts between the moments of utter silence and the shouts in unison of "*¡Olé!*"—truly startling after my experiences in the other bullrings. It is as if the whole public becomes an "arrogant señorito," demanding the ultimate in art and aesthetic beauty in this, the so-called cathedral of bullrings.

On Sunday morning, the last day of Feria, there is a bullfight on horseback (rejoneo). Although in other cities in Spain, rejoneo is often said to be a spectacle for women and children, in Sevilla (due to the role of the horses) rejoneo is considered an upper-class spectacle. My host from the upper-class caseta, Alfonso, returned from the beach Sunday morning to escort me to a corrida de rejones. We had front row seats in Sombra. Alfonso claimed to have been a classmate of three of the rejoneadores, two of whom waved as they circled the ring. (Recall, the rejoneador is thought of as a member of the southern landed gentry, wearing his ranch clothes and working the bulls from astride his marvelous, expensive horses.) He also described two of the rejoneadores as "counts" (*condes*, members of the aristocracy).

If the corrida does not play an essential role in the attendance of Feria, perhaps it is because the images and symbols of the whole phenomenon of los toros are so prevalent in every other aspect of Feria. As noted above, all the streets of the Real are named after famous bullfighters. Thus, names of toreros float around the Feria all day long. Also, the decoration of the caseta includes paintings about the life of the bulls, as well as bulls' heads and bullfight posters. These images represent Sevilla and Andalusia: they are symbols of Southern identity. Furthermore, the two important Feria personalities, the señorito and the gypsy, are intimately tied to los toros. The "typical" señorito, the country gentleman, is often described as owning a ranch where he raises fighting bulls. Meanwhile, the folk image of the gypsy is often that of the torero, the man who fights the bulls from the señorito's ranch.

Analysis

In Feria, symbols of hierarchy have become symbols of Andalusia and thus appropriated by all the classes. The hierarchy itself, the cultural and economic dominance of Sevilla by señores, has been tempered by the growth of Sevilla's middle classes and their access to the symbols of dominance. Rather than rejecting the forms and styles of the landed gentry, the middle classes have accepted them as historical symbols of local identity.

Difference and differentiation are stressed in Feria. Status is celebrated, not denied, and class differences are the most obvious separations emphasized. The casetas are used to separate the upper classes from all other classes, but they now differentiate the middle classes (those with private casetas) from the lower classes (those that use public casetas). The lowest classes, the gypsies, although symbolically central to Feria, actually participate only peripherally. The horse and carriage, present during the longest part of the day, still differentiate and glorify the well-to-do from all the rest of the people. Not only the horse but also the dress and the pose of the riders mark them as superior. To be seen riding in a carriage still confers status.

Sex differences are also emphasized in Feria. There is no blurring of male and female roles except by inversion, when the males serve the food in the casetas. Dress accentuates these perceived differences. Women dress in frivolous, sensual, lower-class costume. Men dress in somber, agricultural work-oriented, upper-class costume. Although in the "morning" upper-class women may ride astride horses, like men, and wear the same clothes as men on the horses, this only underlines their upper-class role as social "men" to the other lower classes, whose women on the sidewalks are dressed as gypsies. At night, however, these upper-class women too dress as "women." The dances in Feria further emphasize differences of maleness and femaleness. All dancing is done in couples, and the dance itself is a sexual confrontation. The female dance style is sensual and provocative; the male style is always more controlled, that is, more masculine in Andalusian terms.

A further differentiation is that of public and private space. Not only are there public and private casetas, but the casetas themselves represent private, domestic space as compared to a public street. Within the caseta, space is further divided, with the trastienda representing private space and the dancing area representing public space. Although the hosts could move freely within both these spaces, guests stayed in the dancing area and the hired help remained in the trastienda.

A final hierarchal difference is the categories center/periphery. The six days of the fiesta have their center, the "equator." These are the days when it is most evident that the upper classes are present: the streets are jammed with horses and traffic comes to a standstill. After the "equator," the upper classes leave Sevilla and the rural proletarian classes invade. The spatial distinction of center/periphery with the respect to the city itself seem to be reversed during the Feria, and the periphery (the Real) becomes the new center, while the city center is abandoned.

Within the fairgrounds there is also a center/periphery division. One of the center streets, Joselito el Gallo, is considered the most prestigious street on which to have a caseta. Three of the most important social organizations in Sevilla have their casetas located there. In the "morning," Joselito de Gallo was always crowded with horses and carriages. If you were to be seen, this was the street to be seen on. The Town Hall was located on Pepe Luis Vázquez, a street that crosses Joselito el Gallo. As one moves away from these "center" streets there was less horse and carriage traffic in the "mornings" and more ambiance of the lower class.

The way in which Sevillanos have appropriated their señores' style is evident in the ethos about drinking in Feria. One must not make a fool of oneself. Drinking is another manifestation of self-control. Elegant composure must be maintained at all times. Even the name of the wine, *fino*, refers to the refined quality of behavior.

Sevillano behavior at the bullring is similar to its drinking ethos. The bulls are taken very seriously. Cheap tricks are not appreciated in a torero, and the silences in the bullring indicate how seriously the public there takes its role. The very fact that the local taurine form in Sevilla is the corrida continues the emphasis on hierarchy. There is no street game with bulls where the crowds jostle and chase ungracefully. The corrida is a morality play where the man's superior intelligence and grace must dominate the animal's brute force.

Despite all emphasis on, and celebration of, hierarchy, especially upper-class hierarchy, there are moments when people seem to think that the hierarchy has become irrelevant. In the late "evenings," when the horses have disappeared from the streets of Feria and all men are señoritos and all women are gypsies, when the bright light of the day has faded and the artificial lights of Feria illuminate a truly fantastic city of splendor, when the symbols of place (versus class) take over and homogenize the population into "Sevillanos" through the singing and dancing of sevillanas and the drinking of fino (two local products), when the casetas are full of three generations of families and friends, when people change their behavior and laugh and drink, when politics and business are consciously avoided as conversation topics, this is when one informant leaned over and told me, "This isn't how we really are, with all our problems of modern life and work. But this is how we would like to be."

In Sevilla social hierarchy is not denied or obliterated. Rather, many participants in Feria seem to feel they have temporarily arrived at the top of the social hierarchy, and in this way the symbols of "class" are turned into symbols of local identity. Similarly, the "elitist" corrida becomes the local taurine fiesta for the South. ¡Olé!

Chapter 8

"SPAIN" RESOLVED: LAS FIESTAS DE SAN FERMÍN IN PAMPLONA

In San Fermín one finds a chorus of male voices under waves of rolled-up newspapers asking for a saint's blessing, a race of boys and bulls down cobblestone streets dappled by early morning sun, an explosion of youths and black horned beasts into a sun-filled ring, red scarves adorning the necks and red sashes around the waists of white-clad participants, music and dancing that fill the streets, and red wine that fills thirsty throats.

In 1986, the bullring in Pamplona discovered the "wave."[1] On Saturday, July 12, members of the youth clubs *(peñas)* started a wave. Spanish television viewers of the World Cup Soccer Championships held in Mexico in June of that year had seen the wave performed for the first time. On that Saturday, members of the peñas were disgusted with the performance of the *torero*, Emilio Muñoz. Bored, the peñas decided to enliven things by attempting a wave. Eventually they succeeded, around and around the whole ring the wave went—*Sol* (sun) and *Sombra* (shade), Sol and Sombra, five times. What better symbol of unity for Pamplona! Everyone seemed quite pleased with themselves.

Navarra as "Spain"

Navarra, located in the north of Spain on the border with France and next to the Basque Country, is an Autonomous Community composed of only one province. Navarra's inhabitants and other Spaniards consistently describe it as a land of contrasts, "a product of contradictions" (Ayuntamiento de Pamplona 1985:1). In a 1982 Spanish tourist pamphlet, Navarra is called the "transition between green Spain and dry Spain." Since in Spain geography is used to speak about perceived cultural differences, this reference to "green" and "dry" Spain implies much more than just climate.

Geographically, Navarra is divided between a rainy, mountainous north, which includes the Pyrenees Mountains, and a southern, dry, fertile plain along the Ebro River valley, which is some of the best wine producing country in Spain. North (called *montañes*) and South (called the *Ribera*) further coincide with different economies (pastoral versus agricultural) and different cultures (Basque versus Castilian-speaking).[2] Pamplona, called Iruña in Basque, is the capital of Navarra and is located on the Arga River in the center of the province. The small population of this Autonomous Community enjoys a rather high standard of living. Navarra was an agricultural region until the last decade when some industry was located in and around Pamplona.

In the nineteenth century Spain was divided several times by civil wars, known as the Carlist Wars. The Carlists were a conservative, religious, almost fanatical, movement that backed a certain pretender to the throne of Spain. These wars were part of the century-long struggle of conservative, regional, rural traditions against the changes imposed by the forms and values of liberal capitalism and the centralization of the state. Navarra became well known as a stronghold of Carlism, although in reality in the nineteenth century, Pamplona and the south of Navarra sided with the Liberals, the opposition to the Carlists. Throughout the twentieth century this same division has existed. Today the north of Navarra votes overwhelmingly for Basque (separatist) political parties in national and local elections, while the south votes for Spanish national parties (Linz 1986). Despite these splits, to quote a collective representation, Navarra's encompassing reputation is as "reactionary, Rightist, and hostile to change" (Ayuntamiento de Pamplona 1985:3).

Historically, Navarra was one of the great medieval kingdoms *(reinos)*. At one time Navarra included parts of what is today Castile, as well as an extensive zone on the French side of the Pyrenees. At times Navarra extended its authority over the three provinces of the Basque Country, but the Basque Country became part of the kingdom of Castile in the second half of the eleventh century, while Navarra remained separate from Castile for five hundred more years. In 1512 the area of Navarra south of the Pyrenees was incorporated into the political union headed by Castile, forming the Spanish state. Nevertheless, the Castilian kings swore to uphold the Navarran statutes of rights and laws *(fueros),* and throughout the sixteenth to eighteenth centuries Navarra maintained its special political institutions with its own parliament and other privileges. In the 1812 Constitution, Navarra was made into a

Spanish province like all the others. But in 1841, after the return of the monarchy and the ensuing civil wars, a special status was negotiated for Navarra, especially in terms of taxes, which was maintained even down through Franco's regime. Franco allowed Navarra to keep its special status because of its loyalty to the rebel cause during the Civil War.

Navarra has a somewhat ambiguous position in the "mental constructions" of "Spain" due to two important, if contrasting, relationships that will be explored below. In the medieval period and earlier, Navarra was culturally Basque, and the Basque language was spoken in most of the area. Politically, however, Navarra always maintained a separate cultural identity from the other Basque-speaking areas. Little by little, the Basque language gave way to Castilian, especially in the nineteenth century. At the present time only 8% of Navarra speaks Basque, mainly in villages in the north. This part of Navarra shares other cultural traits with the neighboring Basque province of Guipuzcoa: architecture, rural lifestyle, and folk traditions of food, dance, and fiestas. In 1979, 7% of Navarra's population said they felt Basque and 31% said they felt as Basque as Navarran (Linz 1986:413). Since Franco's death, some people have wanted to reinstate Basque as an official language. Although only 10% of the Pamplonicas even understand Basque (Ayuntamiento de Pamplona 1985:15), all street signs in Pamplona are now in both Basque and Castilian.[3]

A second important relationship is Navarra's close association with Castile. Navarra appeared in history long before Castile's rise to eminence. In many ways, Castile was born from the western lands of Navarra and the eastern lands of the kingdom Asturias-Leon, and its rulers were born from Navarra's royal families.[4] The first known document written in *castellano,* the *Glosas Emilianenses,* was located within Navarra territory and contained a Basque text as well (López García 1985:44).

These two relationships, with Basque culture and with Castile, often make it difficult for Spaniards to decide whether to place Navarra in the Center or in the Periphery. In its sense of history and regional identity, its "Basque" traditions, egalitarian ideals, and relative prosperity, Navarra is typical of the Periphery. However, its conservatism, strong religious traditions, support of Franco, and relative lack of industry are typical of the Center. Its many associations with Castile confirm this view.

Thus, in many ways, Navarra is a metaphor for "Spain" itself: divided between green and dry, Basque and Castilian, north and south. Yet despite its plural cultures, there is also a long tradition of Navarran identity. Pamplona's fiestas do not emphasize one culture over the other but rather include both.

Feria del Toro: Illusion of Community

Structurally speaking, the fiesta of San Fermín is the fiesta mayor of "Spain," with the nine days of fiesta functioning as a model for the community of "Spains." The fiesta resolves for its province what is problematic in the rest of the state: the opposition between the one and the many "Spains." Although the province has two different cultural traditions, during San Fermín, Pamplona, Navarra, celebrates its unity through the use of plural symbols. Although friction may be just below the surface, the fiestas "act" as if two cultures were not a problem for identity. However, despite the unity theme, antiauthoritarianism characterizes the fiesta. On the one hand, the oppositions in Pamplona are mediated by converting them into two parts of a total process. On the other, those who challenge authority end up submitting to it. Ironically, this "illusion of community" is finally attained by Pamplona's opposing itself to the rest of "Spain" (i.e., the Center), yet all the while using and incorporating symbols of "Spain," namely the bull.

Center

Pamplona is nowhere near the geographical center of Spain, as is Madrid. Located in the north, near the Pyrenees Mountains, it would seem a poor choice of city for Spain's fiesta mayor. However, the fiestas of San Fermín, which run from July 6–14, are almost exactly in the center of the *corrida*/fiesta cycle (see chapter 5), which begins March 19 with Fallas in Valencia and ends October 12 with the fiestas of Pilar in Zaragoza. The fiestas of San Fermín also mark the midpoint of the calendar year, which is July 3.

Origins are also important markers of center. In many contexts the province of Navarra is the origin of "Spain." In los toros, it is said that the earliest form of bullfighting on foot *(toreo a pie)* originated in Navarra, and references to it appear in historical records as early as the tenth and eleventh centuries.[5] The Pamplonicas say that Navarra is the "cradle of bullfighting" *(cuna del toreo),* thus claiming the moral supremacy of the center.

The capital of Navarra, like the capital of Spain, is an administrative city and is located in the center of the province. Pamplona is described as the "head of the kingdom of Navarra" (del Burgo 1982:3). People who live and were raised in the old center of Pamplona are called *castas* (pure), and the traditions of Pamplona are likewise always described as castas (pure, authentic).[6]

Saint Fermín, who lived in the third century, was the first bishop of Pamplona. He left Pamplona to preach to the heathens in what is now France. He was beheaded in Amiens, France, and thus is a martyr of the church. Saint Fermín is not officially the patron of Pamplona (who is Saint Saturnino), but he is the patron of Navarra. Saint Fermín, like Pamplona, represents all of Navarra and does not give preference to one of its cultures. Since his martyrdom took place in France and not in Spanish territory, Navarra is opposed to "France" as outside and not to another part of "Spain." This better enables San Fermín to be the fiesta mayor of Spain.

Feria del Toro

Although the fiesta is named after its patron saint, San Fermín (sometimes the fiestas are called *los sanfermines*), it is also called the Feria del toro, the "Fair of the Bull." To a surprising degree for a northern province, the fiestas of San Fermín revolve around the bulls. Without a doubt for Pamplonicas, and for many people throughout Spain, the morning *encierros* during San Fermín are the most characteristic and important fiesta event. (Spanish television shows the encierro all over Spain several times a day during the fiestas.) However, the afternoon corridas are also some of the most important in Spain, receiving national attention, and Pamplonicas fill the bullring every afternoon. Yet not only the encierro and the corrida but also almost every taurine fiesta celebrated in Spain are offered in Pamplona during San Fermín. Though Pamplonicas say they have no *afición a los toros* during the rest of the year, during San Fermín their fiestas emphasize the bulls.

Although Pamplona offers many taurine activities identified with various parts of "Spain," the fiestas are called the Feria del toro (and not the plural, *de los toros*). This is significant because of the identification of "Spain" with the bull. As noted before, the bull is called the totem of Spain. Given the equation "toro = Spain," the Feria del toro could also be translated as the Feria de España (Fair of Spain), which underlines it as the fiesta mayor of Spain. Of course, since the definition of "Spain" is problematic, only the code language may be used. By switching codes (using taurine vocabulary instead of political vocabulary), confrontation is avoided and unity may be celebrated.

Ethnography of the Fiesta

It is not clear when San Fermín became so important. Ernest Hemingway may have been responsible for internationalizing this fiesta. Indeed, Hemingway is very present in the fiestas of San Fermín. A huge bust of him sits in front of the bullring. Hemingway's well-known book *The Sun Also Rises* uses the fiestas of San Fermín as the backdrop for its drama about the social alienation of a group of American expatriates. The contrast between the anomie of his protagonists and this joyful celebration of collectivity in Pamplona could not have been more evident. Many of the descriptions of the celebration of San Fermín in his book, which was published in 1926, are still valid today.

The San Fermín fiestas attract visitors not only from America and Europe but from all over Spain. Due to proximity, there are perhaps more visitors from the north of Spain, but young people from everywhere talk about wanting to run in the encierros of Pamplona. Special trains leave Madrid for Pamplona during the fiestas. Spanish television makes daily reports on the fiestas, as do national radio and newspapers. Some Spaniards return every year to Pamplona with a group of friends, confirming their reservations in a hotel for the following year. Bars all over Spain celebrate a San Fermín night on July 7. This inundation by outsiders *(forasteros)* has led many Pamplonicas to complain that the fiestas are losing their hometown flavor. Many people who live in Pamplona say they now leave during the fiestas, while others claim that the people who leave are not true Pamplonicas (castas).

History

San Fermín's saint day was originally commemorated in October. But in 1591 it was decided to honor San Fermín in July and to consolidate his celebration with the cattle fairs of San Juan (June 24) and the fiestas de toros of Santiago, patron saint of Spain (July 25). The fiestas of San Fermín have been celebrated continuously, except during civil wars, on July 7 since 1591, and corridas de toros have always been characteristic of these fiestas. These corridas were first celebrated in the Plaza del Castillo, still the center of the fiestas today. In 1844 the first bullring was built. However, two characteristics now considered most typical of los sanfermines, the encierros and peñas, did not appear until the second half of the nineteenth century.

Although for many centuries there was an encierro at 6:00 A.M. every morning of the fiesta, this was simply the way to get the bulls from the corrals outside the city gates to the stalls *(toriles)* in the Plaza del Castillo. No one ran with the bulls. Some horseback riders preceded the herd, blowing horns, warning the citizens to clear the way. The appearance of runners cannot be dated for sure until after 1867, when the equestrian riders disappeared (del Campo 1980:63). In 1876 the streets the bulls used to get to the bullring were definitively chosen and thus became "traditional."

The establishment of the youth clubs (peñas) also occurred sometime toward the end of the nineteenth century. At first the peñas were merely groups of friends who played flutes, violins, and drums through the streets of Pamplona to honor San Fermín and who later attended los toros together. It was not until 1901 that they took on their present-day form (Muez 1986:27).

Giants appeared in San Fermín fiestas from the sixteenth to the eighteenth centuries but then disappeared for several years (Martínez Recari 1985:xxxi). In 1860, eight new Giants were constructed and have lasted until the present. Like many other fiestas in Spain today, San Fermín took its present form in the second half of the nineteenth century.

Overall Unity

The citizens of Pamplona describe los sanfermines much like other fiestas in Spain are described. People emphasize the change that comes over Pamplona during these days: the change from a conservative, rather somber, and "serious" city with little or no nightlife to a light-hearted, open, dancing city, full of music and constant celebration.

Many Pamplonicas told me that the year in Pamplona begins and ends with San Fermín. There is a sense of waiting all year for the fiestas. At the end of the nine days, everyone is so exhausted from all the celebrating that many people take a one-week or two-week vacation and go off to the countryside to "relax."

It is difficult to estimate the level of citizen participation in the fiesta. Pamplona has one hundred eighty thousand inhabitants, and its population triples during the fiestas. The old town is the center of the festivities, but even in the newer residential areas people are singing and dancing in the streets and jamming the bars until 3:00 and 4:00 A.M. The people I met who claimed not to like or enjoy the fiestas happened to be non-Pamplonicas. The people who were most enthusiastic about the fiestas were also described to me as "Pamplonicas for all their lives" and "one of the purest." However, even in towns fifty kilometers away, the young people dress as Pamplonicas and go to the fiestas. In general, participation is massive, and this is the impression Pamplona conveys about the fiesta. Indeed, even in the offices that open on fiesta mornings such as banks and stores, employees dress as Pamplonicas. Posters and bullfighting schedules decorate these offices. In the streets, billboards use fiesta themes in their advertisements. The fiestas take over the city and a kind of collective frenzy reigns for nine days.

Unity is the most important idea projected by San Fermín. The use of the whole city and the same dress (white with red sashes and scarves) for all participants help convey this idea. But this unity is not necessarily based on the concept of one class, as in Bilbao or Sevilla. Rather it is a unity that contains elements of both hierarchy and equality, a cultural unity joining both the Basque and Castilian elements of Navarra's identity. Although only 10% of the population understands Basque, the programs and posters that advertise San Fermín are printed in both Basque and Castilian. Music from both the northern Basque cultural areas and the southern Castilian-speaking areas of Navarra fill the air during San Fermín. The morning is devoted to the encierro, the local form of los toros. But the bulls of the encierro will be used in the afternoon in the corrida, the southern and national form of los toros, and all those who ran in the encierro will also attend the corrida in the afternoon.

Structure of the Fiesta

The Beginning. The fiesta begins with the *chupinazo* (small skyrockets) and the Riau-Riau on July 6. The chupinazo takes place in the Plaza Consistorial in the old city center. Beginning at 10:30 A.M. on July 6, people dressed in their Pamplonica costumes begin filling the plaza in front of the Town Hall. From 11:00 A.M. until shortly before noon the packed square shouts "¡San Fermín, San Fermín!" People spray champagne on each other and drink whatever is left in the bottles. Simple songs or chants are chorused by the crowd, and the ever more frenzied masses hop and dance to the songs. Shortly before noon, the crowd takes off the red scarves from their necks, holding them over their heads in both hands, while the shouts of "San Fermín, San Fermín" take over the plaza. At three minutes before noon drummers and trumpeters get the crowd's attention. A city councilor gives a short welcoming speech from a balcony on the facade of the Town Hall. He then shouts *"¡Viva San Fermín!"* and *"¡Gora San Fermín!"* in Basque and

Figure 8.1. The Giants in the streets during San Fermín. (Photographed by the author)

lights the first rocket. The fiestas have begun, or as Hemingway said "The fiesta exploded. There is no other way to describe it" (Hemingway [1926]1954:152). The crowd becomes delirious. There is hugging and kissing, more champagne showers, and more rockets. Within fifteen minutes the crowd has disappeared to other parts of the city, but now "nothing" can stop the fiestas.

At 4:30 P.M., after lunch, another opening ceremony takes place, again beginning at the Town Hall, where a crowd gathers in the Plaza Consistorial. Out of the Town Hall come the eight royal Giants (figure 8.1), trumpeters, drummers, mace bearers, the band, the city councilors, and the mayor. The mayor and city council members are dressed in coats with tails and top hats. This procession is ostensibly going to the church of San Lorenzo, where the chapel of San Fermín and his statue are located, to pay their respects as the official representatives of the city. However, the objective of the thousands of Pamplonicas is to "detain" the procession, as well as to "accompany" it. In a classical example of a ritual of rebellion (Gluckman 1954), the crowd "prevents" the procession of officials from arriving at their destination by singing and dancing with arms above their heads the Riau-Riau. The Riau-Riau, which first took place in 1915, is a waltz written in the nineteenth century by a Navarran, Astrain, that has the chorus, "for the fiesta has arrived in this glorious city, and in the whole world there is none equal to it. Riau-Riau." The municipal band plays this, and only this, tune over and over hundreds of times. What would usually be a fifteen-minute walk takes the official procession three to five hours during the Riau-Riau. In 1984, after four hours, the city councilors and mayor had not even left the building of the Town Hall, and the Riau-Riau had to be finally stopped.

When the procession leaves the Plaza Consistorial, it enters the small, narrow, main street *(calle mayor)*. The dancing crowd does much pushing and shoving. The temperature rises, and residents in the houses that line the street dump buckets of water or cold champagne onto the officials to "cool them off." The officials, trapped in their ceremonial dress, must keep smiling while the crowd teases and criticizes them in a sometimes playful, sometimes serious, way. Clearly this is a confrontation between authority and the people. Although the authorities submit to this "ritual humiliation," after 1984 it became obvious that they will only go so far before refusing to play the game. When the procession finally reaches the church, the officials enter for a short service (vespers) and the crowd disappears.

The End. The last ceremony, marking the end of the fiestas and the return to everyday life, takes place on midnight of July 14 and is called the *Pobre de mí* (Poor Me). About an hour before midnight people begin congregating in the Plaza Consistorial with small, white candles. The candles are lit and the crowd sings over and over, "Poor me. Poor me. The fiestas of San Fermín are ending." The celebration is less joyful than others: there is less dancing, less drinking, and the atmosphere is more hushed. Fathers carry children on their shoulders. People crowd the balconies around the plaza. Between verses of "Pobre de mí" people in the plaza intone a tune that pleads "We want more. We want more. We want much, much more." At midnight the crowd shouts "¡Viva San Fermin! ¡Gora San Fermin!" and quickly disperses. The fiesta has ended.

The Middle. Beginning July 7, the daily schedule of the fiestas is repeated more or less faithfully for eight days. The only exception to this is the morning procession of San Fermín on July 7, when the image of the saint is paraded around the streets of the town, along with the religious authorities, Giants, and town officials. Otherwise, each day is a repeat of the day before.

At 6:45 A.M. reveille is sounded by small bands in the streets of the city's old section; it is traditional to drink a warm cup of broth in the main Plaza del Castillo before the encierro. The encierro begins at 8:00 A.M. sharp. For half an hour before the encierro, police and clean-up crews have been "sweeping" the streets where the bulls will run. They clean up the debris and drunken and/or sleeping youths. The mayor checks the course, and once approved, the encierro is ready to begin. The runners congregate around a small statue of San Fermín placed in a niche in a wall toward the beginning of the course and ask for his blessing in unison. A firecracker sounds, and the bulls are released into the streets (figure 8.2). The encierro, one of the highlights of the day, lasts only two to ten minutes.

Once the bulls have run across the bullring and are safely in the stalls,

Figure 8.2. Encierro. One bull, Loquillo, has gotten separated from the others. Notice the newspapers in many boys' hands, used for "protection." The graffiti on the wall is about NATO [OTAN]. (Newspaper photograph courtesy of *Diario de Navarra*, July 11, 1986; photographed by Mena)

the cows *(vaquillas)* are loosed in the ring for the runners to "play" with. When the vaquillas are put away, the youths and all spectators leave the bullring to have "breakfast," a hearty meal of fried eggs and bulls' testicles. After breakfast, the Giants and Big Heads come out on the streets to amuse the children and their parents. At 11:00 A.M. every morning there is usually some activity taking place in the bullring: a *fiesta campera* (country fiesta), a *jota* (song contest), *recortadores* (calf dodgers), and log-cutting contests or stone-lifting exhibitions. Musical concerts take place in the city parks and gardens. Then there is a lull in the activities for lunch from 2:00 to 5:00 P.M.

At 5:30 P.M. the mules begin their parade to the bullring from the Plaza del Castillo. The various clubs and their bands join the parade. The corrida de toros begins at 6:30 P.M. After the killing of the third bull, the Pamplonicas bring out an elaborate snack *(merienda)* and eat it in the ring. At the end of the corrida, around 9:00 P.M., the peñas go down into the ring and file out through the main door while singing and dancing.

The peñas make their way back to their clubhouses, all located in the same area, where the night life of the fiesta takes place. About this time a firecracker bull *(toro de fuego)* appears on the streets of the old town. At midnight there is a firework display, but the singing and dancing and celebration continues well into the wee hours of the morning. Soon reveille is heard and the day begins anew.

Despite the order of the above description, there is another perspective on the daily schedule of the fiesta. Certainly for older Pamplonicas, those who sit in Sombra (shade) section of the bullring, especially the women, and the rest of Spain, the day begins with the encierro and builds toward the corrida in the afternoon, culminating in the street celebrations at night. Even those who go to bed late struggle to get up to watch the encierro first thing in the morning.[7]

But for another part of Pamplona, the peñas, those that sit in the Sol (sun) section of the bullring, and especially the men, the day begins with the corrida (the national spectacle) and builds toward the encierro (the local event). The schedule is upside-down. After the corrida, members of the peñas celebrate all night in the streets. At the crack of dawn, they drink some broth, buy a newspaper to use as "protection" in the encierro, and stake out their place on the course. After running the encierro, they have a huge breakfast with their friends, and then at 10:00 A.M. or so, they go home to sleep. Around 3:00 or 4:00 P.M., they get up, shower, change into freshly cleaned and ironed clothes (prepared by their wife or mother), and at 5 : 00 p.m. they again gather with their peña to parade to the corrida. It is, of course, this second schedule that distinguishes San Fermín's fiestas from other parts of Spain.

Peñas

"The fiestas revolve around the peñas and the bull. Without these two elements, there would be no fiestas." People made these statements to me several times. The peñas are the fifteen clubs, with a total of more than four thousand members, originally organized so that groups of friends could go to the corridas together. Each peña has a social center, or clubhouse, where the members meet during the year. During los sanfermines the peñas parade to and from the bullring together along with a band. They also parade with their band periodically throughout the city to "animate" the festivities. At night the streets where the clubhouses are located are the center of the festivities. The Town Hall helps to fund these peñas, in recognition of their "unique and important role" in the fiesta.

The color of the long blouses each peña wears and the emblem sewn on their red San Fermín handkerchiefs worn around their necks distinguish each peña from the others. Members dress as Pamplonicas, and they wear a huge, open blouse over their white clothes. Traditionally the peñas were a male domain, and they still dominate in numbers, but now women form an important nucleus of many clubs, and there is even one woman president.

The active members of the peñas range in age from about seventeen to twenty-five. One never stops being a member of a peña, but with age, job responsibilities and family obligations inhibit one's participation during the year. However, during the fiestas older members usually leave their wives and children to parade with their peña, or party all night long with their peña for one or two nights. However, rarely do they sit with their peña in the bullring. These older members now prefer to sit in the Sombra (shade) section, while the peñas sit in the Sol (sun) section.

Membership in a peña used to be determined by the street or neighborhood where one lived in the old town. Recently, however, with the expansion of Pamplona, peñas are not simply neighborhood based. Nevertheless the connection to the old center remains, and to be a member of a peña "has always been an example of Pamplonesismo" (Barba 1985:xxxvi). Members of the peñas, one woman told me, are the true, authentic Pamplonicas (castas).

Although the peñas "enliven and make the streets joyful," one of the main characteristics of the peñas is their antiauthoritarianism and subversiveness (Goñi 1985:33). Their youthfulness and the fact that traditionally members have been male underline this characteristic, as old age and women are considered more stable and conservative elements in Spanish society. Since the peñas mark the tone of the fiesta, a theme of covert antiauthoritarianism runs through the festivities, which is usually ignored or interpreted as good-humored fun.

Peña members' behavior during the fiestas certainly turns the social order of Pamplona upside-down. Supposedly, the peñas are the main protagonists of the Riau-Riau, where the town officials are kept from their appointment by the boisterous crowd. Thus, when the mayor wanted to prevent a repeat of the 1984 Riau-Riau, when the procession never left the Town Hall, he appealed to the peña leaders for cooperation. Another example of the peñas turning the social order upside-down is their drinking and behavior with women. The "personality" of the Pamplonica is said to be a "serious, hard-working, responsible person," but during the fiestas, although they are not supposed to pass out or behave destructively, the peña members drink and party to excess. Moreover, girls and young women are subject to being grabbed, hugged, and kissed by these drunken Pamplonicas. No offense is taken because the advances are never too overtly sexual. A final example of the peñas subverting the social order is their daily schedule. While for everyone else the day begins with the encierro and builds toward the culminating event of the corrida, for the peñas the "day" begins with the corrida and culminates with the encierro.

Supposedly anyone may run with the bulls in the morning encierro, but the peñas (meaning young Pamplona men) play the most important role. Nevertheless, youths run in an encierro by themselves or with a group of friends, never as an entire peña.

Running, itself, used to be an antiauthoritarian act. For many years during the last half of the nineteenth century, the Town Hall tried to prohibit youths from running in the encierro (del Campo 1980:62). Obviously, the youths paid no attention to these prohibitions. Even today, when running in the encierro is one of the much-publicized characteristics of the fiestas, the authorities try to control the encierro as much as possible, citing safety as their justification. The municipal police rid the streets of people who in their opinion are too drunk, too young, or too old to run; the mayor must approve the course; advertisements are published in the newspapers about the proper behavior during encierros and edicts are published establishing rules; fines are levied on spectators or participants who break the rules. But in Pamplona it is well known that only the runners really control the encierros and punish any transgressors.

The peñas' antiauthoritarian behavior is most manifest in the bullring. Each peña parades to the ring with their band and a huge banner. The banner consists of a biting political criticism in the form of a cartoon with figures and text. Whether addressing local, national, or even international issues, people think this political criticism is so outrageous that it would only be allowed in the context of the fiestas. Usually the cartoons incorporate some symbolic aspect of the fiestas, especially the bull.

The peñas all sit together in the Sol side of the bullring. In Pamplona, to refer to Sol is to refer to the peñas and their behavior in the ring. The peñas' behavior is notorious throughout Spain, and although they only take up the Sol half of the bullring, this behavior has come to stand for and characterize Pamplona's fiestas.

Though each peña is distinguishable by its blouse color and banner, in the bullring all the peñas act the same way. The peña members and their guests arrive drunk and proceed to get more drunk. The fifteen bands play, and the peña members dance and sing in the aisles. Often one peña will begin a well-known chant and all the other peñas will chime in. Some of these chants include standing up, waving, or rowing actions by all those sitting in Sol. Other pranks are also played. A person may be passed from the top seats to the bottom seats. Peñas sitting in the top rows throw bags of flour or bales of hay down upon the peñas seated in the lower rows. Buckets of red wine and champagne shower the peñas. In other words, the peñas claim the protagonism of the bullring—taking it away from, or at least paralleling, the bull and the torero.

Rarely, if ever, do the peñas act as if they are paying attention to the *fiesta nacional.* They *are* paying attention, however, in a negative way. After the performance of every *picador,* the Sol half of the ring must be swept clean of food (e.g., sandwiches and oranges) that the peñas throw at the picador in disgust at his "ruining the bull." And although many members of the peñas actually sit with their backs to the ring, studiously ignoring the torero, the toreros know that they must placate, and play to, the peñas to triumph in Pamplona. This is because the peñas have a "president," who parallels the official president of the bullring sitting in Sombra. The peñas' president will decide if a torero deserves the red San Fermín kerchief for a job well done. If a torero does not perform well—and it is difficult to perform well in Pamplona due to the noise and distractions made by the peñas and to the size of the bulls—the peñas will pelt the torero with food as he attempts to leave the ring, as they do with almost every picador. After all, peña members ran that morning with the bulls, which are killed by the torero in the afternoon in the ring. Thus, they consider the bull as much "theirs" as the torero's, especially after they have risked their own lives with the bull. They, in fact, have identified with the bull.

Pamplonicas sitting in Sombra (shade), although they themselves once sat in Sol (sun), often criticize the action of the peñas during the bullfight. The Town Hall regularly asks the peña leaders to control the actions of their members, especially during the picador's performance. But the peñas define themselves by this behavior, so they do not change.

A final way that the peñas manifest antiauthoritarian behavior is by their associations with Basqueness. Half of the peñas have Basque names, and their banners are often written in Basque, which could be merely considered typical of Navarran culture. Although the peñas claim to be apolitical, their banners criticize the Spanish national government's actions against Basque nationalists.[8] In the bullring, no Spanish national police have been allowed since 1978, nor are there any Spanish flags present. The peñas would not tolerate these symbols of central authority.[9] At every corrida about twenty-five to thirty Spanish traffic police (Guardia Civil de Tráfico) enter the ring and sit at the top of the stands between Sol and Sombra. When they enter, all of the peñas in Sol sing in unison, "Let them go away, let them go away. Tell them to go away." Over and over the people in one half of the bullring, directing themselves to these police in green uniforms, sing this tune.

Although on the streets the peñas oppose some local authorities (officials, politicians, and norms), in the context of the bullring, the peñas oppose the Spanish state. The peñas identify with the Periphery in the Center/Periphery debate.[10]

The peña's central role in the fiestas represents an alternative to the normal power relationship of ruler-ruled. The peña members are careful not to go too far, and a scathing criticism of a peña is to say that it overdoes it. But like the copresidents in the bullring (the official one in

Sombra and the unofficial one in Sol), Pamplona's fiestas propose a sharing of power.

The Process of the Bull

As stated above, many taurine fiestas are celebrated during San Fermín. There is a *novillada* (with a three-year-old calf), a *becerrada* (when the peñas play with the calf), recortadores (cow dodgers), a game of *balón-vaca* (soccer with cows loose in the ring), an exhibition of *rejoneo* (equestrian bullfighting), *toreo cómico* (clown bullfight), *encierros txikis* (children running calves in the streets), toros de fuego (firecracker bulls), and vaquillas (cows loose in the ring). Many of these activities only take place once during the week, and usually local animals (cows and calves) from Navarra are used. Most of these animals are not killed.

The two most important activities, the encierro and the corrida, are part of a process that each bull undergoes. This process is repeated faithfully with different bulls everyday for eight days, thus underlining its importance. Rather than local (Northern) animals, these bulls always come from the Center and South of Spain.[11] The end result of this process is the eating of the bull. This is, of course, what happens to all toros bravos, but in no other fiesta I studied was this fact emphasized as much as in los sanfermines. In other fiestas, the various steps in the continuum of free bull to food do not receive the conscious elaboration that they do in Pamplona.

For a visitor, the two most spectacular steps are the encierro and the corrida. But Pamplonicas have also ritualized several other points. The total process consists of six steps: *encierrillo*, encierro, *apartado*, corrida, *descuartizamiento*, and toro as communal food.

When the bulls arrive by train or truck to Pamplona, they are put in corrals outside the old city gates for four or five days. Like in other Spanish cities, the public comes to view the bulls. About 10:00 p.m. every night, the bulls chosen for the encierro/corrida the following day take part in the encierrillo (little encierro). While the encierro is open to anyone, the encierrillo is a ritual for Pamplonicas only. Visitors rarely know of its existence.

In the encierrillo, the six bulls follow some oxen and a shepherd out of the corrals, across a small bridge, and up a short incline to the corral just inside the city gate, where the bulls and oxen spend the night and from where they start the encierro in the morning. The bulls make the short trip in about thirty or forty seconds, trotting after the oxen up the hill. No one is allowed to line the route. Instead, those who come to view the encierrillo must stand on a sloping road off to the side, which gives people only a glimpse of the animals. Although the crowd gathers thirty to forty minutes before the event, the only noise is hushed talking in the evening darkness. When the bulls pass, there is no talking at all. The crowd consists of families, older couples, and some teenagers. This is Pamplona's private salute to the bulls. Although several Pamplonicas told me in 1985 that the encierrillo was an important part of the fiestas, I did not see one until 1986. The encierrillo does not appear on the fiesta program, and the simultaneous celebrations of the peñas coming out of the bullring detract attention from this event.

The encierro has generated much literature by Pamplonicas (del Campo 1980, n.d.; Echeverría 1983), and descriptions of the encierro abound in the press. Pamplonicas define three distinct sections of the 850 meter course and can explain the dangers and methods of running each section. No runner does the whole course. Although a runner may try out different parts of the course on different days or different years, eventually he chooses a favorite section (e.g., the hill of Santo Domingo Street, Mercaderes Street, Estafeta Street, or the entry into the bull-ring). According to Pamplonicas, it is generally foreigners, those who do not realize the danger of the bulls or the dangers of the different sections of the course, who get hurt. It is common for ten to thirty people to be taken to the hospital in an ambulance after each encierro.

The best runners are known as *los divinos* (the divine ones). A good runner is judged by how close he runs in front of (*en los cuernos,* in the horns) or with one particular bull and for how long. It is not simply a question of running in front of or beside the pack, but to find a bull *(ver toro),* break into the pack and run in harmony with one bull for a period of time, before jumping out of the herd and letting it pass. Few people have the presence of mind to do this in the seconds they have alongside the bulls and in the crowded, dangerously slippery streets, where the behavior of the bulls, the herd, and other runners cannot be predicted.[12]

Those men that manage to run with a bull are captured on film by many professional photographers. Their pictures appear in the two local newspapers and in special poster frames set up in the Plaza del Castillo. These men, the divinos, are admired for their "gallantry, bravery, man-liness" and are the archetype of casta and "fineness" *(majeza)* (del Campo n.d.:7). Although most men quit running with the onset of marriage, I have spoken to some who continue running well into their forties.

Pamplonicas say that the bulls belong to them during the encierro. Although they do not deny the risks that the torero takes, runners stress that they also risk their lives with the bulls in the morning and, thus, are not awed by the afternoon spectacle. Runners I spoke to insisted that they loved the bull—a "pure love" one called it—and implied that they suffered for the bull in the afternoon, especially with the picador. However, even if he does not like the corrida, a young man who runs with the bulls in the morning will necessarily go to the corrida in the afternoon.

The next step in the process of the bull is the apartado. With its upper-class overtones, this is the most blatantly hierarchical taurine activity. At 1 : 00 P.M. every day the bulls, which have been milling around in a corral connected to the bullring, are divided up by lot *(el sorteo)* among the toreros and then put into the individual darkened stalls to wait for the corrida. This small ceremony, called the apartado, is watched from balconies above the corrals by a select public. Because only a limited number of people can watch the apartado for reasons of space, an apartado ticket is a relatively scarce resource, and the mayor and city councilors often give them away as gifts. The apartado, like the encierrillo, is not in the official program. Many non-Pamplonicas are present, but usually by invitation of a Pamplonica. When the bulls are being separated, total silence reigns, as in the encierrillo.

However, fans want to attend an apartado not just to see the bulls but also to be seen. An apartado is like a small cocktail party. The bulls appear for only seconds at a time. Meanwhile people stand around drinking fino (the white wine typical of the South) or red wine from Navarra, eating bulls' testicles *(criadillas)* from the animals killed the previous day, and socializing. Every day in the newspapers are pictures and interviews of the rich, famous people from all over Spain who attended the apartado the previous day: national politicians, tourists, celebrities, bull ranchers, and bullfighters. The fino wine draws a parallel between the apartado and an Andalusian caseta. Even the behavior is the same: dignified, elegant, refined.

After the apartado comes the corrida at 6 : 30 P.M. Everyone goes to the ring dressed in white clothes with the red sash and red kerchief, carrying buckets of ice with bottles of champagne and baskets of food for a snack (merienda).

The antics of the peñas in Sol define the "behavior" or the "personality" of the plaza. On the other hand, the people sitting in Sombra are older, usually couples, or groups of couples. They are well dressed (still as Pamplonicas, but fashionable) and of course, well behaved. Although they only go to los toros during San Fermín, they act interested in what is happening in the ring and often criticize the peñas' barbaric behavior.

Both Sol and Sombra eat the traditional snack (merienda) together after the third bull. As soon as the bull is killed and dragged out by the mules, the spectators open baskets and begin passing out food. In Sol, the boys pass around champagne and drink straight out of the bottles. In Sombra, people bring out plastic cups, or even glass cups, and pour champagne into them. Champagne is always offered to strangers, usually tourists. The merienda can be very elaborate: buckets of bull stew, lamb stew, rabbit stew, or tomatoes and pork stew; or it may be simply the typical Spanish socializing fare (tapa): a cold potato omelette cut in squares, cured ham sandwiches, and slices of cheese. The food is also offered to strangers. The people in Sombra use plates and napkins, as well as cups, and their ham and cheese is good quality and expensive. When I asked what people ate during the merienda, everyone mentioned bull stew *(estofado de toro),* even though I never actually saw anyone eating it. Consequently, I believe all the other food is merely a substitute for the bull.

After the corrida, the next step in the processing of the bull is the butchering (descuartizamiento). Although very few people actually watch this butchering, it has been called a ritual nevertheless ("Cuando el toro . . ." 1986:9). The descuartizamiento begins when the mules bring the dead bull in from the ring. Within ten minutes the job is done and the butchering team is ready for the next bull. The meat has been previously sold to markets and butchers. The "toro-toro" is now *"toro carne"* (bull meat), as one person put it.

In Pamplona this "bull meat" is eaten all day long. It is traditional to eat bull testicles (criadillas) for breakfast after the encierro and at the apartado and bull stew (estofado de toro) at the corrida and for dinner. Many other dishes are also typical for breakfast, the snack at the corrida, and dinner in restaurants during los sanfermines. Therefore, how many people actually eat any bull meat during the fiestas is unknown. Nevertheless, everyone consistently told me that it was "traditional" to eat the bull; this dish appeared on the menu in many of the places where I ate, and I ate it! If the bull is the totem of Spain, Pamplona eats the totem that it sacrifices during its Feria del toro.

The encierro is the powerful indigenous symbol of local identity for Pamplona during the fiestas. In contrast, the corridas, despite their definite Pamplonan characteristics, function as a symbol of "Spain," and hence the peñas "ignore" the "center" of the ring. But in Pamplona the encierro and corrida are not exactly two separate events like, for example, the *sokamuturra* and corrida in Bilbao. The corrida is the reason for the encierro. The goal of the encierro is the corrida. Both events are part of the same process: the sacrifice and consumption of the bull. Furthermore, the animal is the same throughout the process. As the bull moves through the rituals of the encierrillo, encierro, apartado, and corrida, he moves through rituals of local identity to rituals of national identity. The encierrillo and the encierro "belong" to Pamplona and are peculiar to Pamplona. The apartado and the corrida point to identification with the rest of "Spain." In the encierro there is identification with the bull; in the corrida the bull is controlled and dominated. The themes of equality and hierarchy are present at the opposite ends of the process of the bull. Notwithstanding the oppositions (local/national, equality/hierarchy, participation/spectacle) inherent among the various rituals, the rituals together form a process whereby what is local becomes national.

Community

The image Pamplona projects during the San Fermín fiestas is one of unity: unity of the Pamplona community and perhaps of the whole province of Navarra. This unity encompasses aspects of both equality and of hierarchy. Perhaps the most obvious characteristic of equality is the dress or costume that everyone wears. All of Pamplona is dressed as a Pamplonica: white pants and shirt (older women often wear a white skirt and blouse), red sash, and red kerchief. Furthermore, there is equality between Navarra's two cultures: the Basque and the Castilian speakers. The programs are printed in both languages, the "¡Vivas!" are shouted in both languages. The music of both cultures echoes in the streets.

Despite this emphasis on equality, hierarchical relations are neither mystified nor ignored. Unity encompasses these relationships. For example, most informants, especially older ones, stress that this is a male fiesta. There is a noticeable asymmetry in the relations between men and women: men are the protagonists in the peñas, men run in the encierro, men grab and kiss girls, husbands leave their wives to go party. There is also a hierarchy between the Pamplonicas and the visitors: activities are rated for hometown people and for the foreigners. Within

Pamplona there are los castas (the pure) and the immigrants. Within the ranks of the runners of the encierro, there are the divine ones (divinos) and the others.

Class divisions are also evident. Even though the dress is white and red, members of the different social classes dress differently. The upper-middle class dresses elegantly in white designer clothes. Different bars cater to clientele from different classes. Upper-middle-class professionals party and celebrate together. That is, there is no real mixing of the classes. The apartado is a ritual reserved for people with the right connections. Even the much-beloved Giants are royalty.

Perhaps the most obvious symbol of asymmetrical relations is the division of the bullring into Sol (sun) and Sombra (shade) and the significance of these divisions. Although Sol and Sombra repeat some of the above divisions—in broad terms, Sol is men, Sombra is women; Sol is unmarried, Sombra is married; Sol is the runners of the encierro, Sombra is the nonrunners; Sol is the castas, Sombra is the visitors; Sol is Basque, Sombra is Castilian; Sol is poor, Sombra is rich—basically Sol and Sombra reflect an age hierarchy. Sol is young and Sombra is old. This is the uniqueness of the bullring in Pamplona.

Elsewhere in Spain, Sol and Sombra refer to two inherently opposed social classes. Sol and Sombra have become a metaphor for the "two Spains." One cannot be the other. In a conversation in Madrid about the San Fermín fiestas, an informant described Sol and Sombra in Pamplona as totally opposed. He used a new metaphor when he said, "They are like North and South." But in Pamplona, *with time* Sol will become Sombra. Sol and Sombra are opposed, but at the same time they are part of a process: aging. The young in time will leave Sol, get married, make money, and go to sit in Sombra. The people sitting in Sombra criticize the behavior of those sitting in Sol, but ten or fifteen years earlier they also sat there. In Pamplona, Sol and Sombra are two points of the same process, like the bull who runs in the encierro to die in the corrida. Sol and Sombra together form the round plaza de toros.

This unity of Sol and Sombra is very tenuous and subject to disruption. Everyday life in Pamplona is a series of political, social, cultural, and economic confrontations, which are left aside during the communitas of the fiesta. Thus, the social divisions are there, ready to appear at any notice. The following discussion of the "wave," described at the beginning of the chapter, is an example of this.

The day after the first wave newspapers editorialized them, complaining that such behavior showed a lack of respect for the torero, who after all, was risking his life in the ring. Nevertheless, the wave was repeated on Sunday, July 13.

On July 14 at 8 : 00 A.M., a car bomb exploded in Madrid as a busload of traffic police (Guardia Civil de Tráfico) passed by. Eight young police trainees were killed and fifty-six police and other people were wounded. ETA, the Basque separatist terrorist organization, claimed responsibility for the act. The official reaction in Madrid was shock and outrage. The public was especially disgusted that the targets had been nineteen- and twenty-year-old traffic trainees.[13] Televisions all over Spain were tuned to the news.

In Pamplona, it was the last day of fiestas. At 6 : 00 P.M. the bullring was filling up. As usual, Sol was full of pranks and antics: the last bash before the sad Pobre de mí (Poor Me). The group of Traffic Guardia Civil filed in. Sol sang its song, "Let them go away." But this time the people in Sombra stood up and directed themselves toward the group of Guardia Civil and applauded. Sol tried again to sing its song. Again Sombra stood up and applauded the Guardia Civil. Three times this happened before Sol gave up and went on with other pranks.

I was stunned. It had been a very emotional moment. I was sitting in Sombra with a visitor from Madrid. The fiestas of San Fermín are a definition of Navarra in opposition to Spain. The symbols of "Spain," the flag and the colors red and yellow, are nowhere to be seen during los sanfermines. Thus, the incident in the bullring was quite significant. The Guardia Civil, without a doubt, is a symbol of "Spain," especially in the Periphery. Not only is it a symbol of "Spain," but it is frequently thought of as a symbol of the oppressive aspect of the state, since it was closely associated with the Franco regime.[14] The fact that Sombra stood up and applauded the Guardia was a demonstration of solidarity with "Spain" in the face of Sol's rejection of "Spain."

The atmosphere was tense. The corrida began with the ceremonial parade of the toreros. Sol, on this last day of fiestas, was being especially obnoxious. Somewhere in the middle of Sol, a peña decided to start a wave. All of Sol picked it up, and the wave started to the left. However, when the wave reached Sombra, no one—not one person—stood up. The peñas tried again. This time the wave went toward the right. Again when the wave reached Sombra nobody stood up. It was not a question of lack of enthusiasm on the part of Sombra, or lack of cooperation. Rather, it seemed as if Sombra had come to a collective, unanimous decision. They would not identify with Sol. Two days earlier the wave had signified Pamplona's unity as it circled around the ring five times.

On Monday, the "nonwave" pointed to Pamplona's underlying structural opposition, Sol and Sombra, North and South.

Nonetheless, the corrida continued and so did the fiestas. That night at midnight in the plaza of the Town Hall, all of Pamplona was represented by the thousands of people with candles singing "We want more, we want more, we want much, much more" and "poor me," lamenting the end of their fiestas. Unity had been regained.

Analysis

The fiestas of San Fermín function as a fiesta mayor for Spain because they serve as a model that incorporates two cultural traditions in a nonproblematic way. Rather than choosing one culture over another, Pamplona celebrates its unity by consciously utilizing aspects of both cultures in the fiestas, Basque and Castilian, while stressing its identity as Navarra.

The function of the fiesta mayor is not overt, but it is clear that in many ways Navarra is a metaphor for all of Spain. The attention focused on los sanfermines, the place of the fiestas in the collective consciousness, the constant pilgrimages of Spaniards from all over to the small northern capital, and the desire of many young men to run in the encierro are not due merely to the intrinsic attractiveness of the fiesta itself, though informants may say this. Instead, I suggest it is because Pamplona's fiestas offer an illusion of community, based on more than one culture, not found elsewhere in Spain.

Within this fiesta stressing unity, however, all authority is constantly under challenge. Those on the outside of political power (peñas, Sol, young, Basques) claim the protagonism of the fiestas over those on the inside of official power (city officials, Sombra, elders, Spanish). It is a Center/Periphery dialogue. In Pamplona, this dialogue is changed from merely stagnant opposition to a dynamic process that creates community. In time, the members of the peñas (los castas) will become city officials, Sol will go sit in Sombra, the young will get old, and the bull in Pamplona's encierro will be killed in Spain's corrida. If aging is the process that unites Pamplona, "history" is the process that unites the many Spains.

Despite the overt theme of unity and the challenge to authority mediated by time, another message also comes out of the fiestas. In Pamplona, in contrast to the Basque Country, the peñas go to the corrida. And although Sol turns its back on the center of the ring, their bull—the bull they ran with in the morning—is sacrificed. Furthermore, along with Sombra, Sol also partakes of the totem during the communal meal (merienda). In this subtle way, Sol accepts the hierarchy of Center/Periphery.

Ironically, this illusion of community is obtained at the expense of "Spain." Pamplona does not declare itself "Spanish" in these fiestas. Rather, it declares itself "Navarra." "Spain" is conspicuously absent from the fiestas, thus, "Spain as problem" continues.

However, when one switches to taurine vocabulary and ignores the political vocabulary, another message is heard. The bull is "Spain." The many different taurine fiestas represent the many differentiated parts of Spain. People in some parts of Spain do not want to be part of the Spanish nationality. Sometimes they refuse to have anything to do with los toros, while other times they reject the national form, yet celebrate a local form. Yet, no part of "Spain" is politically homogeneous, as some people in those same areas do identify with "Spain." San Fermín speaks to them.

San Fermín is the Fair of the Bull. Although the many taurine fiestas, representing the "many Spains," are offered during San Fermín, the most important taurine activity is the encierro/corrida process. This process can be seen as the transformation of a regional activity into a national one, the transformation of a regional tradition (the encierro) into a national rite (the corrida). Furthermore, the conflagration of the bull in the ring is the sacrifice of the Periphery to Center. However, in this case, the relationship periphery to center is not a relationship of part of Spain to another part of Spain but rather of part to whole. Center now stands for the whole, the totality of the parts. And the black bull is the symbol of this relationship.

CONCLUSION

This book connects Spanish identities to the bulls. It explains why bulls and taurine games and all their attendant imagery play such a prominent, yet ambiguous, role within Spain.

With the expression *the bulls,* I do not want the reader to think only of the national bullfight, the *corrida*. It is a mistake to focus primarily on that singularly evocative event if we want to understand why bullfights persist in Spain. Thus, this is not a description or analysis of the corrida. It is not a discussion, psychological or otherwise, of that spectacle. Neither is it a history nor social history of the corrida.

The expression *los toros* includes, and indeed is dominated by, the corrida, but this spectacle forms only a small numerical part of "the bulls." More numerous are the thousands of lower-level local taurine games that take place every year during patron saint festivals and other celebrations in Spain. Moreover, these local games seem to oppose directly the meaning and use of the corrida and the few other national formats. Rather, it is the *relationship* between the many formats that is the subject of this book. Towns all over the peninsula make use of the many formats of "the bulls" and all that surround them to talk about and make manifest other important Spanish concerns, contradictions, and social tensions such as urban/rural, male/female, upper class/lower class, North/South, local/national, political left/political right, and tradition/modernity.

Spaniards feel ambivalent about "the bulls" because in some contexts *los toros* means the corrida, while other times *los toros* refer to a cherished local tradition (e.g., *encierros* or *toros embolados*). For many of those who aspire to be recognized as European and modern, corrida implies the opposite: backward and anachronistic Spain. Yet some Spaniards feel great ambivalence about their newly "Europeanized" and "modern" country. They wonder if they have lost something valuable. At the same time, as Spain becomes more obviously "Europe," especially for the young generations, other Spaniards fill the bullrings proclaiming that

Spain is "more than Europe" and that los toros are part of the quality of life missing in northern Europe. Meanwhile, for others, the corrida, the national fiesta, is the symbol par excellence for the nation-state "Spain." At the same time certain Spaniards feel intensely ambivalent about "Spain." Will they lose their own local distinctiveness if they identify with "Spain?"

Even while rejecting the corrida, many Spaniards see no irony in promoting other games with bulls and cows in the setting of their local fiestas. These are as dear and traditional as the special foods, music, and dress worn during festive days; as cherished as the little saints and virgins paraded through the streets during fiestas, though few worship these icons any longer during the rest of the year; as necessary as the ludic moments that are the community fiestas themselves. These rural games are attacked by urban animal protection leagues. Yet many Spaniards feel some ambivalence about these attacks on such cruelty to their bulls. Are the attacks sponsored by a condescending "Europe" that deigns to pronounce what culture is?

Finally, one cannot talk about the bulls without talking about regionalism in Spain. Perhaps the most important subject since the death of Franco has been how politically to construct the Spanish state. This political problem is due to the perception that the different parts or regions of Spain are represented by different cultures, several of which have political parties or movements that aspire to nationhood. Consequently, it is only to be expected that the contrast between the national forms of the bulls and the local taurine formats will get carried into the discourse on nationalism. I show how this discussion is mapped onto the use of the taurine games in town fiestas. Ambiguity arises when a large metropolitan area in the Periphery, like Bilbao, offers corridas despite the corridas' national (i.e., Spanish) resonance, as after all, corridas are "traditional" for urban areas. In the 1978 reorganization of the fiestas, Bilbao tried to make them more "Basque" by, among other things, incorporating local Basque forms of the bulls (sokamuturra). As rural, village forms, these games seem at times out of place in the giant cities—again creating ambiguity and logical scandal.

On the other hand, ambivalence is created in Andalusia when towns add vaquillas to their fiestas not for the sake of cultural authenticity but to allow more participation on the part of townsfolk. For in Andalusia, the corrida was born in these lands, it is the local form. To bring in new forms, albeit for festive purposes, is to pollute a celebration of local identity with an outside tradition.

Despite the many Spanish citizens who feel only "Catalan" or only "Basque," even in Catalonia and the Basque Country many people feel only "Spanish." The Spanish fiesta cycle speaks to them. This cycle weaves the attention and attendance of people and the press all over the country into an annual circuit that draws together, as well as delineates, the many parts of Spain as represented by five important cities. The cycle condenses within itself a model of egalitarian relationships, as well as a suggestion of hierarchy. In some references, North and South are used as complementary, but equal, parts of the cycle. In other references, North, Center, and South are used. Center, while sometimes simply a third division equivalent to North and South, can also become the hegemonic part of the Center/Periphery dyad. These two models embody the ambivalence Spaniards have about the construction of the state. Should it be hierarchical and governed from the center or should it be a totally federated association of equal parts?

The last three chapters give examples of how taurine games were used and what they mean in three different fiestas. In Bilbao, contrary to expectation, taurine games play a prominent and framing role in the festivities. In this northern Basque city, with supposedly little *afición*, taurine activities begin and end the day. In a fiesta that stresses Basque identity and the common man, the corrida (representing Spanish identity and the upper class) has a problematic place in the fiesta. Nevertheless, it is at the bullring for the corrida that the opposing sides of Bilbaino identity (Basque/Castilian, upper class/working class) are mediated momentarily.

In Sevilla the bulls actually play a rather small role in the festivities. Nevertheless, their images decorate the tents *(casetas),* and the fairground streets are named after bullfighters. This fiesta turns all Sevillanos into *señoritos,* if only for a moment. The corrida, already so identified with Andalusian culture, is the only taurine event offered during Feria. This spectacle about hierarchy, control, and domination seems a good symbol for this celebration of upper-class forms and fancy.

I describe both these fiestas in some detail to show the different, but integral, role of the bulls in each. I explain how the bulls were fit into the other preoccupations and concerns being expressed in the fiestas. Consequently, I describe the larger fiesta context and its rituals to show how the taurine games were manipulated to speak to each site. Each city celebrates its "identity." This identity consists of regional and local traditions, symbols, and in the examples studied here, a preference for class. In other words, class (the common people, in the case of Bilbao;

the gentry, in the case of Sevilla) becomes one of several elements that define regional identity. This helps explain why in Bilbao the popular taurine fiestas predominate and why in Sevilla only the elegant and elitist corrida is celebrated.

A fiesta cycle that tracks public attention and attendance across and around the many Spains, of course, does not create a national identity as much as recreate it—point it out, underline it, again and again every year. It is only one of a series of institutions that nod to the existence of "Spain." As mentioned, there are fiesta cycles that recreate the "Basque Country" (e.g., Korrika [del Valle 1988]) as an entity separate from "Spain." The Spanish fiesta cycle competes for some of that same territory (i.e., Bilbao, representing the Basque Country) as part of "Spain."

Yet despite fervent Basque nationalism, for some Spanish citizens, "Spain" is their "imagined community." Poll after poll attests to this (del Campo et al. 1977; Linz 1986). These Spaniards, although being "of" the region they were born in and without a doubt identifying culturally with that area, also take pride in, celebrate, and enjoy recognizing and participating in other aspects of their shared "nationality." The fiesta cycle parallels this plural vision, articulating many cultures rather than emphasizing only one. As J. W. Fernandez (1965:923) has said, ritual can promote social solidarity without implying that people share the same values or even the same interpretation of the rituals: "the moral community created by coordinated interaction such as ritual may actually be threatened by an attempt to achieve moral community on the cultural level where the dimensions of interaction must be made explicit."

The use and implicit understanding of the whole cycle's symbols, especially the "bulls," by many participants underscore the existence on one level of a "Spanish community," a shared culture. Recall Antonio Gala (1985:7) saying, "It is because of what it has that is not learned that I consider the fiesta culture." He is referring to those things that are simply absorbed passively, rather than those things taught or actively learned, that put you in a relationship of identity with others.

The importance of Navarra's San Fermín is that it offers in the North (i.e., "European Spain") an "illusion of community" based on two cultures. Moreover, it is a fiesta where the bulls do most of the talking. Community unity, rather than one particular group or social class, is emphasized. Almost all the taurine fiestas celebrated in the peninsula are offered in Pamplona during San Fermín. In this case the northern,

local forms (encierros, vaquillas, and *toros de fuego*) do not take precedence over the national corrida. Instead one literally leads to the other.
The bulls of the encierro are used in the corrida. Moreover, while running in an encierro is a rite of passage of sorts for Pamplonan identity,
attendance at the corrida (where the bulls of the local encierro are sacrificed for the national spectacle) is the centerpiece of this fiesta. Even
the scandalizing boys in Sol, acting up against authority and the state,
in the end defer. With literally all of Spain watching, the bulls are run to
the plaza for the *fiesta nacional*.

Clearly, there are other areas, other moments, when for many Spanish
citizens the problem of "Spain" is resolved. I can think of the two weeks
of the 1992 Olympics when Spaniards won thirteen gold medals and
shocked the nation into a celebration of nationalism. This was especially
evident on the last evening of the games when Spain played for the gold
medal in soccer in the huge stadium in Barcelona. (The team had not
dared to play there until then, due to Catalanist fervor, which implied
anti-Spanish sentiment.) Many fans, Catalan and others, were aston-
ished at themselves as they cheered "¡España! ¡España!" and waved
Spanish flags enthusiastically. This was Barcelona! These were the Catalan Games! All of Barcelona was draped with Catalan flags! Yet over the
course of the two weeks, for many particularism had given way, momentarily, to pride in "Spain." Cynicism had given way to a giddy
patriotism.

The Olympics, and other such events, affected millions of people
throughout Spain due to media exposure. A fiesta such as Pamplona
perhaps only affects those in attendance. Nevertheless, it exists in Spanish folklore as an ideal, a model of communitas, where for a week two
cultures join to form one. Significantly, it is in the bullring where Sol
and Sombra, North and South, modernity and tradition, local and national are joined. "Because the bull is not an animal for us; it is much
more: a symbol, a totem, an aspiration, a eucharist with those around
us and our forefathers" (Gala 1985:7).

After I had written this book, I was present during the following conversation. It was the end of a hot, sultry July in Charlottesville, Virginia.
I was eating dinner with four Spaniards. One was my husband, a fifteen-
year U.S. resident originally from Madrid. Our host was a young cardio-
vascular surgeon visiting the University of Virginia hospital for three
months. Juan was from Valencia and would be returning home soon.
The others were a couple from Pamplona: he was a university econom-

ics professor, also visiting the University of Virginia for the summer, she was a student of English. The conversation was about Spanish regionalism. Things were getting "animated," as the Spanish say. Finally, Juan from Valencia said, "You can say whatever you want, but when you hear the music from San Fermín and see the clips of the running of the bulls on American television, you get goose bumps. That's you! That's yours!" The two from Navarra—what else could they do?—deferred.

The principal tension that "the bulls" evoke above all, however, is that between "modernity" and "tradition." These are the terms that swirl in and around all discussions of the bulls. These social constructs have provoked and driven much of Spanish history for the last two hundred years. The definitions of the terms are not self-evident, but as used by the Spanish they seem opposed. For many Spaniards, the arbitrators of modernity are "Europeans." For "Europeanized Spaniards," the symbol of all the stumbling blocks to Spain's modernity has been the bulls. Avid taurine fans have inevitably been described as conservative traditionalists. Despite a desire to be recognized as "modern," many Spaniards feel ambivalent about giving up their "traditions." Local and regional traditions are the bedrock of identity. They are history still lived. Traditions differentiate a Spaniard from a German, an Andaluz from a Basque, one villager from another. Tradition, informants say, is what makes Spanish life richer than northern-European life. These "traditions" are celebrated, transformed, made manifest, and reified in the patron saint festivals of towns and cities all over the country—festivals that contradict "Europe" by sacrificing productivity. These celebrations have "from time immemorial" included taurine games and spectacles. How can one give these up without giving up identity?

Some Spanish citizens see no irony in saying, like Javier, the young Catalan, "I don't like the bulls" *(no me gustan los toros)* and minutes later proclaiming their aspiration to run with the bulls in Pamplona *(correr los toros en Pamplona)*. In this conversation, Javier can be "modern" by rejecting los toros as corrida, which represents hierarchy, the Center, the Right, Franco, and "Spain." At the same time he can be "traditional" by identifying with los toros as encierro, which represents egalitarianism, democracy, the Periphery, regionalism, and youth. In this equation one format, the encierro, actually equates with the folk definition of modern "Europe."

Recently, however, other Spaniards simply proclaim that not all is rationality and attend corridas by the millions. They have decided that

"Europe's" definition of modernity is deficient. For them Spanish modernity includes the bulls and all that they entail. "Who decides what civilization is? And above all, who decides what our civilization is? Because if we are bloody and crazy and crude, it isn't because of los toros; on the contrary, los toros make the violence delicate, golden and silky; they make it mystical and magical" (Gala 1985:7).

NOTES

Chapter 1, The Bull and Bull Festivals

1. When castrated, male *toros bravos* are called *cabestros* (oxen) and are used to control the *toros* and *vacas*. Oxen are more manageable than bulls and cows and so are used to lead them, for example, across the countryside, through the streets of towns, and in and out of bullrings. Bulls and cows will spontaneously follow a lead ox. An ox of another breed is generally called a *buey.* These work animals pull carts and plows. I have never heard of using a toro bravo for work.

2. *Manso,* which means domesticated and tame, also implies in a male animal that it is castrated. Because in the human sphere the definition of manliness *(hombría)* is intimately linked to having testicles *(cojones)* (Brandes 1980:92–94; Gilmore 1987:9–13), to be called a manso is to imply a lack of testicles, and thus manliness. It also implies a meek, controllable man (by a woman, especially [Marvin 1982: 230]). A cooperative, or "tame" *toro bravo* is called "noble." To be called manso is an insult to a toro bravo.

3. Miguel Hernández, a well-known Spanish poet who died in a Nationalist jail during the Spanish Civil War, used these metaphors in the poem "Vientos del pueblo me llevan," which was cited to me several times in the 1970s by opponents of the Franco regime. The following are some relevant passages:

> *Los bueyes doblan la frente,*
> Oxen bow their heads,
> *impotentemente mansa*
> impotently tame
> *delante de los castigos:*
> before affliction:
>
> . . . .
> *No soy de un pueblo de bueyes,*
> I am not from a people of oxen,
> *que soy de un pueblo que embargan*
> I am from a people that seizes
> *yacimientos de leones,*
> fields of lions,
> *desfiladeros de águilas*
> gorges of eagles
> *y cordilleras de toros*
> and mountain ranges of bulls

> *con el orgullo en el asta.*
> with pride in the horn.
> *Nunca medraron los bueyes*
> Oxen never prospered
> *en los páramos de España.*
> on the plains of Spain.
>
> *¿Quién habló de echar un yugo*
> Who spoke of putting a yoke
> *sobre el cuello de esta raza?*
> on the neck of this breed?

Hernández then calls upon all the peoples of Spain (Asturians, Basques, Valencians, Castilians, Andalusians, Extremeños, Galicians, Catalans, and the people of Aragón and Murcia, Leon, and Navarra):

> *yugos os quieren poner*
> People of the weed
> *gentes de la hierba mala,*
> want to put yokes on you,
> *yugos que habréis de dejar*
> yokes which you have to
> *rotos sobre sus espaldas.*
> break over their backs.
>
> . . . .
>
> *Los bueyes mueren vestidos*
> Oxen die dressed
> *de humildad y olor de cuadra:*
> in humility and in the smell of the stall:
> *las águilas, los leones*
> eagles, lions
> *y los toros de arrogancia,*
> and bulls (die of) arrogance,
> *y detrás de ellos, el cielo*
> and behind them, the sky
> *ni se enturbia ni se acaba.*
> does not get dark nor end.

Miguel Hernández 1937; 1968:85, my translation

4. In the nineteenth century it was typical to put on spectacles in the bullrings, where a Spanish bull would confront lions, Bengali tigers, or elephants and the Spanish press would praise the bravery of the native bull (Cossío [1947]1965[2]: 691–703).

5. By the adjective *serio* Spaniards mean "dignified," "reliable," and "grave." The fiestas at the top of the hierarchy are "grave" because of the presence of death in the ring—that of the bull and the possible death of the *torero*. Thus *serio* means "sober," not light or gay, not showy.

6. Since the 1920s and 1930s the *afición a los toros* has constantly compared and measured the bullfighting public and publicity with the public and publicity of soccer. These two spectacles are often used to represent different aspects of "Spain" (see chapter 4). In this sense it is significant that the two spectacles occupy different halves of the Spanish calendar. Soccer season begins in September and runs through June, the month the championships are held. In June 1986 bullfighting fans complained that the televised World Cup Championships were keeping people at home in front of their television sets instead of out at *corridas de toros*.

7. For many Spaniards in all five provinces studied here, "sun" is one of the defining characteristics of "Spain." There is a definite sense that Spain has a lot of sun, as compared to northern Europe. Since 1970, Spaniards of many regions have "explained" to me that the thirty-six million to forty-four million tourists a year that visit Spain come to get Spanish sun. I know several Spaniards who have gone to other countries in Europe such as England, Sweden, and Switzerland to live. Their critiques almost always end up with the complaint that there is not enough sun in those countries; then the person would emphasize that he/she needed "sun." Where there is no sun, life is "sad." Spain, of course, is advertised for tourists as "sunny Spain," and millions of Europeans flock to Spain's Costa del Sol (Sun Coast). A recent tourist poster shows a giant abstract sun drawn by Joan Miró with the words "Everything under the Sun." During the oil crisis in the 1970s, a topic of discussion in Spain was the need for Spain to develop solar power, since the sun was Spain's "principal natural resource."

8. In 1984 there were *novilladas* in Sevilla every Sunday after June 23 (San Juan), however, there were no more *corridas* in Sevilla city again until the *feria de Septiembre* at the end of September.

9. The earliest recorded *fiesta de toros* took place in the eleventh century. Although there has been much speculation, the origin of these taurine festivals is simply unknown. Almost from the beginning there was evidence of two traditions: an aristocratic tradition where bulls were fought from horseback and a village tradition where bulls were chased on the ground. The aristocratic tradition attracted many spectators, especially in the sixteenth and seventeenth centuries when the aristocracy fought bulls in Madrid's Plaza Mayor. Bullfights were celebrated to honor the visit of a dignitary, the birth of a royal child, a marriage, or a military victory. In 1700 the French Bourbon King, Philip V, came from France to take over the Spanish throne. This French king was revolted by bullfights and discouraged his nobility from participating in such events. The decline of aristocratic bullfights led almost immediately to the rise of a new plebeian form of fighting bulls. In Ronda and Sevilla in the south, men from the lower classes thrilled publics by fighting and killing bulls from the ground. To slow down the bull, the role of the horseman was retained, but now under the orders of the man on the ground. This form of bullfighting rapidly spread to all of Spain in the second half of the eighteenth century.

10. What other national government is in charge of keeping a spectacle dangerous?

11. There is another category of animal that is fought in a *novillada*. These are known as *novillo-toros*. These animals may be as big or as old a *toro*, yet they were disqualified from that category by not passing the *tienta* (test for bravery) on the ranch, or by being "defective," that is, not physically perfect enough for the *corrida*.

Such animals might have uneven (asymmetrical) horns or have vision problems in one eye. Although these characteristics make them quite difficult to "fight," their status as "defective" makes them much less expensive to buy than a true "toro."

12. A *novillero* is not paid as highly as a *torero*. A torero may appear in a *novillada* (although a novillero may never appear in a *corrida de toros*), but he is paid much less than he would be to kill a real "toro."

Chapter 2, "Mental Constructions" of "Spain"

1. When speaking of Spain as a cultural construction, or cultural concept of one or another group, I use "Spain." When speaking of Spain as a geographical entity on maps (which are also cultural constructions, I realize) I use simply Spain.

2. Portugal was part of Spain in the seventeenth century, and Catalonia tried to withdraw in 1640.

3. For many authors and speakers, especially in the Basque Country and Catalonia, the terms *nación* and *nacionalidad* are equivalent (Solé Tura 1985:22). However, the Constitution of 1978 (Article 2) distinguishes between the two terms. In the Constitution *nación* refers to nation-state, such as Spain or Germany, whereas *nacionalidad* is the term used to refer to those Autonomous Communities that do not call themselves regions and claim to have "historical and cultural identities" but which are legally equivalent to regions (Fernández Vega and Mariscal 1983:250). I use the word *nacionalidad,* realizing that I have chosen one indigenous term over another, without implying preference, nor pointing to any "reality."

4. There is a total Basque population of 2.1 million, which is about 0.056% of the total Spanish population (Instituto Nacional de Estadística 1985:64).

5. Juan Linz, a Spanish sociologist at Yale University, sums the question up as follows, "Today we could say that Spain is, for a large majority of Spaniards, a nation-state, for significant minorities (of different 'nationalities') a binational state, and for very small minorities (only significant in the Basque Country) a state opposed to the Basque nation. Even among the latter, only a sector put into doubt the legitimacy of the authority of the Spanish state" (Linz 1986:27, my translation).

6. The town or city where a person was born is also said by many to be the primary source of identification and a powerful force in shaping a person's worldview, or personality (del Campo et al. 1977:122). However, the town always implies a region that, together, creates one's essential personality. If someone is from the capital city of a region (e.g., Sevilla, Valencia, Bilbao), the name of the city almost always replaces that of the region.

Most anthropological work in Spain has taken note of (Lisón-Tolosana, pers. comm.) or dissented from (Gilmore 1980) the importance of intense identification with towns. The phenomenon is known as that of *patria chica* (little homeland or country), in contrast to the *madre patria* (motherland or "Spain"). The stated objective of Pitt-Rivers' book *The People of the Sierra* (1971), the first Spanish village ethnography, was to place the village within the context of the nation-state. Furthermore, the prominent Spanish anthropologist Julio Caro Baroja (1957) wrote extensively on the phenomenon of extreme identification with local communities, which he calls the "sociocentrism" of these towns. Caro Baroja claims sociocentrism is an essential aspect of "Spanish" life. It pits one village against a neighboring one in a kind of competition. Larger cities are also opposed in this way. For many authors, it is this extreme version of local identification that prevents, or inhibits, the wider national identification with "Spain."

7. Children of immigrants pose particular liminal categories: children born in Catalonia of Andalusian parents, for example. The parents, no matter how long they have been in Catalonia, are Andalusian, but the children's regional identity is problematic for the first generation.

8. "Differentiating element" *(elemento diferenciador)* is the term used by Spanish anthropologists del Valle (1985) and Lisón-Tolosana, who has made them the subject of a research project in eastern Spain. Another term used is "differential fact" *(hecho diferencial)*. Informants also use "characteristics" and "identity."

9. Islamic historic, linguistic, and cultural influences are freely, even proudly, acknowledged—whole schools of history are based on reincorporating the Islamic additions to Spanish history (see Castro 1954, 1961). However, in general one can say that the Islamic permanence in Spain is perceived as one of invading foreign forces (regardless of whether historians emphasize that much of the native population quickly converted to Islam and during the five centuries probably identified and merged with that culture). The adjective *moro* (moorish) is a negative characterization in much of colloquial speech, despite an appreciation of Islamic culture. The essence of all the "Spains" is always emphasized to be European and Christian, not Islamic.

10. For two millennia this part of Spain has produced wheat, wine, and olive oil for various markets. Recently soybean and sunflower oil have begun to be produced.

11. Rioja is a good example: of 174 municipalities, 156 have a population of under two thousand people; fifteen more have a population of under ten thousand (Instituto Nacional de Estadística 1985:488).

12. Noble status was enjoyed by a large part of the northern society in earlier times. Over one half of the nobility lived along the northern coasts in the seventeenth century. The whole population of Vizcaya in the Basque provinces was declared to be "noble." This compares to one or two percent of the population in the South (Domínguez Ortiz 1955).

13. Gilmore categorizes as "agro-cities" towns with populations from three thousand to thirty thousand inhabitants (Gilmore 1980:1).

14. In the 1980s people in Madrid celebrated this ambiguity by stressing Madrid's urbaneness and sophistication (*la movida*, a vanguard cultural movement, is an example of this), all the while calling their city a *villa*. This title was emphasized by the late Tierno Galván, mayor of Madrid from 1978–1986, when he used it in his speeches to refer to Madrid. Now that Madrid is the largest and one of the most industrialized cities in Spain, to call it a rural town is a paradox. Nevertheless, the use of the phrase, along with many other traditions Tierno brought back to Madrid, is an attempt to reforge a community identity after a demographic upheaval and cultural conflict. It is an attempt to give a village sense of identity to a disparate population whose various generations had just undergone the cultural shock of industrialization to varying degrees.

15. Although I link *ser* and *estar* to the Spanish categories of Center and Periphery, the two forms of "to be" are not the cause of the categories but rather are

coincidental with them. The whole Mediterranean culture area elaborates the variations on the categories Inside/Outside. Much anthropological research has been directed recently to pan-Mediterranean categories of Inside/Outside (see Dubisch 1986; Herzfeld 1986).

16. Empirically these divisions cut across every province and region in Spain to varying degrees. In Andalusia the landless peasants and anarchists were numerically very strong, and certainly the Left won the 1936 elections in Andalusia, but the landowning ruling classes with the help of the rebel armies were able to quickly reestablish control of the South at the outset of the war. Navarra was a stronghold of the Nationalists. Its definition as Center or Periphery varies by author.

17. In this definition Andalusia is obviously part of the "Center" despite its position on the geographical periphery.

18. In the mid-1970s Spain became the tenth most industrialized nation in the world.

19. Generally in the center/periphery relationships, which are characteristic of many nation-states, the problem is similarly about how to incorporate the periphery into the nationalism of the center. However, the periphery is usually the poorer, underdeveloped areas with respect to the center, for example: Quebec in Canada, Bavaria in Germany, Scotland in Great Britain, and Sicily in Italy. It is the opposite in the case of Spain.

20. In the 1986 national elections, the party headed by a man from the Periphery (a Catalan) with presidential ambitions failed to win even one seat in Parliament.

21. Catalans told me many times that "Catalonia pays for the rest of Spain," thus voicing their frustrations about perceived inequities between the Center and Periphery.

22. Already in the first half of the nineteenth century there was abundant literature that described "a definite dualistic Spain: on one side, *interior Spain*, dry, agricultural, sick from *latifundismo*, one crop, fallow land and absenteeism, extensive cultivation, crops dependent on the weather, low yield, weak industrialization, seignorial, reactionary, turned to the past, centralist, and bureaucratic; on the other side, *peripheral Spain*, of intensive agriculture, in the process of industrialization, vigorous commerce, bourgeoisie, progressive, and looking toward the future" (summarized in Lacomba 1969:100, my translation).

This is a good example of how the geographical characteristics of North/South categories transform into the moral descriptions of the Center/Periphery (i.e., "dry" becomes "reactionary" and "intensive agriculture" implies "looking toward the future").

23. The Socialist Party, in a much disputed move, removed the word *marxist* from its title. Nevertheless, in the 1980s the party would probably have lost many of its members if it had not identified primarily with the Spanish Left.

Chapter 3, From Rented Cows to Virgin Bulls

1. These figures were given to me by the three organizations that provide animals for these many fiestas (ADETA, ANOET, and UNETE). These, like many of the statistics that include lower-level taurine fiestas, are not very "trustworthy," as the president of one of these organizations told me. The figures, certainly for the *corrida de toros* and usually for *novillada con picador,* are quite reliable since these

spectacles are under strict government control and are kept track of by national magazines. However, even at this level there are some discrepancies in figures, which have to do with definitions of the spectacles, more than number fabrication. One agency will call a spectacle a corrida and another institution will list the spectacle on the same dates as a novillada. Most of the problems, however, come with the lower-level formats *(capeas, vaquillas,* and *encierros).* According to Sr. Moreno of UNETE, the errors, if any, are on the low side. It is because many towns "especially in Valencia and Vizcaya, do not ask permission of anybody." Many of these towns celebrate their fiestas with any kind of animal they can obtain locally without going through one of the above organizations. Sr. Moreno said he had once calculated the number of vaquillas probably celebrated in the province of Teruel alone at 826, which is well above the official statistics of 200.

2. This causes the animal to misjudge his distances. Furthermore, since the nerve is often exposed, goring and charging become more painful for the bull. After banging the sides of the ring and the horses a couple of times, the bull quickly learns to avoid goring anything.

3. It is said that in the twenty minutes the bull has in the ring, it will learn quickly. If it has ever been caped before, it will know not to charge the cape and will charge the man instead.

4. The first free-standing *plaza de toros* building was constructed in Ronda in 1795. Sevilla had a temporary round, wooden ring by 1733. But the plaza de toros is a direct descendent of the city plaza, or town square (Vázquez Consuerga and Díaz Recaséns 1985). In fact, many of the earliest plazas were square or rectangular shaped. The plaza de toros is not a copy of the Roman amphitheater or circus, of which there are many examples in Spain. Rather, it is an adaption of the arched Castilian *plaza mayor* that developed as a marketplace in the Middle Ages and became the scene for religious and other public spectacles such as jousts and bullfights. As bullfighting began to change to a plebeian spectacle in the eighteenth century, so did the plaza evolve. The rectangle shape was left behind in favor of an octagonal, and later, round shape. However, it was not until 1795 that the bullring was conceived as a completely separate and exclusively civic public building.

5. Sevillanos often talked about Sevilla's *afición* for the bulls although they often disassociated themselves personally from the bulls, scorning the "mass hysteria" that sometimes develops there, especially about its bullfighters. (On the occasion of the torero Paquirri's death in September 1984, it was estimated that one million people attended his funeral.) In a national news magazine, a letter to the editor from someone in Sevilla put it well in reference to Sevilla's *afición a los toros:* "If there are two Spains, there are also two Sevillas" (Ereza Díaz 1985 : 10).

6. I want to expand a little more on the category "North" and *fiestas taurinas.* Not all that is true for Navarra and Vizcaya is true for the rest of the "North." In general, all of the regions of the North share many similarities. However, not all of the North has a tradition of taurine fiestas. Although these other regions fall outside of my comparative study, I will refer to them at this point.

The North, as pointed out in chapter 2, is also coincident with the Spanish category of the "periphery." The periphery is defined as a group of culturally heterogeneous regions or "nations" *(naciones).* Therefore, each region of the North is culturally "distinct" from the others; this is certainly true as far as taurine fiestas are concerned. If we start from the extreme west and go east across the north of Spain

(Galicia, Asturias, Cantabria, País Vasco, Navarra, Aragón, and Catalonia), it is only in the central regions—País Vasco, Navarra, and Aragón—that we find any tradition of *afición a los toros.*

Galicia, Asturias, and Cantabria are the Spanish regions with the lowest numbers of *corridas* and *novilladas* in 1984 (see table 3.4). I have no numbers for the lower-level fiestas in these regions, but there is no evidence in the literature of any taking place there. According to the 1983 Alef poll, afición a los toros is the lowest in Galicia and the third lowest in Asturias. Thus the 1983 poll reproduces the social facts already established by the eighteenth century. Jovellanos, an Enlightenment figure, published a "Report on Agrarian Law" in 1796, where he said that corridas de toros were "totally" unknown in Galicia and Asturias (Cossío [1943]1980[1]: 143). Although Cantabria has very few corridas and novilladas, its afición a los toros is rather high (39.6%). I attribute this to this region's historical and cultural ties with Castile. (Originally it was considered part of Castile.) These three regions (Galicia, Asturias, and Cantabria) and part of the Basque Country compose what is known as "Green Spain" *(la España verde).* Traditionally this part of Spain produces milk products from cows. Each household has a domesticated ox, or two, which is often also yoked to pull a plow. (It is said that the terrain in the North is unsuitable for raising the *toro bravo.*) It has been noted before that where cattle are used to produce milk there is no "true" afición a los toros (Mirá 1976). One must recall that the bulls are sacrificed ultimately to be eaten as meat in the rest of Spain. Although most of the regions in Green Spain have some corridas, Galicia has two provinces where there were no corridas at all in 1984. These were the only two provinces in Spain without corridas that year. In another Galician province, La Coruña, a corrida was held in the town of Noya (population 5,672), thus contradicting the characteristic of the corrida in the rest of Spain (i.e., that they are held in cities). Of these three regions, only Galicia has its own language (Asturias also differentiates itself with its dialect, Asturiano) and is usually considered to be more culturally distinct, although either as "Green Spain" or "the periphery," these three regions are opposed with others to *"castiza"* Spain, that is, Castile.

7. In reality these Spanish stereotypes (hierarchy associated with Southern agrocities, egalitarianism associated with Northern villages) are oversimplifications. Much literature shows egalitarian forms in the "South" (Collier 1982; Pitt-Rivers 1971) and hierarchical forms in the "North" (Douglass, W. 1969; McDonough 1986).

8. Madrid has more *corridas* than any other province, even subtracting the corridas that take place in Madrid city.

9. It is important to recall that for the South the local form *is* the *corrida.* When I asked in Sevilla why there were no *encierros,* people looked at me as if they thought the question was outrageous: "We don't do those things here." Thus, in the South, towns celebrate corridas or nothing at all. I was quite surprised to find that in the province of Sevilla many towns do not celebrate their major festivities with *toros.* Since the only forms they identify with are the expensive national-level spectacles such as corridas and *novilladas,* many years they cannot or do not offer these fiestas. *Fiestas mayores* and *ferias* (fairs) in the South are, thus, much less associated with los toros than the Center and North. (Southern fiestas use other symbols of identity, such as *vino fino* and flamenco dancing.)

10. In 1986 there were two national state-controlled channels as well as local channels in Catalonia and the Basque Country that had existed since 1980.

11. In another context Brandes (1980) draws an opposition between control and absence of control in his description of Giants and Big Heads in town festivals. Brandes emphasizes that the Giants represent the upper class and control. Big Heads stand for the working class and absence of control.

12. Thirty-five of the best *ganaderías* were affected. Eight lines of pure bred bulls disappeared forever. Twenty-three ganaderías saved some of their animals, but not necessarily their best (Gutiérrez Alarcón 1978:229).

13. I have found no historical record of this connection before 1978.

14. The change was justified in the following way: "A process of profound changes in Spanish society has taken place. These changes were motivated by the dynamic of the population and the influence of the media of social communication on the thinking of that population. These changes have affected these spectacles in such a way that they now become one of the ways to use free time" (Ministerio del Interior 1982). Therefore it should be clear that the numbers I obtained for the taurine fiestas from the various regional governments for the years 1984–1985 do not imply similar relationships earlier than 1982, since the lower-level spectacles were illegal then. Historically, however, the North was said to have more *vaquillas* than the South.

15. When I asked the same question about the *corridas,* the answer was *"desde hace siempre"* (always).

Chapter 4, The Bull that Ravished Europa

1. The classical understanding of modernity (individualism, secularism, science, and nationhood, along with urbanization and industrialization) is not the Spanish reference. As we shall see, the colloquial use of "modernity" in Spain means "European"—democratic, efficient, socially progressive, liberal, and rational.

2. This was the first time the World Championships had been inaugurated outside of a swimming pool.

3. Whether *los toros* are cruel or not is debated among the *taurinos* themselves, with many admitting it is a cruel, but still beautiful and artistic, spectacle. Other *aficionados* deny that the animal suffers in its fifteen to twenty minutes in the ring. They claim that due to the excitation of the moment the animal does not feel any pain until the very end. They say that this opportunity for a moment of glory for the bull surely compensates for any pain and insist that this is better than walking complacently to one's death in an impersonal, mechanized slaughterhouse.

4. England is home to dog lovers, fox hunters, and boxers.

5. One person complained that it was not necessary to propose an ideal of European Spain in the battle to eliminate tauromachy from Spain. This only exposed the "argument to the Spanish and Europe-hating banner of sacrosanct traditions and the sacred national character." This writer claims that Isabel, queen of Castile, was an enemy of the bulls (Sánchez Ferlosio 1985:13). His implication is that one need not be European to hate the bulls. Even the most Spanish of the Spanish (i.e., Isabel) can hate them.

6. These images of the savage as "authentic" and as controlled by aesthetic canons or civilization point to the contrast in *ser* and *estar,* essential/peripheral.

7. In 1753 the Toro de San Marcos was prohibited in all of Spain. From 1754–1759, Fernando VI prohibited all *corridas de toros.* In 1758 a Royal Order prohibited the *corridas de toros de muerte.* In 1785 Carlos III prohibited corridas de toros in all of Spain, except for charity benefits. In 1786 all corridas were unilaterally prohibited, except in Madrid. In 1790 Carlos IV prohibited running bulls in the streets of towns, day or night. In 1805 Carlos prohibited all corridas and *novilladas* in the whole realm (Boado and Cebolla 1976; Cuevas 1976:63–65; Rojas and Vidal 1976; San Juan de Piedras Albas 1927:138–41).

8. It is beyond the scope of this work to investigate the reaction of other Europeans to the Spanish *fiestas de toros* in the eighteenth century, although initial perusal would indicate that there were both supporters (Jean-Jacques Rousseau) and detractors.

9. Defense of *los toros* took place especially during the nationalist revival in the first half of the nineteenth century, during a general reaction against the French invasion and foreign ways. Later, the Novecentista Generation, a reaction against the excessive pessimism and Europeanizing of the Generation of 1898, also defended los toros.

10. The Andalusian culture complex consists of such things as *toros, flamenco,* dark-haired women, bandits, and gypsies.

11. Many say that the Islamic invasion in 711 and occupation of the southern part of the peninsula until 1492 also effectively isolated Spain from Europe. However, Christians in the north began the Reconquest in the tenth century and participated in European cultural forms from then on.

12. "Spain Is Different" was a slogan used in Spanish tourism in the 1960s and 1970s. For many Spaniards it had a double meaning.

13. "Rationalism was attacked by the Romantics not on the grounds that the intellectual results yielded by it would fail, but rather on the grounds that they were inadequate, or in other words, that an essential part of human nature was being starved" (Schenk 1966:6–7).

14. Recall the Basque magazine with the *torero* on its cover that asked the question, "Are we Basques Spanish?" (chapter 1). The underlying assumption is that torero = Spanish.

15. *Rapto* can be translated as "abduction," "ravishment (of a woman)," "rape," "kidnapping," or "rapture."

16. Furthermore, the organization of the *corrida* at the end of the eighteenth and the beginning of the nineteenth centuries points to another aspect of "modern" life: the professionalization of the *torero,* who was now paid for his work and often trained in tauromachy schools to perform it. The torero himself was the incarnation of bourgeoisie values, since the profession of torero enabled the poor boy to rise to riches. The ultimate imposition of the Andalusian form of fighting bulls is further indication of the nationalization and centralization (i.e., rationalization) of the Spanish state.

17. The dialectic is sometimes expressed as northern Europe opposite southern Europe (or the Mediterranean). In Spain, it most often takes the symbolic formula "Europe versus Spain," even though much of urban Spain has adopted the north-

ern, or European, worldview. Recall that the categories North and South, as well as Periphery and Center (chapter 1), are differentiated in this same way in Spain: the North and the Periphery are called "European," while the South and Center are "Spanish."

18. Some Spanish historians have stressed this factor in Spanish life as a constant throughout history and as a differentiation from the rest of Europe. "It was always a great quality, as well as a great defect, of the Spaniard to attend to idealistic motives more than economic pursuits. The incentives of gain and material well-being are always postponed by the Spaniard for other ideal goals 'of the lofty and glorious spirit' " (Menéndez Pidal 1951:14). Others have dismissed this as nothing more than an idealistic vision of Spain's poverty (de Miguel 1976). Of course, Menéndez Pidal represents the "Spanish" mentality, while de Miguel, educated at Yale, represents the "European" mentality.

19. A reference to Strabo's metaphor about the physical appearance of the map of the Iberian Peninsula: a bull's hide.

20. Since the death of Franco (a symbolic return to Europe in itself), Spanish intellectuals of the Left have begun to deal with *"castizo"* subjects in art, film, and song, subjects they ignored as "Spanish stereotypes" *(España tópica)* during the Franco years. Bullfighting is one of the "castizo" subjects to reappear in the films *El Matador, Carmen,* and *Tú Solo* and in the rock group Los Toreros.

Chapter 5, The Fiesta Cycle

1. Winter fiestas have disappeared or have been transferred to the summertime as an additional day in the patron saint festivities, usually coinciding with a weekend.

2. In some cases the *fiesta mayor* is not the patron saint day.

3. In fact, the absence of people is the worst blow a fiesta can suffer. Another blow is to have bad (i.e., rainy) weather. Velasco notes that *fiestas mayores* are described in terms of "brilliance" and "splendor" and that weather serves as a metaphor for this social time (Velasco 1982b:21). Recall that *los toros* also require good weather. There are many Spanish expressions for fiestas destroyed by rain, for example, *se aguó la fiesta* (the party was washed out).

4. In the Middle Ages towns would pledge to "run a bull" in thanks to its patron saint's sparing the town from the plague.

5. Some towns in Andalusia free a bull in the streets or in a ring for boys to cape, but these are usually small villages, found in the Sierra. Some larger agro-cities may have added a lower-level form one year to their fiestas, in the spirit of participation, but since that form was not part of the "local identity" (i.e., history), it was not continued (see chapter 3). I have heard of a new phenomenon in Sevilla, a kind of *becerrada* offered at country restaurants and bars, where for a fee you can enter the ring with many other people for the chance to cape a *becerro*. Obviously this is outside the framework of a *fiesta mayor.*

6. The Basque Country is a good example of overt manipulation and rejection of the urban symbols of Spanish nationalism with respect to *los toros.* The fiestas of Vitoria (Alava) take place in the first week of August. Vitoria's fiestas take over the streets of the city with much singing, dancing, and drinking. Traditionally, a *corrida*

takes place every afternoon. Vitoria's youth clubs are known as *blusas* for the long shirts the members wear. Their existence outlasts the fiestas and the toros, but they were originally organized for attendance at los toros. (Blusas are similar to other *peñas* north of Madrid.) Normally the blusas gather and parade group by group to the bullring before the corrida. Later they leave the bullring, also in a kind of parade. As mentioned in the text (chapter 2), while parading to the bullring several years ago, an argument began over whether the corrida was the *fiesta nacional*. In response, the blusas arrived at the ring and, en masse, refused to go in, thus refusing to participate in Spanish national culture. Every year from then on, the blusas have still paraded to the bullring and then refuse to enter.

The fiestas of San Sebastián (Guipuzcoa) take place the second week of August. Guipuzcoa is considered the center of Basque nationalism and the nucleus of Basque culture (along with parts of northern Navarra). In 1973 the bullring in San Sebastián was torn down, and nothing has been built to replace it. Consequently, there are no corridas in San Sebastián's fiestas. Although there is no question about the strong *afición a los toros* in San Sebastián back in the nineteenth and early twentieth century (Solera Gastaminza n.d.), the lack of corridas in the fiestas is indicative of San Sebastián's relationship with the rest of Spain since the early 1970s. Guipuzcoa is perceived as the center of Basque rejection of Spanish culture.

It has been noted, however, that recently San Sebastián's fiestas have not been characterized by the delirium and street festivities of fiestas in other Basque capitals (Vitoria, Pamplona, and Bilbao). Some critics suggest that the lack of festive enthusiasm is precisely because San Sebastián does not have toros. A local debate about the construction of a new bullring takes place every year during the fiestas. Ring supporters and *aficionados* say that the corridas and *encierros* would return the sense of festivity present in the other capitals to San Sebastián's streets (Barbería 1986: 13). (Perhaps San Sebastián is not as homogeneous as implied.)

Although San Sebastián does not celebrate with corridas, other towns in Guipuzcoa do. Furthermore, Deva (Guipuzcoa) is the home of the ranch that has supplied cows for *vaquillas* and *sokamuturra* in the many *fiestas mayores* in Vizcaya and Guipuzcoa for almost forty-five years. In Bilbao the press referred to the cows as "Guipuzcoanas" or "the calves from Deva," thus emphasizing their origin. I spoke to one of the cow herders from this ranch, who assured me that the cows were of Basque-Navarran origin and that crossing them with blood lines from the Center or South produced weak, spiritless cows (an example of speaking about "the Spains" through los toros). He also assured me that the cows work everyday in the summer, and "go to all the fiestas in the Basque Country." San Sebastián may disassociate itself from one form of los toros (the corrida), which it considers symbolic of Spanish nationalism, but it cannot disassociate itself from all forms (sokamuturra, vaquillas), which seen structurally are also representative of "Spain" (i.e., the use of one form or another of los toros as a differentiating element of identity).

The fiestas of Bilbao (Vizcaya) are the third week of August. According to Linz and others, Bilbao is the periphery of the Basque Country, geographically, demographically, and morally. In 1983 there were some "incidents" with *toreros* during Bilbao's fiestas (their cars were surrounded, while crowds jeered and insulted them as anachronisms from "Spain"). Nevertheless, corridas continue to be celebrated there during the fiestas, and the ring is full on the days of the best *cartel*. This bullring's distinctions and differences are emphasized. Since 1978, youth groups *(comparsas)* have been reorganized, some of which attend the corridas as a group, parading together to and from the ring. More important has been the addition of, and massive attendance at, the various sokamuturra and vaquillas in the fiesta program. Thus, the ambiguity of Bilbao (the large "Spanish" population [immigrants] side by side with the "Basque" population) is symbolically stated in the forms of los toros celebrated during Bilbao's fiestas.

7. I remind the reader that this is a generalization made from the empirical data. As shown in chapters 1 and 3, all forms of taurine fiestas are celebrated in all parts of Spain, but in the North the local-level forms dominate, while in the South the national-level forms dominate.

8. In Pamplona and Valencia I was told that the bull was the most beautiful animal in the world.

9. Karl Deutsch (1953:71) proposes a functional definition of nationalism based on "social communication." "Membership in a people essentially consists in a wide complementarity of social communication." Thus, ethnic complementarity is not merely subjective, "but based on performance."

10. Each fiesta is the *fiesta mayor* of its town fiesta cycle, as well as of its province.

11. I use the word *community* for two reasons: to avoid the word *nationality* and to liken the functioning of the community of the nation to the functioning of community of any other size (neighborhood, city, province). I agree with Handler (1985, 1986) and others who define nationalism as a social product formed by the arbitrary selection of differentiating elements (which may or may not have objective reality) to form a distinct "culture." Ethnic groups form similarly, in response to the nationalism (i.e., ethnicity) of a nation-state. Ethnic groups have no more natural basis of existence than nationalities. I also agree with Davydd Greenwood (1985) that proof of a longer "history" of an ethnic group makes it no more genuine than a recently emerged or formed ethnicity. Nationalisms, we know, were formed (or recognized) and promoted (or created) in the mid-nineteenth century. As an identity, that fact makes nationality no less genuine today than an ethnicity that claims deeper historical roots. I believe "Spain" exists for some people, as much as "Basqueness" exists for others. They are both social constructions and both "real."

12. It is not clear when this cycle appeared in history. In the 1920s Hemingway followed the cycle around Spain.

13. In Valencia the directors of the Oficina Cultural Taurina insisted that *los toros* during Fallas and Fallas, itself, were two different things and that some people did not even know there were bullfights going on. One of these men did, however, point out that the most important corrida always took place on March 19, the high point of the fiesta and that, furthermore, many people attended the bullfights dressed as *falleros.* I would add that the bull also played a prominent role in many of the *fallas* (structures to be burned). "The Rape of Europe" was the theme of one falla in 1986. In 1984 a store window in the center of Valencia showed a bull's head coming out of a huge fire, thus likening the sacrifice of the bull with the sacrifice of the falla.

14. The *presencia* (presence, appearance or outside) is equivalent to the *estar* (to be) or peripheral characteristics of the animal (see chapter 2).

15. The *esencia* (essence, core or inside) is the *ser* (to be) or moral characteristic of the animal.

16. If the public's booing and whistling is loud and long enough, the president will signal to have the bull taken out of the ring.

17. The *peñas* exist all year long and function somewhat like young men's clubs. They each have a locale for weekly meetings and for a place to have refreshments during the fiestas. Although they were traditionally male-only organizations, in the last ten years girls and young women have been admitted or are invited to join during the fiestas. The peñas' activities and importance far outlast the fiestas, however, and they serve as organizations for athletic competition and public service. Service and participation decline with age (and marital status), although during the fiestas older male members leave their wives and families to spend time with their peñas.

The word *peña* also refers in other contexts to groups dedicated to the bullfight itself and all of its technical aspects *(peña taurina)*, or to a specific bullfighter. These clubs are not connected to the town fiestas in any way but rather discuss the national cycle and bullfighters' performances around the country.

18. In fact, "personality" is often used to justify roles in the division of labor: for example, why Catalans make good businessmen and Andalusians do not.

19. Supposedly even the taurine literature and poetry follows this pattern, with writers and poets in the North writing about the bull and writers and poets in the South writing of the bullfighter (Martínez Remis 1963:12).

20. The date a *novillero* "graduates" *(tomar la alternativa)* to *torero* determines his order of entry into the rings, vis-à-vis the other toreros. But the date he "confirms" his graduation in Madrid is also a source of measurement. Cordobés waited several years before he went to Madrid, where he failed miserably the first time.

Chapter 6, The North

1. Fear of violent reprisals by the Basque radicals was clearly a valid reason for these people to lower their voices.

2. Marijaia's name is a combination of *Mari* and *jaia*. *Mari* means "María" (Mary) in Basque and therefore may refer to the original mother and so-called matriarchy of the Basques. Although it has a Latin etymology, *jaia* means "to celebrate" in Basque.

3. Stanley Brandes devoted a chapter in his book *Metaphors of Masculinity* (1980) to the symbolic meaning of Giants and Big Heads in Monteros in southern Spain. The Giants in Monteros were royalty. Brandes sees the relationship between the Giants and Big Heads as similar to those of class (upper and lower) and age (parents and children). If the Giants in Bilbao are not royalty but instead represent the *pueblo*, then the only hierarchy stressed in Bilbao is age (see Fernandez 1986:287).

4. Basque peasant society is idealized as a society made up of small landowners and, thus, not stratified. Even in the Middle Ages, Basque ideology says that kings were held in check by *fueros* (rights) of the people.

5. Logistically, it is easier to contain these cows, which wear no ropes, in a permanent bullring, as compared to the rickety fences of the *sokamuturra*. Furthermore, more people can watch in the stands of a bullring.

6. However, the *corrida* is not the only activity programmed for the afternoons.

There are alternative activities for the parts of Basque culture that reject the corrida as "Spanish."

Chapter 7, The South

1. During the national elections in June 1986, I watched an exchange on Spanish television where representatives from an Andalusian cultural organization claimed to be the "most Spanish of the Spanish, the heart of Spain." This claim provoked the representative of Asturias to respond that they too were Spanish. Asturias, part of the North, was never effectively conquered by the Arabs in the seventh century. It is the province from which the Reconquest began. People there like to say, "Asturias is Spain, the rest reconquered land" (James Fernandez, pers. comm.).

2. Both the week-long fiestas in Sevilla (called *fiestas de Primavera,* the fiestas of spring) should actually be studied together since in many ways they are exact opposites of each other. Semana Santa (Easter Week) is considered as an "interior" fiesta for Sevilla only; Feria, an "exterior" fiesta for Sevilla and the rest of Spain. Semana Santa exalts Sevilla's spiritual side, while Feria celebrates its material side.

3. The aesthetics for decoration of the *caseta* itself was set between the turn of the century and the 1920s in the theater plays of the Quintero brothers, and in some other literary works, as they described what became the official "Andaluz image" (Burgos 1972:20).

4. A livestock market is still held during Feria with a minimal number of animals and activity.

5. Several factors impede free entry by people from the street. Although the front flap is open, the gate delimits the private space from the street. Also, often a hired man sits at the "door," who "lets" people in and out of the entry way. Furthermore, the purpose of entering the *caseta* is to visit, not just to sit, eat, or watch. Thus, if you have no one to visit, there is no sense in entering the caseta.

6. The horse, since the Middle Ages, has always been a symbol of the upper classes. Horseback riding and raising remains the patrimony of the upper classes in Spain.

Chapter 8, "Spain" Resolved

1. A "wave" occurs when a section of a stadium from top seats to bottom seats stands up and sits down, followed by the next section, followed by the next section and so on, around the stadium, creating a wavelike effect.

2. In 1985 in Navarra, *corridas de toros* took place only in towns and cities south of Pamplona. To the north of Pamplona there were only the lower-level forms of taurine fiestas such as *vaquillas.*

3. In the Basque Country the three nationalist parties all consider Navarra as part of Euskadi but vary in their approach to the question. The most extreme position says that Navarra belongs to Euskadi; for them the question is "not negotiable." Other parties are willing to let a referendum in Navarra settle the question. There is no evidence that a referendum in Navarra on the question of becoming part of Euskadi would be won by the pro-Basque forces. (During the Second Republic, Navarra had initially formed part of the Basque Autonomous Government [1932] but withdrew in six months over disagreements and differences.)

4. At the beginning of the eleventh century Castile was ruled by the king of Navarra, Sancho III. Upon his death in 1035, his lands were divided among his sons: Ferdinand I (Castile), García (Navarra), and Ramiro I (Aragón). In the battle of Alpuerca, Ferdinand defeated his brother García and Castile no longer belonged to the crown of Navarra. From the time of Ferdinand I on, Castile became the most dynamic kingdom in the peninsula, initiating the Reconquest and relations with Europe.

5. The *corrida,* although on foot, is considered an evolution of aristocratic bull-fighting on horseback. Paralleling the aristocratic spectacle was a plebeian foot-form of bull-baiting ascribed to young men from the North.

6. *Casta* is a noun used consistently to describe Castilian culture. When I asked Pamplonicas about this, they differentiated between *castizo* (Castilian) and *casta* (pure).

7. Many of my married informants now program their VCRs to tape the *encierro* so they can sleep in and watch it when they get up.

8. In any other context, like all Spanish fiestas, overt politics is not allowed. In 1985, right before the *chupinazo,* someone tried to unfurl a banner on the Town Hall that demanded amnesty for (Basque) political prisoners. The banner was quickly pulled down.

9. On July 8, 1978, Spanish national police entered the bullring in Pamplona with the pretext of putting down some disturbance. The police started firing live bullets into the crowd. A nineteen-year-old youth, Germán Rodríquez, was killed, and dozens of people were injured. People fled the bullring and hid in nearby homes and buildings. Panic struck the city. There were street clashes, and it was decided to cancel the rest of the fiestas. The police were never brought to trial.

Since then, on July 8, the *peñas* and their bands do not parade in the streets, and in the bullring there is a minute of silence in memory of Germán. This police action only underlined the peñas' sense of opposition to "Spain."

10. Physically in the ring, the bull and *torero* occupy the "center," while the public sits on the "periphery."

11. The South and Center is where the ranches with the most prestige are located. Since the organizers want the "best" bulls available, they go to these ranches to get bulls for the fiestas.

12. If a bull falls and becomes separated from the other animals, it is very dangerous, and the youths can no longer "run" with it but must try to lead it or entice it on to the ring.

13. ETA used to gun down only suspected police informers or police torturers.

14. The Guardia Civil are a national paramilitary police. No member of the Guardia Civil is assigned to his own region. Rather, the guard is sent to another region of Spain, specifically, it is said, so that he will not identify with people of his region over Spain. The Guardia Civil was often used by Franco to put down labor and student unrest. Even in the 1970s and 1980s, the Guardia Civil was used by the central government to confront pronationalist (i.e., regionalist) demonstrations. Especially in the Basque Country, the presence of the Guardia Civil is a source of much friction, often making it the target of terrorist attacks. The Guardia Civil is considered an invading force by many Basque nationalists.

LITERATURE CITED

Aceves, Joseph. *Social Change in a Spanish Village.* Cambridge: Schenkman Publishing Co., 1971.

"La adhesión de España a la C.E.E." *Provincas* (Valencia), 31 March 1985, 18.

Aguilera, Francisco E. *Santa Eulalia's People: Ritual Structure and Process in an Andalusian Multicommunity.* New York: West Publishing Co., 1978.

"Agur (Adiós)." *Correo Español–El Pueblo Vasco* (Bilbao), 26 August 1985, 5.

Alef, S.A., Gabinete de Estudios Económicos y Sociales. "Ocio y Cultura. Investigación Cultura E/724. Diciembre 1983." Public Opinion Poll. Madrid: Alef, S.A., 1983.

Algañaraz, Juan Carlos. "La España de la ikurriña." *Cambio 16* nº 637, 13 February 1984:52–54.

"Algo más que un mercado." *Levante* (Valencia), 30 March 1985, 21.

Almirall, Valentí. *España tal cual es.* 1886. Reprint, Madrid: Seminarios y Ediciones, 1972.

Alvarez de Miranda, Angel. *Ritos y juegos del toro.* Madrid: Taurus, 1962.

Amon, Santiago. "La fiesta del toro." *Iberia Magazine* (n.d.):14–17.

Arauz de Robles, Santiago. *Sociología del toreo.* Madrid: Prensa española, 1978.

Arévalo, José Carlos. "Ortega y los toros." *Revista de Occidente* 36 (1984):49–59.

Armas Marcelo, J. J. "Europa: El lugar común." *Correo Español–El Pueblo Vasco* (Bilbao), 10 March 1985, 49.

Ayuntamiento de Pamplona, ed. *Boletín de Información Municipal.* Nº 26. Pamplona: Navarra de Prensa y Comunicaciones, S.A., 1985.

Azcona, Jesús. *Etnia y nacionalismo vasco: una aproximación desde la antropología.* Barcelona: Anthropos, 1984.

Barba, Andoni. "Las peñas." *Navarra Hoy* (Pamplona), 4 July 1985, xxxvi.

Barbería, José Luis. "La elegante vitalidad de San Sebastián." *País* (Madrid), 14 August 1986, 13.

Barquerito [pseud.]. "El Cordobés, un revulsivo del toreo." *Diario 16,* Revista del Domingo (Madrid), summer 1985, 541.

Bateson, Gregory. "Morale and National Character." In *Steps to an Ecology of Mind,* edited by Gregory Bateson, 88–106. New York: Chandler Publishing Co., 1972.

de Bengoechea, Javier. "Fotografía española." In *Poesía hispánica del toro,* edited by Mariano Roldán, 270. Madrid: Escélicer, S.A., 1970.

Bennassar, Bartolomé. *The Spanish Character: Attitudes and Mentalities from the 16th to the 19th Centuries,* translated by Ben Keen. Berkeley: University of California Press, 1979.

Boado, E. and F. Cebolla. *Las señoritas toreras: Historia erótica y política del toreo femenino.* Madrid: Ediciones Felmar, 1976.

Boffe, Charles [pseud.]. "Contra la barbarie." *País Imaginario* in *País* (Madrid), 1 June 1986, 2.

Bonifaz, Juan José. "Panorama del toreo hasta 1979." In *Los Toros: Tratado técnico e histórico.* Vol. 5, edited by José María Cossío, 27–198. Madrid: Espasa-Calpe, 1980.

Brandes, Stanley. *Metaphors of Masculinity.* Philadelphia: University of Pennsylvania Press, 1980.

Brenan, Gerald. *El laberinto español,* translated by J. Cano Ruiz. París: Ruedo Ibérico, 1962.

del Burgo, J. *Pamplona, Navarra.* Madrid: Ministerio de Transportes, Turismo, y Comunicaciones and Rotedic, S.A., 1982.

Burgos, Antonio. *La feria de Sevilla.* León: Editorial Everest, 1972.

Caba, Pedro. "Lo mágico y el toreo." In *Los toros en España.* Vol. III, edited by Carlos Orellana, 10–18. Madrid: Orel, 1969.

Cambria, Rosario. *Los toros: Tema polémico en el ensayo español del siglo XX.* Madrid: Gredos, 1974.

Cambria, Rosario. "Bullfighting and the Intellectuals." In *Blood Sport: A Social History of Bullfighting,* edited by Timothy Mitchell, 199–227. Philadelphia: University of Pennsylvania Press, 1991.

del Campo, Luis. *Historia del encierro de los toros en Pamplona.* Pamplona: n.p., 1980.

del Campo, Luis. *Psicología del corredor en el encierro de los toros en Pamplona.* Barcelona: Talleres Gráficos SET, S.A., n.d.

del Campo, Salustiano, Manuel Navarro, and José Félix Tezanos. *La cuestión regional española.* Madrid: Editorial Cuadernos para el Diálogo, 1977.

Caro Baroja, Julio. *Los vascos.* 1949. Reprint, Madrid: Istma, 1972.

Caro Baroja, Julio. "El sociocentrismo de los pueblos españoles." In *Razas, pueblos y linajes,* edited by Julio Caro Baroja, 261–92. Madrid: Revista de Occidente, 1957.

Caro Baroja, Julio. "The City and the Country. Reflections on Some Ancient Commonplaces." In *The Egalitarian Society,* edited by Julian Pitt-Rivers, 27–40. Paris: Musée de l'Homme, 1963.

Caro Baroja, Julio. *Estudios sobre la vida tradicional española.* Barcelona: Ediciones Península, 1968.

Caro Baroja, Julio. "Toros y hombres." *Revista de Occidente* 36 (1984):7–26.

Castro, Américo. *La realidad histórica de España.* México: Editorial Porrúa, 1954.

Castro, Américo. *De la edad conflictiva.* Madrid: Taurus, 1961.

Claramunt López, Fernando. "Los toros desde la psicología." In *Los toros: tratado técnico e histórico.* Vol. VII, edited by José María Cossío, 1–181. Madrid: Espasa-Calpe, 1982.

Cole, John W. "Culture and Economy in Peripheral Europe." *Ethnologia Europaea* 15(1) (1985):3–27.

Collantes de Terán Delorme, Francisco. *Crónicas de la Feria I (1847–1916).* Sevilla: Servicos de Publicaciones del Ayuntamiento de Sevilla, 1981.

Collier, George. *Socialists of Rural Andalusia: Unacknowledged Revolutionaries of the Second Republic*. Palo Alto: Stanford University Press, 1982.

Comaroff, John and Jean Comaroff, eds. *Modernity and Its Malcontents: Ritual and Power in Postcolonial Africa*. Chicago: University of Chicago Press, 1993.

Conrad, Jack R. *The Horn and the Sword: The History of the Bull as a Symbol of Power and Fertility*. New York: E. P. Dutton, 1957.

Corbin, J. R. and M. P. Corbin. *Compromising Relations: Kith, Kin and Class in Andalusia*. Hampshire, England: Gower, 1984.

Cossío, José María. *Los toros: tratado técnico e histórico*. 8 vols. Madrid: Espasa-Calpe, 1943–1986.

Cossío, José María. *Los toros: tratado técnico e histórico*. Vol. 1. 1943. Reprint, Madrid: Espasa-Calpe, 1980.

Cossío, José María. *Los toros en la poesía*. Buenos Aires: Austral, 1944.

Cossío, José María. *Los toros: tratado técnico e histórico*. Vol. 2. 1947. Reprint, Madrid: Espasa-Calpe, 1965.

Cossío, José María. *Los toros: tratado técnico e histórico*. Vol. 5. Madrid: Espasa-Calpe, 1980.

"Cuando el toro ya no es toro." *Navarra Hoy* (Pamplona), 15 July 1986, 9.

Cuevas Villamanán, Tomás. *Evolución y revolución de la fiesta de toros*. Albacete: Imp. Gráficas Fuentes, 1976.

"Dejad que los niños vengan y se acerquen a mí." *Correo Español–El Pueblo Vasco* (Bilbao), 18 August 1986, 23.

Delgado Ruiz, Manuel. *De la muerte de un diós: La Fiesta de los toros en el universo simbólico de la cultura popular*. Barcelona: Nexos, 1986.

Desmonde, William H. "The Bullfight as a Religious Ritual." *American Imago* 9 (1952):173–95.

Deutsch, Karl W. *Nationalism and Social Communication*. Cambridge and New York: Technology Press of the Massachusetts Institute of Technology and John Wiley, 1953.

Domínguez Ortiz, Antonio. *La sociedad española en el siglo XVII*. Madrid: Consejo Superior de Investigaciones Científicas, 1955.

Domínguez Ortiz, Antonio. *Sociedad y estado en el siglo XVIII español*. Barcelona: Editorial Ariel, 1976.

Douglass, Carrie B. "Toro muerto, vaca es." *American Ethnologist* 11(2) (1984): 242–58.

Douglass, William. *Death in Murelaga*. Seattle: University of Washington Press, 1969.

Dreissen, Henk. *Agro Town and Urban Ethos in Andalusia*. Nijemen: Katholieke Universiteit, 1981.

Dubisch, Jill, ed. *Gender and Power in Rural Greece*. Princeton: Princeton University Press, 1986.

Echeverría, Javier. "Del arte de correr toros a pie: el encierro de Pamplona." In *Arte y tauromaquia*, edited by Universidad Internacional Menéndez Pelayo, 127–85. Madrid: Ediciones Turner, 1983.

Ereza Díaz, Carmen. Letter. *Cambio 16* n⁰ 701, 16 May 1985:10.

"España, desde fuera: Toros, flamenco, paella y sangría." *Diario de Navarra* (Pamplona), 30 April 1985, 14.

Fernandez, J. W. "Symbolic Consensus in a Fang Reformative Cult." *American Anthropologist* 67 (1965):902–29.

Fernandez, J. W. *Persuasions and Performances: The Play of Tropes in Culture.* Bloomington: Indiana University Press, 1986.

Fernandez, J. W. and R. Fernandez. "El escenario de la romería asturiana." In *Expresiones actuales de la cultura del pueblo.* Madrid: Centro de estudios sociales "Valle de los Caídos," 1976.

Fernández Flórez, Wenceslao. *Relato inmoral.* Madrid: Atlántida, 1927.

Fernández Vega, José and Jaime Mariscal de Gante, eds. *Diccionario de la constitución.* Barcelona: Planeta, 1983.

"Fiestas sin espectáculos taurinos." *Navarra Hoy* (Pamplona), 20 April 1985, 10.

Floristán, Alfredo. "Evolución intercensal de la población española: 1960–1970." *Geográfica* 14(3) (1972):157–77.

Frank, Waldo. *Virgin Spain: Scenes from the Spiritual Drama of a Great People.* New York: Boni and Liveright, 1926.

Freeman, Susan Tax. *Neighbors: The Social Contract in a Castilian Hamlet.* Chicago: University of Chicago Press, 1970.

Gala, Antonio. "Piel de toro." *Club Taurino–Pamplona* 6 (1985):7–9.

Gallup Spain. "SAMTLIGA. ICSA Gallup-Encuesta periódica, 5 Febrero 1971." Public Opinion Poll. Madrid: Gallup, S.A., 1971.

Gallup Spain. "IDSA Gallup: Estudio 869, Marzo 1977." Public Opinion Poll. Madrid: Gallup, S.A., 1977.

Gallup Spain. "IG 2349, Septiembre 1985." Public Opinion Poll. Madrid: Gallup, S.A., 1985.

Gallup Spain. "Toros IG 2482, Abril 1986." Public Opinion Poll. Madrid Gallup, S.A., 1986.

García, Victoria. "La fiesta nacional vive su edad de oro." *Levante* (Valencia), 8 March 1985, 11.

García-Baquero González, Antonio, Pedro Romero de Solís, and Ignacio Vázquez Parlade. *Sevilla y la fiesta de toros.* Sevilla: Servicio de Publicaciones del Ayuntamiento de Sevilla, 1980.

García de Cortázar, Fernando and Manuel Montero. "Una historia común." *Cambio 16* n° 637, 13 February 1984:55–57.

García Lorca, Frederico. "Teoría y juego de duende." 1954. In *Obras completas.* Vol. 1, edited by Arturo del Hoyo, 1067–82. Reprint, Madrid: Aguilar, 1974.

Garrigues, Elena. "La calle es una fiesta." *Cambio 16* n° 669, 9 September 1984: 74–79.

Geertz, Clifford. *Interpretation of Cultures.* New York: Basic Books, 1973.

Gilmore, David. *The People of the Plain: Class and Community in Lower Andalusia.* New York: Columbia University Press, 1980.

Gilmore, David. "Introduction: The Shame of Dishonor." In *Honor and Shame and the Unity of the Mediterranean,* edited by David Gilmore, 2–21. Washington D.C.: American Anthropological Association, 1987.

Gluckman, Max. *Rituals of Rebellion in South-East Africa.* Manchester: Manchester University Press, 1954.

Gómez Mardones, Inmaculada. "La piel que cubre España." *País* (Madrid), 23 June 1985, 33.

Gomis, Lorenzo. "Europa, idea de superación." Editorial. *Correo de Andalucía* (Sevilla), 30 April 1985, 4.

Goñi, Fermín. "El espacio de la fiesta y la subversión." *País* (Madrid), 9 July 1985, 33.

Greenwood, Davydd. "Castilians, Basques and Andalusians: An Historical Comparison of Nationalism, 'True' Ethnicity and 'False' Ethnicity." In *Ethnic Groups and the State*, edited by Paul Brass, 202–27. London: Croom Helm, 1985.

Gutiérrez Alarcón, Demetrio. *Los toros de la guerra y del franquismo: El transfondo político de la fiesta nacional durante los últimos cuarenta años*. Barcelona: Caralt, 1978.

Handler, Richard. "On Dialogue and Destructive Analysis: Problems in Narrating Nationalism and Ethnicity." *Journal of Anthropological Research* 41 (1985): 171–82.

Handler, Richard. "Authenticity." *Anthropology Today* 2(1) (1986):2–4.

Handler, Richard. *Nationalism and the Politics of Culture in Quebec*. Madison: University of Wisconsin Press, 1988.

Hemingway, Ernest. *The Sun Also Rises*. 1926. Reprint, New York: Scribner's Sons, 1954.

Hemingway, Ernest. *Death in the Afternoon*. 1932. Reprint, New York: Scribner's Sons, 1960.

Hernández, Miguel. *Antología*. 3rd ed., edited by María de Gracia Ifach. Buenos Aires: Editorial Losada, 1968.

Herzfeld, Michael. "Within and Without: The Category of 'Female' in the Ethnography of Modern Greece." In *Gender and Power in Rural Greece*, edited by Jill Dubisch, 215–34. Princeton: Princeton University Press, 1986.

Herzfeld, Michael. *Anthropology Through the Looking Glass: Critical Ethnography in the Margins of Europe*. Cambridge: Cambridge University Press, 1987.

Hidalgo, Manuel. "Por fin, ríase de la guerra civil." *Cambio 16* n° 694, 18 March 1985:112–15.

Hill, Christopher. *Reformation to Industrial Revolution: The Making of Modern English Society*. Vol. I, *1530–1780*. New York: Pantheon Books, 1967.

Holtzman, Wayne H. *Personality and Development in Two Cultures*. Austin: University of Texas Press, 1975.

Hunt, Winslow. "On Bullfighting." *American Imago* 12 (1955):343–53.

Ibañez Escofet, Manuel. "Europa y nosotros." *Correo Español–El Pueblo Vasco* (Bilbao), 26 March 1985, 30.

Ingham, John. "The Bullfighters." *American Imago* 21 (1964):95–102.

Instituto Nacional de Estadística. *Censo de la población de España de 1981: Nomenclator*. Madrid: INE, 1985.

Irizar, Ignacio. "Vuelvo a los toros con mi hijo Rafael." *Correo Español–El Pueblo Vasco* (Bilbao), 1 April 1985.

Jiménez Lozano, José. "De la Europa de Erasmo a la del zoco." *País Internacional* (Madrid), 30 December 1985, 10.

Lacomba, Juan Antonio. *Historia económica de España contemporánea*. Madrid: Guadiana, 1969.

de Larra, Mariano José. "El Día de difuntos de 1836." In *Obras de Mariano José de Larra*. Vol. 2, edited by Carlos Seco Serrano, 280. Madrid: Atlas, 1960.

Leiris, Michel. *Miroir de la tauromachie, précédé de tauromachies*. 1937. Reprint, Paris: GLM, 1964.

Lévi-Strauss, Claude. *La totémise aujourd'hui*. Paris: Presses Universitaires de France, 1962.

Lévi-Strauss, Claude. *Structural Anthropology*, translated by Claire Jacobson and Brooke Grundfest Schoeph. New York: Basic Books, 1963.

Linz, Juan J. *Conflicto en Euskadi*. Madrid: Espasa-Calpe, 1986.

Linz, Juan J. and Amando de Miguel. "Within-Nation Differences and Comparisons: The Eight-Spains." In *Comparing Nations: The Use of Quantitative Data in Cross-National Research*, edited by Richard Merritt and Stein Rokkan, 267–320. New Haven: Yale University Press, 1966.

"La llegada de Marijaia." *Correo Español—El Pueblo Vasco* (Bilbao), 17 August 1985, 5.

López García, Angel. *El rumor de los desarraigados: Conflicto de lenguas en la península ibérica*. Barcelona: Anagrama, 1985.

López-Morillas, Juan. *The Krausist Movement and Ideological Change in Spain, 1854–1874*. Cambridge: Cambridge University Press, 1981.

López-Valdemoro, Juan [Conde de las Navas]. *El espectáculo más nacional*. Madrid: Rivadeneyra, 1900.

MacDonald, Sharon, ed. *Inside European Identities*. Oxford: Berg Publishers, 1993.

Machado, Antonio. "El Mañana Efímero (1913)." In *Obras Completas: Manuel y Antonio Machado*. 5th ed., edited by Heliodoro Carpintero, 828–29. Madrid: Editorial Plenitud, 1967.

Machado, Antonio. "Juan de Mairena (1936)." In *Obras Completas: Manuel y Antonio Machado*. 5th ed., edited by Heliodoro Carpintero, 1136. Madrid: Editorial Plenitud, 1967.

Marco-Gardoqui, Ignacio. "Hoy, por fin, somos menos diferentes." *Correo Español—El Pueblo Vasco* (Bilbao), 30 March 1985, 35.

Martínez Recari, Iñaki. "Hay ocho gigantes sueltos." *Navarra Hoy* (Pamplona), 4 July 1985, xxxi.

Martínez Remis, M. *Cancionero popular taurino*. Madrid: Taurus, 1963.

Marugán, J. A. "Las vaquillas, los ponys y los espontáneos se adueñaron ayer del ruedo de Vista Alegre." *Correo Español—El Pueblo Vasco* (Bilbao), 16 August 1985, 5.

Marvin, Gary R. "La Corrida de toros: An Anthropological Study of Animal and Human Nature in Andalucía." Ph.D. diss., University of Wales, 1982.

Marvin, Gary R. *Bullfight*. Cambridge: Basil Blackwell, 1988.

McDonald, Maryon. *We Are Not French! Language, Culture, and Identity in Brittany*. London: Routledge, 1990.

McDonough, Gary Wray. *Good Families of Barcelona: A Social History of Power in the Industrial Era*. Princeton: Princeton University Press, 1986.

Mead, Margaret. "National Character." In *Anthropology Today*, edited by A. L. Kroeber, 642–67. Chicago: University of Chicago Press, 1953.

Méndez, Manuel A. "Superado el complejo de inferioridad internacional." *Navarra Hoy* (Pamplona), 30 March 1985, 26.

Menéndez Pidal, Ramón. *Los españoles en la historia y en la literatura: dos ensayos*. Buenos Aires: Espasa-Calpe Argentina, 1951.

de Miguel, Amando. *40 millones de españoles 40 años después.* Barcelona: Ediciones Grijalbo, S.A., 1976.

de Miguel, Amando. *El rompecabezas nacional.* Barcelona: Plaza & Janes, 1986.

Ministerio de Agricultura, ed. *Geografía española del toro de lidia.* Madrid: Publicaciones Agrarias, 1980.

Ministerio del Interior, ed. *Boletín Oficial del Estado.* N° 118. (Madrid), 18 May 1982.

Mintz, Jerome R. *The Anarchists of Casas Viejas.* Chicago: University of Chicago Press, 1982.

Mirá, Joan F. "Toros en el norte valenciano: notas para un análisis." In *Temas de antropología española,* edited by Carmelo Lisón-Tolosana, 107–30. Madrid: Akal Editor, 1976.

Mitchell, B. R. *European Historical Statistics, 1750–1975.* 2nd ed. New York: Facts on File, 1981.

Mitchell, Timothy J. "Bullfighting: The Ritual Origin of Scholarly Myths." *Journal of American Folklore* 99(394) October 1986:394–414.

Mitchell, Timothy J. *Violence and Piety in Spanish Folklore.* Philadelphia: University of Pennsylvania Press, 1988.

Mitchell, Timothy J. *Blood Sport: A Social History of Spanish Bullfighting.* Philadelphia: University of Pennsylvania Press, 1991.

Mitchell, Timothy and Lila Abu-Lughod. "Questions of Modernity." *Items* 47(4) (1993):79–83.

Mocholi, Mikel. "Pienso seguir caminando hacía la gestión directa." *La Revista* n° II-21, April 1986:9.

Moreno Navarro, Isidoro. *Andalucía: Subdesarrollo, clases sociales y regionalismo.* Madrid: Manifiesto Editorial, 1978.

Muez, Mikel. "El poderío de la calle." *País* (Madrid), 10 July 1986, 27.

Ninyoles, Rafael. *Madre España.* Valencia: Editorial Prometeo, 1979.

Noel, E. *El flamenquismo y las corridas de toros.* Bilbao: n.p., 1912.

"Novillada." *Correo Español–El Pueblo Vasco* (Bilbao), 13 May 1985, 45.

Onega, Fernando. "Ya estamos a las puertas de Europa." *Correo de Andalucía* 22 March 1985:4.

"Opinión." *País* (Madrid), 18 July 1986, 8.

Ortega y Gasset, José. *Invertebrate Spain,* translated by Mildred Adams. New York: W. W. Norton & Co., 1937.

Ortega y Gasset, José. "Afterword: Enviando a Domingo Ortega el retrato del primer toro." In *El arte del toreo,* by Domingo Ortega. 1950. Reprint, Valencia: Artes Gráficas Soler, 1985.

Ortega y Gasset, José. *An Interpretation of Universal History,* translated by Mildred Adams. 1960. Reprint, New York: W. W. Norton & Co. Inc., 1973.

Papell, Antonio. "Al fin, en la CEE." *Correo Español–El Pueblo Vasco* (Bilbao), 30 March 1985, 39.

Pérez de Ayala, Ramón. *Obras completas.* 3 vols. Madrid: Aquilar, S.A., 1963.

Pitt-Rivers, Julian. *The People of the Sierra.* 2nd ed. 1954. Reprint, Chicago: University of Chicago Press, 1971.

Pitt-Rivers, Julian. "Le sacrifice du taureau." *Le Temps de la Reflexion* 4 (1983): 281–97.

Pitt-Rivers, Julian. "La identidad local a través de la fiesta." *Revista de Occidente* 39 (1984):17–35.

Pitt-Rivers, Julian. "The Spanish Bullfight and Kindred Activities." *Anthropology Today* 9(4) August 1993 : 11–14.

Prado, Angeles. *La literatura del casticismo.* Madrid: Editorial Moneda y Crédito, 1973.

Prat Canos, Joan. "Aspectos simbólicos de las fiestas." In *Tiempos de fiesta,* edited by Honorio M. Velasco, 151–68. Madrid: Tres-catorce-diecisiete, 1982.

Press, Irwin. *The City as Context.* Urbana: The University of Illinois Press, 1979.

Rabinow, Paul. *French Modern: Norms and Forms of the Social Environment.* Cambridge: MIT Press, 1989.

Reglamento de espectáculos taurinos. 1962. Reprint, Madrid: Academia Editorial LAMRUJA, 1982.

Robles, José Luis. "Queridos convecinos." *Correo Español–El Pueblo Vasco* (Bilbao), 17 August 1985, 25.

Roda, María Antonia. Letter. *País* (Madrid), 27 August 1986, 7.

Rodríquez Becerra, Salvador. "Métodos, técnicas y fuentes para el estudio de las fiestas tradicionales populares." In *Tiempo de fiesta,* edited by Honorio Velasco, 27–42. Madrid: Tres-catorce-diecisiete, 1982.

Rodríquez Becerra, Salvador. *Las fiestas de Andalucía.* Sevilla: Editoriales Andaluzas Unidas, S.A., 1985.

Rojas, Carlos and Manuel Vidal. *Cuernos para el Diálogo.* Madrid: A. Q. Ediciones, 1976.

Roldán, Mariano, ed. *Poesía hispánica del toro (Antología, siglo XIII al XX).* Madrid: Escelier, S.A., 1970.

Roma, J. *Aragón y el Carnaval.* Zaragoza: Guara Editorial, 1980.

Romero de Solís, Pedro. "El papel de la nobleza en la invención de las ganaderías de reses bravas." In *Arte y tauromaquia,* edited by Universidad Internacional Menéndez Pelayo, 34–64. Madrid: Turner, 1983.

Saiz Barberá, Juan. *España y la idea de la hispanidad.* Madrid: Asociación española de Lulianos, 1982.

de Salas, Juan Tomás. "Paula." *Cambio 16* nᵒ 698, 15 April 1985 : 5.

"San ferminización de las mascletáes." *Provincias* (Valencia), 15 March 1985, 24.

San Juan de Piedras Albas. *Fiestas de toros: Bosquejo histórico.* Madrid: n.p., 1927.

Sánchez, María Angeles. *Guía de fiestas populares de España.* Madrid: Editorial Tania, S.A., 1982.

Sánchez-Albornoz, Claudio. *España: un enigma histórico.* 2 vols. Buenos Aires: Editorial Sudamericana, 1956.

Sánchez Bardón, Luis. "El Mercado Común puede dar la puntilla a los toros." *Tiempo* nᵒ 174, 9–15 September 1985 : 24–29.

Sánchez Ferlosio, Rafael. Letter. *País* (Madrid), 30 July 1985, 13.

Santa Cecilia, Carlos G. "Dalí dibuja el rapto de Europa." *País* (Madrid), 12 June 1985, 30.

Schenk, H. G. *The Mind of the European Romantic: An Essay in Cultural History.* London: Constable, 1966.

Serrán Pagán, Ginés. "El ritual del toro en España." *Revista de estudios sociales* 20 (1977):87–100.

Serrán Pagán, Ginés. "El toro de la Virgen y la industria textil de Grazalema." *Revista española de investigaciones sociológicas* 5 (1979):120–35.

Serrán Pagán, Ginés and A. Muntadas. *Pamplona-Grazalema: From Public Square to the Bullring.* New York: Enquire, 1980.

"El Sesenta por ciento de los españoles, a favor de la fiesta taurina." *Ya* (Madrid), 30 May 1986, 46–47.

"Sevilla perdonó a Paula." *Cambio 16* nº 698, 15 April 1985:128–33.

"El sexto Gargantúa decepciona a los bilbainos." *Gaceta* (Bilbao), 18 August 1986, 2.

Solé Tura, Jordi. *Nacionalidades y nacionalismos en España: autonomías, federalismo, autodeterminación.* Madrid: Alianza Editorial, 1985.

Solera Gastaminza, Antonio. *Los toros en Guipúzcoa.* San Sebastián: n.p., n.d.

Tamames, Ramón. *The Spanish Economy, an Introduction.* London: Hurst & Co., 1986.

Tierno Galván, Enrique. *Desde el espectáculo a la trivialización.* Madrid: Taurus, 1961.

"Toros: arte o barbarie." *Cambio 16* nº 698, 15 April 1985:132–33.

"Los toros en el siglo XX en España." *Aplausos-Extra* nº 946, 13 November 1995:3.

Torres, Gloria. Letter. *País* (Madrid), 27 August 1986, 7.

Tuñon de Lara, Manuel. *Medio siglo de cultura española (1885–1936).* 3rd ed. Madrid: Editorial Tecnos, 1973.

del Valle, Teresa. *La mujer vasca: imagen y realidad.* Barcelona: Anthropos, 1985.

del Valle, Teresa. *Korrika: Rituales de la lengua en el espacio.* Barcelona: Anthropos, 1988.

Vázquez Consuerga, Guillermo and Gonzalo Díaz Recaséns. "La fiesta de toros y la ciudad." *ABC-Sevilla* (Sevilla), 19 May 1985, 56–57.

Vázquez Montalbán, M., ed. "Paella." *País* (Madrid), 26 August 1986, 32.

Velasco, Honorio M., ed. *Tiempo de fiesta.* Madrid: Tres-catorce-diecisiete, 1982a.

Velasco, Honorio M. "A modo de introducción: Tiempo de fiesta." In *Tiempo de fiesta,* edited by Honorio M. Velasco, 7–25. Madrid: Tres-catorce-diecisiete, 1982b.

Vicens Vives, Jaime. *Approaches to the History of Spain,* translated by Joan Connelly Ullman, 2nd. 1952. Reprint, Berkeley: University of California Press, 1970.

Vidal, Joaquín. "La seriedad y el toro." *Deía* (Bilbao), 21 August 1985, 25.

Villán, Javier. "Fuera de cacho." *País* (Madrid), 8 June 1985, 35.

Newspapers Used and Abbreviations

Bilbao:

El Correo Español–El Pueblo Vasco (CEPV)
Deía (Deía)
Egín (Egín): published in San Sebastián
Gaceta (Gaceta)

Madrid:

> *ABC* (ABC)
> *Alcázar* (Alcázar)
> *Diario 16* (DI6)
> *El País* (País)
> *Ya* (Ya)

Pamplona:

> *Diario de Navarra* (DN)
> *Navarra Hoy* (NH)

Sevilla:

> *ABC-Sevilla* (ABC-S)
> *Correo de Andalucía* (CA)
> *Diario 16* (DI6-S)

Valencia:

> *El Levante* (Levante)
> *Las Provincias* (Provincias)

INDEX

ABOUT THE AUTHOR

Born into a military family, Carrie B. Douglass lived and went to school in Japan and Germany. After earning a B.A. in history at the University of Nebraska, Douglass participated in archaeological digs in Israel and England. Interest in the Mediterranean area began in Israel. Douglass later lived for eight years in Barcelona, Spain, in the 1970s during the transition from the Franco regime to democracy. She returned to the United States to get a Ph.D. in cultural anthropology at the University of Virginia. Douglass's fieldwork took place in five provinces in Spain in the mid-1980s. Presently, she is an assistant professor of anthropology and Spanish at Mary Baldwin College in Staunton, Virginia.